BATTLE BELOW

THE WAR OF THE SUBMARINES

By ROBERT J. CASEY

WAR

The Cannoneers Have Hairy Ears
I Can't Forget
Torpedo Junction
This Is Where I Came In

MYSTERY

The Secret of 37 Hardy Street
The Secret of the Bungalow
Hot Ice
News Reel
The Third Owl

TRAVEL

Four Faces of Siva
Baghdad and Points East
Easter Island
The Land of Haunted Castles
The Lost Kingdom of Burgundy

ROMANCE

The Gentleman in Armor
Cambodian Quest

SATIRE

The Voice of the Lobster

TECHNICAL

Manual of Radio Interference

VERSE

The Vest Pocket Anthology

BIOGRAPHY

Such Interesting People

BATTLE BELOW

THE WAR OF THE SUBMARINES

By

ROBERT J. CASEY

THE BOBBS-MERRILL COMPANY

INDIANAPOLIS   **NEW YORK**

BATTLE BELOW
The War of the Submarines

MA..NOW IT MAY BE TOLD

First Edition

THE CORNWALL PRESS, INC., CORNWALL, N. Y.

To the Men Who Go Under
the Sea in Ships

PUBLISHERS' NOTE

THIS BOOK was written in the spring of 1943 with facilities supplied by the Navy Department and the Navy. Permission for its publication was then withheld by the Navy on grounds of national security.

The permission to publish was granted two years later, in June 1945.

Except for the appreciable deletions and other alterations made by the Navy censorship, the book is now published exactly as written. The reader will understand that where the present tense is used, as for example in the account of the German U-boats, the reference is to conditions existing in the spring of 1943. And if a commander today was a lieutenant then, he will accept our apologies for the use of his old title.

THE BOBBS-MERRILL COMPANY.

ACKNOWLEDGMENTS

THIS BOOK has been made possible through the kindness of Admiral Freeland Daubin (Comsublant), Captain J. B. Longstaff, Commander Lewis Parks, Captain Elwin F. Cutts, Lieutenant Robert Johanson, Admiral Thomas Withers (formerly Comsubpac), Captain C. M. Elder, Commander Robert A. Knapp, Lieutenant John Steele, Admiral Wilhelm Friedell, Commander Walter E. Andrews, Ensign Dan Clark, and all the other submarine officers and men who put up with me in my researches. For this my heartfelt and everlasting thanks.

ROBERT J. CASEY

CONTENTS

CONTENTS—*Continued*

APPENDIX

LIST OF ILLUSTRATIONS

PART ONE

THE WAR

1

MEN WHO WALK APART

IN THE days when with other war correspondents I loitered about Honolulu, waiting with polite skepticism for the Pacific fleet to work its miracle, submarines held interest only as mysterious gadgets that had no real part in the war we lived with. We would see them slide into the harbor occasionally, salt-caked, battered and ugly-looking—long, black sewer pipes covered with patches of white. We were struck by the pomp and circumstance of their arrival, with a busy-looking four-piper ahead and sometimes another behind them. We had heard the legend of how one of them had to work for two days to get the channel patrol to quit dropping depth charges on it, so we weren't surprised at the escort.

For a long time submarine men were as rare in our jittery little community as visitors from Mars. After a while when we came to see more of them we marked them instantly as creatures apart. They were for the most part pale and nearly always thin young men who walked quietly aloof with others of their kind. High-hat, some of the gobs from the surface ships called them, but they said it without resentment or unkindness. If these lads considered themselves a special breed of Navy men—well, so did everybody else. The boots looked at them with obvious awe, the older men with grave respect. For, whatever the current status of the submarines as warships, nothing had lessened their hold on the imagination of men in the less secret services. It was tradition in the Navy that only the most intelligent applicants were ever selected for the submarines, that only the men without fear volunteered for the duty and that only the strong survived.

For my part, I was struck with the extreme youth of the submariners. The skippers were all lieutenant commanders, few of whom seemed to be more than thirty years old. The crew men, you felt, might average nineteen or twenty. The CPOs of the service, the graybeards and high priests of this highly exclusive sect, were usually twenty-five or twenty-six.

One thing about them, strikingly obvious to those who lived next door to them in the close confines of wartime Honolulu, was their resilience. Uniformly when they came off patrol they were pallid and strained-looking and tired. All of them were thin, some positively emaciated, as you might expect in men who had just passed a couple of months locked away from sunlight inside an iron barrel. They were alert and pleasant and interested in their surroundings, but so far as my own observations went few of them in their first two or three days ashore ever laughed out loud.

If any of them went out and got drunk, which certainly seemed a good and excusable idea, they did it like everything else they did, in their own way and at their own convenience. Even after the provost's antiliquor order had been repealed you never saw one of them in any of the local dives. I, for one, was too old a hand to figure that this indicated they had been recruited in Sunday schools of the stricter order, but it did seem to hint at least that they were fastidious.

They would come ashore and for two or three days disappear from sight, which I suppose was not remarkable inasmuch as in those days they were quartered on the base. But in a matter of some seventy-two hours they'd be in circulation again and we'd stand and look at them as they passed, wondering at their metamorphosis. By some miracle of the Hawaiian sun, or more likely of their tough youthfulness, they would have lost their corpselike whiteness and with it their grave reserve. You knew, while doubting the evidence of your own eyes, that they were ready for sea duty and in another day or two they'd be gone again—once more on their way to Japan or the mid-Pacific islands or the chill deadliness of the Aleutians.

None of them talked to us, and since we shared some of the fleet's awe of them we made no effort to break down their reserve. They were kids, of course, like the average run of American kids, and there was no shyness about them. But they weren't supposed to talk about themselves or their work and they didn't. Whether or not we felt that they might have anything important to say if they had chosen to talk, we somehow respected the delicacy of their position chiefly, because we instinctively respected the men themselves.

One surprising thing about them—and even now after I have lived with them and eaten in their messes and shared to some small extent their lives aboard the submarines, I still wonder at it—was their mutual tolerance. It had long been my conviction that two of the best friends on earth weather-bound in a lonely cabin, or marooned on a sand bar somewhere, would most likely be at each other's throats in a week. Yet here were men who lived virtually in each other's laps for months on end *saecula saeculorum*, and ashore, where they had every opportunity to separate and enjoy a few hours of privacy, were seldom out of one another's company. Where you saw one of them you seldom saw less than half a dozen. And while they would fight willingly—individually or collectively—with members of the lesser services, they seldom so much as raised their voices to any of their own kind.

I heard a correspondent mention to a submarine skipper one time that they were more like a family than a ship's crew and the captain snorted.

"A family!" he said. "Listen, we couldn't live in one of these pipes if we acted like a family. Brother, we're all in there together and we have to get along!"

We didn't know much about the submarines in those days but we were certainly learning something about the men who sailed in them and we were beginning in a vague way to understand why they thought themselves *different*. The main reason seemed to be that they *were* different.

2

THEY UNDOGGED THE HATCH

CURIOSITY is one vice seldom cured by repentance and the higher life. So, as time went by and the Pacific fleet moved on about its complicated business—taking me with it as a war correspondent—I could never get the submarines and the men who worked them completely out of my mind.

We kept on seeing them from afar as we steamed in and out of Pearl Harbor. Once we almost manned the rails of the old *Swayback Maru* to greet a battered boat following a four-piper through the slot, in the erroneous belief that she was the *Shark*, even then thirty-two days overdue. Two or three times the correspondents assembled on the slippery decks of submarines in dock, for conference with visiting brass hats or to witness the award of medals. But always we were outside the boats themselves and even farther outside the lives of the personnel.

The decks we could have—unrevealing expanses of iron that might have belonged to submarines, or platforms at the entrance to a coal mine. We were allowed to look at the artillery—unimposing guns that seemed little different from all the other ordnance in the world. But never once did we get to look down through a hatch into the mysterious world below the surface of the oily water. We could walk in and out through the doorless portico of the conning towers—the "fairwater," they call that open cavern under the bridge—but the watertight doors leading to the cluttered laboratory inside were always dogged down before our arrival. And there were no doorbells or welcome mats.

This studied secrecy may have increased our respect for the service—as a matter of fact it did—for one always must stand in awe of something beyond his experience or comprehension. But it became more and more disconcerting, as we plowed into battles and discovered through operations messages that these strange iron fish were actually our companions in times of stress, and valuable companions. We went against the impossible odds of Midway somewhat cheered by the thought that they were out there unseen in the front line, and for several hours our sole hope for getting out with our lives was centered in them. And we came to wish that someday we might tell them about it. You like to see the men you are cheering.

We never did see them—not out there. Admiral Withers, who made one notable attempt to get the story of his submerged heroes into the daylight, seems to have got little encouragement at the time. I turned in my suit to the Navy and came home to read the augury of North Africa in the tank maneuvers of Southern California, and adjusted myself to a life that was far away from the sea and dive bombers and roaring turrets. On a blistering desert where water had to be hauled in fifty miles on a truck it should have been reasonably easy to forget all about men-of-war and similar unrealities. And it might have been, save for one thing—the unsolved and seemingly unsolvable mystery of the submarines.

So one day I went to Washington and rapped on the door of another sealed conning tower—the Navy Department.

This time somebody undogged the hatch.

It seems that out on the Pacific and elsewhere a lot of the boys were getting tired of being the war's unknown sailors. More particularly they were bored with news releases that tended to show how the aviators and the men in the PT-boats were winning the war for them and, presumably, taking over a difficult job that they had somehow failed to do for themselves. Captain Merrill Comstock and Captain Tully Shelley in the Submarines Operation Office thought it might further the war effort if the people back home were given some idea of how important this service had really become. Admiral Richard S. Edwards, himself an experienced submariner, agreed. Secretary Knox gave the matter his blessing, and I set out to visit the places where submarine boats are made and manned, the ports from which they sailed in times of peace and which they still call "home," the schools where the crews are trained. Little by little I came to meet the officers and men who had been shadows on the edge of the war a year before in Honolulu—literally hundreds of them. I questioned them pointedly and even impertinently, ate at their messes and lived in their barracks, and I discovered one day that the old reserve in which the service had been muffling itself for thirty years had suddenly disappeared.

They told their stories modestly and factually—so factually at times that it took days of work and the piecing together of many fragments of information to provide background and atmosphere —but stories the like of which I had not yet heard in this war. They spoke frankly of their own limitations, their own errors in judgment, and without jealousy or disparagement of the work of others. Uniformly they minimized the importance of what they had done and seemed to fear publicity only in that it might give to them the credit that rightly belonged to somebody else. I listened to them in astonishment, not only at the picture they gave of the war below the surface but at themselves. I had been right in my first judgment of them as men in a special category. I may say truthfully now that I have never met another group like them.

They took me aboard the submarines—the old O-boats, the R-boats, the ubiquitous S-boats, and the magnificent new ones. They accepted me as a passenger, without question, and I rode with them on training trips into the Atlantic and dived with them day and night in the ice water of Long Island Sound. They explained to me patiently every device used in the diving and navigation, and propulsion and gunnery of a submarine. And I was flattered and touched. When they decided to take me in, there were no strings attached to their welcome.

When I set out to ask questions about the service, I proceeded at first with no particular plan. I felt that anything they might say about it would be news to me who knew nothing at all. Later the inquiry took definite form. I wanted to know something of how this strangely complicated weapon had come into being, something of its technical operation, its endurance, its strategy. And finally I wanted to know a lot about the strange race of people who made it work—what manner of men they were, what sort of talent they took into battle, what sort of lives they lived.

What I discovered is set forth in this book as they told it to me in New London and Portsmouth and Mare Island, in the messes, aboard a dozen or more of the new submarines, on trips with Captain Ralph C. Lynch and Captain W. O. Kinsella, and others, in some twenty-five dives and in some three months of close association. I have put it all down here as they told it to me, with little comment and no embellishment of my own. It has been suggested by some critics who read my notes, and whose opinions I respect, that I have approached the subject with too many superlatives. My only answer is that no other approach is possible. This is one branch of the military services in which I haven't been able to find a damn thing wrong.

3

MR. WHITEHEAD'S TORPEDO

IN THE HAGUE, no more than a guilder taxicab ride from the International Palace of Peace, there used to be a building which might have been listed in the guidebooks as a monument to Irony. The brass tablet over the door read: "Whitehead Torpedo Company, Ltd."

There is no way of telling whether or not it is still there. It probably is, set back from the tree-shaded street in dreamy shadow grown more dreamy now that business is bad. Probably some fourth assistant *gauleiter* occupies its offices now and has long since made pipe spills out of the elaborate line of catalogs that used to decorate the anteroom table. Very likely he has removed the pictures of the British King and Queen from the wall, together with any signs of the firm's nationality—if sudden death may be said to have any nationality. But, if he knows his history, this *gauleiter*, whoever he is, will tip his hat each morning to the whiskery chromo of Robert Whitehead, and he will say the Nazi equivalent of a prayer of gratitude. For without the aid of Mr. Whitehead it is very likely that no nation in the world—including Germany—would be in the submarine business. And that, from the point of view of a Nazi, would be a major tragedy indeed.

When you go back through the dizzy history of the submarine —Alexander's diving bell, Fulton's *Nautilus*, Bushnell's *Turtle*—you find that hundreds of years of ingenuity never got anywhere until, almost simultaneously, the storage battery arrived to supply power enough for a practical electric motor, Dr. Rudolf Diesel devised a revolutionary internal-combustion engine, and somebody invented the periscope. When these three elements were combined with hulls already designed by Holland and Lake, the submarine

22

was definitely with us. But what to do with it would have been something to worry the builders from then on, had not Mr. Whitehead appeared with a weapon. Until then the world's experiments in slaughter had been fumbling and amateurish.

The history of the Whitehead torpedo leads one to suspect that its real designer may have been E. Phillips Oppenheim.

Mr. Whitehead in 1864 was director and designer for an engine works in Fiume. There came to him one day Captain Lupuis of the Austrian artillery who had with him the model of a contraption to destroy ships.

"I inherited this thing from a brother officer who was the inventor of it," Captain Lupuis said. "It is a torpedo, as you see—a moving torpedo actuated by a little compressed-air motor. But in its present form it is steered by strings in the hands of some operator ashore. And the Austrian government representatives to whom I have shown this device think it is too clumsy. They say that they would be interested in it if we could get some better steering device. . . . And I shall admit that the present engine *is* a little clumsy."

Concerning this historic meeting we have no record save in reports of what both Whitehead and Lupuis later told their friends. But tradition has it that the Scotch engineer saw his own destiny right then, even though he could have had no inkling how closely it was to be linked with the fate of Europe in the early twentieth century.

"And what have I to do with such murderous things as this?" Whitehead wanted to know. "I am a designer of steamboat engines and I don't know anything about war or gunpowder. . . ."

"You are the only one hereabouts who can do the mechanical work that will make this thing practical," said the captain simply. "It is a device which will make a weak navy strong and make peaceful nations as strong as their aggressors. It can very well restore the old Austrian empire to its onetime grandeur. It can be made to keep the Prussian upstarts in their place. . . . If you will do the work of perfecting it, I'll give you a half-interest."

"No," said the simple Scots engineer. "I'm buying this thing from you outright except for a royalty agreement to run for a period that we'll talk about presently. . . ."

This is a story that was told to me one night in The Hague while the German panzer divisions were still wandering about the border, fostering the war of nerves. It may not be exactly true. But it is close enough. The main thing is that a Scotchman in Fiume got the idea for what they called a "mobile torpedo" and that presently the thing was loose on the world.

Up to the time when Lupuis brought his sketches to the Fiume engine builder, torpedoes were actually bombs, grenades, mines. Bushnell had had an idea for screwing a charge to the bottom of wooden ships. The Civil War had seen some experiments with powder charges sent against enemy men-of-war at the end of long poles by rammers, some of which were craft that ran virtually submerged. Between the Revolutionary War and the coming of iron ships at Hampton Roads there had been repeated experiments with blasting devices to be towed under the target on ropes and exploded on contact.

Whitehead demonstrated his first practical mobile torpedo in 1866. Significantly, the first Whitehead ever put into the water was a successful one. Today with a better motivating device, greater size and TNT instead of gunpowder in the war head, it is probably a hundred times more deadly. But it is very little different. That first one wasn't merely the best mobile torpedo that had ever been built. It was the only one that had ever been built—and it was all Whitehead's.

The original torpedo came out of the Fiume shop in 1866. It was fourteen inches in diameter and about twelve feet long, with a war head that consisted of eighteen pounds of powder. Compressed-air motors drove it more than a mile at a six-knot speed.

It was a little slow, a little weak, and it tended to plunge. But four years later a depth-keeping device had been worked out—a pendulum actuating fins; the diameter had been increased to sixteen inches; the speed was already stepped up to seven and one-half knots. A war head containing 67 pounds of guncotton made it very nearly the most vicious projectile ever devised.

Whitehead brought his invention home then. Great Britain reluctantly bought a share of it for $60,000 and thereafter it developed rapidly to its modern form. Ludwig Obry gave it greater stability by adding a gyroscope to its complicated insides. A group of English specialists put in a little motor to control the steering, and substituted steam for compressed air in the main power plant.

By 1915 the size of the torpedo had grown to a 21-inch diameter, with a length of 21 feet. The outer hull of it remains virtually unchanged today, although it can carry 300 pounds of TNT nearly seven miles at a speed of from 28 to 60 knots.

We make our own torpedoes now, and at the moment the Whitehead Company, whose connection with the British government did not prevent its doing a fine international business, is supplying none to several of the world's largest users. But whether you call them Capablanca in Spain, or Têteblanche in the Axis factory at Toulon, or Weisskopf in Wilhelmshaven, they are still Robert Whitehead's little tin fish from Fiume.

Our torpedo works with twin turbines of remarkably high efficiency—but so, probably, do everybody else's. In ours when the torpedo is discharged from the tube, a mixture of alcohol and air is injected under pressure into a little boiler, where it is turned into steam instantly by a burner like an alcohol blowtorch. The little engines are working at full speed before the torpedo is well out of the tube. A gyroscope wheel set spinning at the same time holds the torpedo on its course. The whirling gyro by its nature will not move out of the plane in which it is set moving, but it may be placed at a predetermined angle through which the whole projectile will have to move before proceeding on its straight course . . . thus making it possible to shoot torpedoes around corners.

The torpedo is so designed that if it misses its target it will travel on to the end of its run and then sink. The modern tin fish weighs something around two tons, and the force necessary to drive a mass like that through water at 60 knots must run up into hundreds of horsepower. Yet the power plant, aside from the flask containing the air supply, occupies scarcely more than a cubic foot of space. It is still one of the world's mechanical marvels.

Whitehead's shark, despite its general adoption by the navies of the world—for surface craft as well as submarines—and despite the rapid development of submersible boats to make fuller use of its destructive powers, was, until the beginning of the First World War, a terror only in theory. Then it immediately proved itself, as everybody seems to have expected it would. From September 1914, when Lieutenant Hersing and the *U-21* sank four British cruisers, until the end of the war, fourteen hundred British ships were destroyed by torpedoes. In this war it looks as if the score might run higher.

The torpedo has gone about its work of breaking up the world's shipping under a couple of severe handicaps. In the first place, it has been so slow until recently that a ship with fair speed and a short turning radius could get out of the way of it. In the second place, whether powered by steam or compressed air, it always leaves a feathery froth in its wake. The fact that it is generally a quarter of a mile ahead of this white plume does not keep the enemy observers from getting plenty of warning of its approach.

4

THE SUBMERSIBLE IRISH

THE submarine began in fantasy—Alexander the Great submerging himself in a diving bell to look at a whale. It developed through a series of purposeless dreams—Leonardo da Vinci planning a sort of superhelmet for a study of underwater plant life—the Reverend John Wilkins hoping to breed a race of men who could live without air in a submersible cask. It became an accomplished fact as a terrible agent of war because of the genius and persistence of a lot of humanitarians and patriots who hoped to make a better world—Bushnell the scholar, Fulton the engineer, Holland the gentle schoolteacher. In the form in which it was to become a menace to existing fleets it was made possible by the collection of pennies from American school children with the promise that the invention would be used against Great Britain, a nation with which we had been at peace for seventy-five years. It derived from no properly organized scientific research. It got no assistance from the thought and experience of practical men. It was fostered for dubious purposes by people who, for all their zeal and good intentions, had a weird idea of neutrality and national obligations, not to mention ethics.

Bushnell designed his *Turtle* in 1776 to "rid the colonies of European tyranny forever and restore the air of America to a race of free men." He was going to do this, of course, by sinking the visiting fleet of His Majesty George III. Fulton, who sailed a practical submarine in the Seine in 1805 and worked up a lot of French interest in his project, was never concerned with helping Napoleon. He was attempting, as his letters home show, to strengthen the position of his own country (the young United

States) on the seas. And the technique, of course, was the destruction of the British.

The semisubmersible *Davids* of the Civil War that drowned their crews with startling regularity, although one of them damaged the USS *New Ironsides* and another contrived to sink the *Housatonic* outside Charleston Harbor, differed from their prototypes in that they were not directed toward the English—and also in the fact that they actually sank ships. But they, too, were the product of a great and heroic idealism, the gesture of a weak nation against a strong. For the South didn't have any navy and the North had—and without looking any farther than that through the archives of sea warfare you get a pretty good picture of why submarines came to be invented in the first place.

Finally you get John P. Holland, a gentle, learned, Irish pedagogue whose youth had been made bitter by memories of the great potato famine, and whose Irish technique for fixing responsibility for all the suffering he had witnessed was simple and direct. He came to the United States in the sixties to teach school in Paterson, New Jersey, but principally to think of a way to benefit humanity and establish the rights of small nations by, of course, destroying England's sea power.

It is difficult to say whether John P. Holland was a great genius or merely a good mechanic who correlated some good ideas at the right time. In either case, as in that of Robert Whitehead, whose work he brought to its greatest usefulness, he was the father of the modern submarine.

Before Holland, Fulton had worked out the uses of the diving plane or horizontal rudder for submerging and raising the boat while at neutral buoyancy. Bushnell had worked with variable water ballast and a vertical screw, and had demonstrated the use of a "depth gauge"—a barometer extending through the hull. The several *Davids* had provided a library of information about things that can be wrong in submarine construction.

Holland arrived at the idea that a cylinder is the strongest form of construction, and his first boat was a long wooden barrel with a cone at either end. Unfortunately the plans of it have been lost. The boat itself, a badly built affair, finished in 1875, was out of existence long before anybody in authority ever heard of Holland.

She was not, properly, a submarine at all, but a sort of torpedo boat designed to run awash rather than submerged. But it is interesting to note that she had many of the characteristics of later subs. For instance, she had a double hull with ballast tanks between, diving planes and screw propulsion. The motive power was actually a bicycle mechanism and the conning tower was a diver's helmet. The whole outfit was 16 feet long.

The second Holland boat was similar but had a four-horsepower gasoline motor. Holland was dissatisfied with the trials and sank this specimen in the Passaic River. For many years the gentle schoolteacher and his rabid Fenian friends poured what money they could get into the building of trial boats, three or four more of which were completed without particular menace to the British fleet.

During all this time, Holland was enjoying a bit of luck not given England's other inventive enemies. Fortune had already provided him with the gasoline engine, which was going to make submersion a simpler problem. And while he was toiling at his patriotic work over in New Jersey, some other lad who presumably didn't care a hoot about the British navy was producing a workable storage battery. Things like that are what make one man a successful inventor and another just an experimenter.

Holland's friends tried to arouse some attention in Washington. They had no success. Britain's change-over to an iron fleet was progressing very well when, along about 1888, the Navy got interested in the Whitehead torpedo and, also in something that might use it to the best advantage. Nordenfeldt, the gunsmith, had been experimenting with submarines, and he put in a bid against Holland for the United States government contract. Holland won and for some years wished that the luck had gone the other way!

He started to build the boat according to the plans he had submitted and to meet the specifications set out by the government. He was immediately beset by naval architects and inspectors who forced him to revise his blueprints as he went along, and the *Plunger*, as the boat was called, was on her way to obsolescence before she was ever launched. In the meantime Holland's experimental dockyard had expanded into a fair-sized shipbuilding plant, and alongside the frequently revised *Plunger* he put down the keels for some other boats which he could construct as he pleased while official committees disputed each rivet in the work under their direction.

The *Plunger* was never finished. As she neared her launching day and the breakup yard simultaneously, Holland offered to replace her with one of his new boats. The government gladly accepted and paid over $150,000. The Holland Company's loss at the moment was about $200,000 but it turned out that a lot of that could be charged against advertising.

The new ship was by all standards a success. She was 53 feet 10 inches long and 10 feet 3 inches in diameter and 75 tons displacement. She had a 50-horsepower gasoline engine which gave her a surface speed of seven knots, and a battery of 1,400 ampere hours' capacity which would give her a maximum speed of eight knots submerged. She had a range of 1,500 miles on the surface and 50 submerged. Her tank arrangements, controls and internal design weren't very different from those of the most modern submarine. Japan bought a couple of Holland submarines, for instance; so did Russia. Germany looked at Nordenfeldt's blueprints and Holland's, and bought the Nordenfeldt boat but kept Holland's designs. And nobody was much surprised when they found out what the first Krupp submarine looked like.

So, in an indirect way, you might say that Holland eventually got a good start with his weapon to destroy the sea power of England. At one time, twenty-six years ago, it looked as if the job had been completed. Holland had died unnoticed just before that. (The Germans were coming into Belgium on the day of his death.)

But there was at least one spot of irony in the world-revision plans of John Philip Holland. About the time he was finishing the boat which he was to deliver to the United States in place of the *Plunger*, the die-hards in England decided that the British fleet ought to have some submarines, and in view of the development in Germany, France and the United States it seemed a little late to start experimenting. So, by way of short cut, the Vickers Company bought the designs of *Holland No. 9,* and that became the model on which the British submarine fleet has been based from that day until this.

QUICK DIVE

Under momentum of her engines the boat goes under in what used to be called a "crash dive." With perfect timing at all controls she will get completely submerged in less than sixty seconds.

THE EYES OF THE SUBMARINE

This is the lower end of the periscope. The officer who studies the sea through it in brief glimpses may raise or lower it or turn it around through an arc of 360 degrees.

You read the history of the submarine with increasing wonderment. And when you have laid down the books it's an exhilarating thing to hurry out to a base and watch the pig boats nosing into their slips. You feel that they have no business being there at all—that they have an existence only in your imagination and in the imaginations of hundreds of visionaries who have gone before you. Almost you feel that when you go away from them they won't be there any more.

5

THE THINGS THAT NEVER HAPPENED

HARDLY a man is now alive who does not remember the story of the U. S. submarine that lay for a month under a dock in Tokyo Bay, and the sad but interesting fate of the *Yawata Maru*. But at the risk of boring those who do not know that Paul Bunyan was a submarine man, we shall tell it again, (a) because the test of time has proved it a very fine story, and (b) to keep somebody from lamenting that it was not included in this study of how war looks from the underside.

A famous submarine commander—so goes the story as they used to tell it in Pearl Harbor—was sent out on the Honshu Island patrol, and like numerous other skippers before and after him, made his way under the patrol vessels into Tokyo Bay. He had been in there another time, it appears, and so knew just where he was going. There was a dock with an unused slip alongside it and a deep draft of water beneath. And if you contrived to get in there without being hoisted by the murderous ash cans, you could stick up your periscope undetected at virtually any time of the day and see all of the activities of the harbor, not to mention the Yokohama water front.

This unnamed skipper got in all right, spent an evening on the surface, charging batteries and "jamming air" and looking at the pleasant sights. The next morning he stuck up the periscope and saw another pleasant sight. He was squarely in front of a big shipyard, and on the ways, with workmen swarming over her, was a ship of the *Yawata Maru* class just about to enter upon a new existence as an aircraft carrier.

The skipper looked at this spectacle slaver-mouthed, because he knew that no matter how good his luck he was never going to be able to make a torpedo slide up onto dry land. There was nothing he could do about it but look. So he looked and worried and eventually maundered.

Each day for a month this routine was repeated. Each day the skipper retired to meditate in silence and work over his brain for an answer he knew wasn't there. On the last day of the thirty assigned his patrol he was just as far from knowing what to do with the carrier as he had been on the first. But it was no longer given him to concern himself about it. His supplies were running down. His men needed a rest after the confinement of more than four weeks on the bottom of Tokyo Bay, and that night he would have to pick his way out through the ash-can barrage and, with luck, get started for home. So it was merely through force of habit that he stuck up the periscope for the last time at noon that day and took a final yearning look in the direction of the shipyard.

The first thing that struck his consciousness was a bandstand and then the glint of the sunshine on the waving baton of a band leader. Presently he noted that flags were flying and people cheering, and a Japanese lady of quality, dripping with champagne or sake, was standing on a platform amid a forest of wooden beams. And in front of the lady, already well on her way to the sea, the *Yawata Maru* was moving and gathering momentum.

"Well I'll be doggoned, or words to that effect," said the submarine skipper. And then, as the carrier came whipping the oily surface of the bay into white froth with her eager keel, he put two fish into her. And she didn't hesitate. She kept right on going—to the bottom. The submarine took on more ballast, turned over the motors a bit, and went down to rest there beside her, while the ash cans crashed in futile frenzy.

The only criticism that anyone could possibly make of so beautiful a story is that it probably never happened. One regrets that the fact that Navy men tell it to each other all over the world does not make it any truer. Sundry archivists of the submarine service, including some censors, point out that the *Yawata* was sunk on such and such a day *outside* Tokyo Bay, and they are sorry that the facts should interfere with any such chronicle of achievement.

However, at the moment that doesn't seem to make much difference. The sailors will continue to tell the story to one another until eventually a full file of patrol reports will fail to controvert it. And in the meantime nature imitating art or submarines arriving a little behind the schedule set for them by their admirers seem to be making it all come true . . . in pairs perhaps instead of singly, but nevertheless producing a reasonable facsimile of what we wanted to believe a year ago. Maybe nobody sank the *Yawata* in Tokyo Bay but something very much like her was definitely sunk by Lieutenant Commander Lew Parks just about the time Captain William Brockman was bouncing up off the bottom to blast an 18,000-tonner with a full load of troops.

So, all things considered, as the facts pile up and more and more news becomes available about the war in the deep, you no longer doubt that anything can happen to a submarine. Admit they exist and you have already attested the impossible.

Once perhaps you might have listened with politeness and a half-smile to the story of the submarine that surfaced off Hawaii and caught a lot of fish in the open vestibule of the conning tower. . . . (Only you wouldn't have smiled if you had ever smelled the aroma of fish clinging with the green slime and barnacles to every submarine that ever came back from patrol to Pearl Harbor.) You might have lifted an eyebrow about the one that came up and bumped a Japanese destroyer, or the one that slid a torpedo onto a beach and killed an unfortunate horse that just happened to be passing by. There are elements in those stories that make them resemble the chronicle of the skipper who sat under the dock off Yokohama. Yet neither is much more fanciful than the authenticated report (of which more later) concerning the submarine that came back from Guadalcanal with a Japanese seaman's coat wound around the second periscope.

One may confess to a certain hesitancy over a recent yarn from the Aleutians. . . .

In this case the boys were somewhere off Kiska. They had sunk a supply ship and in diving had stranded themselves on a ledge that barely put their conning tower under water. The rush of the destroyers passing over them to drop the depth-charge barrage had virtually lifted the water away from the top of the hull.

Unable to move forward or back or down, they had stayed there expecting the worst, which seemed to have arrived when there was a terrific thud like the smash of a pile driver on the deck just above the forward battery compartment. There was no accompanying explosion—just a metallic smash as if, perhaps, something had come apart. The shocked crew looked hesitantly for the leaks that they had every reason to believe they would find. But there was no drip from above, no rush of ice water from below.

They went back to their vigil and presently the sound of the screws and the exploding bombs died out in the distance. They blew all ballast and surfaced. And up there imbedded in the wooden deck of the superstructure they found an unexploded ash can. . . .

The report doesn't say what they did with it, which is unfortunate inasmuch as the disposal of such a present might involve many interesting features. The best guess is that somehow they carried it gently aft, got the boat moving full speed ahead, and rolled it overboard. If the ledge hadn't been there holding them, they might have gone on to the end of their dive to have it explode and destroy them at the depth for which it was set.

Submarine men discussing this story never tell you that it couldn't have happened. They are probably remembering the seaman's coat on the periscope. What they say is that they haven't heard any official comment on it. In the main I think they believe it. Tomorrow's patrol reports will probably give a verified account of some submarine that surfaced with two depth charges aboard, or possibly a part of a destroyer's keel.

Toward the end of the last war there used to be much conversation about a ghost ship, a sort of submersible *Flying Dutchman*, which appeared on the German register as the *UB65*. The story went that she was haunted by the ghosts of men she had slaughtered . . . and while nothing should have appeared more silly than that to a submarine man, the story gained a lot of credence around Kiel, and crews mutinied rather than serve aboard her. The last seen of her was off the coast of Spain in 1918 when the U. S. submarine *L2* sighted her on the surface. The *L2* made an approach for a torpedo shot, apparently unobserved, and got close enough to read the numbers on the U-boat's conning tower. But before she could release a fish the *UB65* obligingly exploded with no outside help.

Until recently it has been difficult for most people to believe any more of the story than that the *UB65* blew up while the *L2* was looking at her. Now you can't be sure.

A classic story of the old submarine service had to do with a sort of last man's club, its hero a young skipper who sacrificed himself to get his men out of a sunken E-boat. This yarn had so much popularity that the publishers of pulp magazines distributed a synopsis of its plot to all their readers with the notation that the trade had grown tired of printing it. "Probably true," was their laconic observation, "but we believed it the first time and will try to remain convinced."

The story was one of those simple though harrowing tales of the unknown world only just beginning to be explored beneath the sea. The submarine, with a crew of ten or twelve men, a couple of underofficers and the brave skipper had gone under for a trial dive and, as was not unusual with boats of her kind, had refused to come up. That part of it was worthy of the detail with which it was presented, for if submarine accidents in those days failed to take the toll of later tragedies they certainly provided as now the most horrible way to die that human imagination had yet devised. But there was more to give it a place in the lasting literature of the services—calm bravery in the face of the ultimate catastrophe, the rise of the young officer unhesitatingly to meet the greatest demand that would ever be made upon him, to give his own life that other, lesser men might live.

The skipper, not to repeat too much of a narrative still so widely circulated that it may have lost some of its original power, assembled his men in the torpedo room. One after another he shot them out of the torpedo tube until finally he alone was left. There was nobody, of course, to pull the trigger that would release him so, one judges, he sat down calmly to await the terrible end.

I did not try to check up the antecedents of this story, either as a bit of submarine rescue lore or as a glowing tradition of the service. Because by the time I had got that far in a study of the submarines, I knew better. I had seen torpedo tubes work, and I had learned a little about Momsen lungs and the "bends." The brave skipper had become something like the brave little Dutch boy who put his finger in the leak in the dike. And I recalled what Irvin S. Cobb once said about the little Dutch boy—that he had plenty of courage but no knowledge of hydraulics.

Yet, as I have mentioned, you never know. One night at Portsmouth I met a sailor who had been long in the submarine service, and without my asking him he volunteered the story of his weirdest experience. It was aboard one of the early S-boats at Newport News or some such place and something had gone wrong. The boat was down by the stern, the stern planes were jammed and a pump went out of commission. And the personnel, including the skipper, had crawled or hauled one another out through the torpedo tubes.

The boat, it seems a shame to add, was almost on the surface and her bow, after the accident, was sticking up out of the water. But they did come up out of the torpedo tubes to lend verisimilitude to an otherwise bald and unconvincing narrative.

And that isn't the end to the evidences of the uses to which torpedo tubes may be put, other than the routine job of expelling torpedoes, not by any means. The most gruesome story of all that the men in the trade tell to one another may be placed in this category. I have heard it three times now at submarine bases and more recently over the radio from a commentator who might have done better with it.

If we may believe this report, the Germans have been extending themselves in recent months to make the evasive tactics of their U-boats more effective. Long ago they discovered that the best way to make an enemy stop dropping depth charges on you is to convince him that he has blown you apart. So they tried numerous tricks to provide misleading evidence. It was they who first tried releasing quantities of fuel to make oil slicks on the surface, and then sent up streams of bubbles to indicate fatal leaks. In a later maneuver they shot out chunks of cork lining and unidentifiable wood, all of which were duly picked up and cataloged. But by that time the escort commanders of the Allied Nations were getting a bit skeptical about easy hits. The depth charges continued to go down at the old rate and reports of sunken submarines were always well qualified.

One day, however, an American destroyer dumped over a spiral of ash cans and got a reward. Oil came up, and air bubbles and chunks of debris and then, presently, a corpse in dungarees. Nobody, no matter how coy, would have declined to read a meaning into such an exhibit as that—or rather nobody but the American commander.

"I'll believe that's a corpse only when it tells me it is," he said. "Haul it in."

So they hauled it in and had a look at it and transferred it to a cruiser, where a doctor performed an autopsy on it. A signal came back in fifteen minutes:

"Your corpse has been dead about three months and pretty well embalmed." The destroyer proceeded with the dumping of the ash cans.

Every now and then we hear the story of the submarine that came up under the keel of a ship, and conceal our sadness that nobody is ready to say what submarine or what ship or where or when. Only the persistence of the yarn gives one any hope for it, but it is certainly the sort of accident that everybody in the service has been expecting to happen for years.

As basis for it one may have to go back to the last war, but there one comes to fact attested by twenty witnesses and incontrovertible. A British submarine went out to operate off Revelstoke, reached a rendezvous point and submerged.

If the skipper and diving officer had not been well acquainted with the spot as a favored underwater haven, the incident might have turned out differently. As it was, when they scraped bottom at a point where the depth gauges showed they should have had fifteen feet of water under the keel, they suspected something wrong. Sound apparatus in 1917-1918 had plenty of lacks but it was good enough for the job at hand. With all power cut off the operator of an affair like a stethoscope listened to what he might hear against the hull and confirmed a suspicion already well settled in the captain's mind.

"Metallic grinding, sir," he reported, "and running motors. I think we're on top of another submarine."

"So do I," said the captain. "And if it's another submarine it's none of ours. We're the only Allied submarine in these waters."

So they moved forward a bit and backed a bit, and weighted the ballast tanks first on one side and then on the other, and felt a series of shocks through the lead ballast over their keel. Something was giving way beneath them. When they came up two hours later they were in a sea of oil pock-marked with odds and ends of cork and similar rubbish. Everybody, including the Admiralty, thought the evidence was conclusive.

More reasonable than some of these tales but no less difficult to trace is the one about the American sub that was bombed by a friendly plane off the coast of Australia. Submariners accept it readily and without rancor, for it is part of their code that they are likely to be bombed at times by planes on their side. With the speed of planes what it is, and the necessity for immediate action against submarines what they themselves know it has to be, they are never sanguine that a recognition signal is going to be seen and identified in time to do them any good. Starting off from home in the belief that they have no friends, they are not disappointed when they turn out to be right.

In this case the submarine, homebound from patrol, sighted the plane as it came through a low-lying cloud rack and flattened out at the bottom of its dive. The bomb, which missed being a direct hit by inches, was off the stern. Stern planes jammed, the hull itself lifted up out of the water, the submarine started down like an express elevator. The diving officer thought he'd been holed forward and he surfaced. The plane came back and put another bomb where the first had gone off. The submarine went down even faster.

Somehow the crew got into position and flattened the boat out before it could get to the bottom, but it was a near thing. When they finally got the lights back on and the electrical gear straightened out, they discovered that a lot of their instruments including depth gauges had quit. It was two hours before they could repair enough of the damage to get back onto the surface. Some of the bridge was gone and the radio antenna had been smashed but they were able to rig up a couple of wires and report the attack.

In the meantime the two aviators who had bombed them had

reached their base and announced the sinking of a Jap submarine. They were in the officers' club celebrating when the report of the target was brought to them. . . .

There remains only the typical turn to this story. Days later the submarine arrived and was met at the dock by a distinguished flying officer. To the skipper he tendered profuse apologies and the skipper made a characteristic reply.

"Don't mention it, sir," he said. "Those boys were damned good shots."

It may not be true, of course, not any of it. But it sounds to me very much as if it might be. . . . There was that report of a bomber at Midway who dropped a bomb and saw what he thought was a cruiser go under in forty seconds.

In the officers' messes you hear many odd echoes like that of torpedoes that ran hot at the wrong time . . . of mirages by day and of shadowy convoys that weren't there by night . . . of weird pursuits and strange targets. You get little data, few details, nothing much save the general plot and the almost universal belief that is the beginning of all folklore. Maybe Lieutenant Commander Blank didn't really hear screws passing over him in an empty sea. Maybe Captain Doe wasn't really deceived by the silhouette of a dead whale. But submarines find it hard to reject entirely such rumors as the one about the "Sitting Pigeon of the Java Sea."

Of course there is no cast of characters to the drama. Like all the others it is anonymous. But you will hear in almost any club on the Pacific coast the odd story of how the USS *Sardine* came onto this prize at the end of a successful patrol. The target was a pure gift. No ships had been reported in that vicinity. Sound had picked up no screw noises. So far removed from the war was this peaceful stretch of ocean that the submarine had not even bothered to submerge with the dawn. It was shortly after sun up that the lookout discovered the Sitting Pigeon.

"It's a steamship," he reported. "She looks to be at anchor off a small island with no steam up. . . ." He gave the bearing.

The captain took a look and agreed. The ship was in the haze that covers such waters in the early dawn, but her outline was plainly visible and the lookout's original report seemed correct in all detail.

"Clear the bridge," the captain ordered. "Stand by to dive."

The klaxon rasped and the ship went under. Warily the captain directed his approach. The bow tubes were loaded. The torpedo men stood tense. They had "rubbed Buddha's belly" for luck—which is to say they had placed gentle hands on the well-described protuberances on the torpedo-tube doors.

In the control room the captain was chuckling as he leaned up to the periscope. The approach was going magnificently. The submarine had not been detected. The mist was clearing . . . 4,000 yards, 3,000 yards, 1,000 yards, 500 yards . . . "Stand by to fire torpedoes. . . ."

And then the mist parted entirely and the captain got another look at the Sitting Pigeon.

"Oh, hell," he said. "Secure torpedo tubes. . . . Stand by to surface. . . ."

He was looking even then at the fine clear silhouette of a merchant ship that had gone aground there twelve years before, her gaunt, empty frame golden against the gentle rise of sunlit coral behind her.

6

"IT AIN'T NECESSARILY SO"

ONE day, in the era of the old pig boats, the skipper started for his bridge after a submerged run and as he opened the hatch the air pressure behind him blew him clean off the boat. They tell of it now occasionally in the messes, generally without names, for it was no isolated case in those days, and they smile at the suggestion that it is ever likely to happen again. Contrary to a general belief, the air pressure in a modern submarine hundreds of feet below the surface remains just what it was when the ship was corked up for the dive. So men go down and men come up with never any danger from nitrogen bubbles in the blood and the paralysis of the bends. They can open the hatches and go to work with the deck guns without any preliminary decompression.

There could, of course, be leaks in the compressed-air lines inside the boat. But it is not possible that the change in the barometers would go unnoticed. Air pumps would take the vagrant pressure out of general circulation and lock it up somewhere else, and the ship would surface as usual with no greater discomfort than a pop in the ears.

The old-timers in the submarine service—most of them ashore—speak with nostalgic concern of those adventurous days when captains were always getting blown out of hatches and the continuous bouquet of a submarine was part of its inherent charm. (In those days the air, like the eggs, was unfit for human consumption unless it had a fine ripe aroma.) And they mention among other things the body that a bit of gasoline gave the coffee, and the sustaining qualities of a diet of hardtack and corned beef in the iceless tropics. More technically they talk of the craziness of the plane controls, the flimsiness of the hulls, the leaky torpedoes, the ubiquity of battery gases, the fatalistic conviction throughout the service that what went down quite frequently stayed there. And as they mention these things you become aware not only that you don't know much about submarines but that what you do know about them generally isn't so.

There was the matter of internal pressure aforementioned. The average civilian, and quite a number of Navy men, figure with some logic that submarining is after all only another form of deep-sea diving, and that therefore the sub itself is just another extra-roomy diving suit subjecting its wearers to all the inconveniences that sea pressure brings.

With less logic there has grown up the belief that sub designers have worked out some intricate device for reworking secondhand air over and over again, so that there is virtually no limit to the time a submarine may be submerged without damage to the crew. It would be nice if that were true.

Simon Lake discovered by test a generation ago that a man needs fifteen cubic feet of air an hour. And the most modern device we have in submarines for supplying each man with fifteen cubic feet an hour is to take that much aboard before dogging down the hatches. A few things are done to this air in the course of its use and reuse. The air conditioners cool it off and take the moisture out of it and distribute it through the compartments uniformly so that, for instance, the Diesel oil fumes won't be any thicker in the engine room than in the forward torpedo compartment. When indicators show that the carbon-dioxide content of the air is dangerously high, a chemical absorbent is tossed about the ship—a crude scheme but effective. And in the ultimate pinch oxygen can be released from the flasks reserved for the Momsen lungs.

Just how long a crew could last under seal with one charge of air is something on which there is no official United States figure. Men have lasted a long time in wrecked subs by lying still to conserve oxygen—a man quiescent doesn't require so much as a man active. But the point is that when the first supply of air wears out there are no reserves.

It is surprising, however, how long a boatful of air will last with no manipulation or care whatever. One of the landsman's beliefs is that smoking is taboo aboard subs at all times and particularly when submerged. As a matter of fact smoking is allowed some of the time on all submarines submerged or surfaced, the length of time depending on operating conditions. On all trainers, and on more than one submarine of the battle line, there have been no rules at all against smoking. One may smoke until he can no longer keep a cigarette going or until so little oxygen is left in the air that a match won't light in it. Your lungs—which presumably are of better material—will keep going for twelve or sixteen hours in air so thick that it can be used to put out fires.

When we were diligently strewing the floor of the Pacific with ash cans in the early months of the war we gave no thought to the mathematics of submersion. If the sound apparatus located a suspected submarine in a particular spot one day, we'd still be dropping depth charges on it two or three days later.

And if we figured that Jap submarines could stay on the bottom forever, we were no better informed about how fast or how far they could move without coming up for air or showing a periscope. Once a cruiser officer told me that he suspected a sub had been following us submerged since we had left Pearl Harbor five days before. I saw nothing wrong in that. Submarines were supposed to travel submerged, weren't they? Very well, then, why not be realistic about it and accept the fact that they were a tangible menace always at our heels?

Well, looking back at it now from a submarine base, I can see a lot of reasons why we need have had no fear of submarines submerged or otherwise. We had been doing about 23 knots since leaving port. Conceivably a modern submarine might do as well on the surface if her skipper didn't mind the air patrols, which would most certainly have spotted her the first day out. Submerged, no submarine in the world can do better than eight knots and at maximum submerged speed no submarine can travel longer than two hours. At an economical speed of two knots the sub can travel forty-eight hours, or very nearly 100 miles, before the battery is exhausted . . . but that talent is of small use in tracking down fleets.

The uncanny ability of the sub to get her bow under water

has fostered other strange beliefs, one—a bit stranger than the others—to the effect that if a boat is watertight and under control there is no limit to the depth at which she may rest submerged. For such a theory, of course, there is no hint of defense, although there may be the excuse that underwater caissons are operated hundreds of feet below what would be the periscope depth for even a large submarine. There is, of course, the important difference of internal pressures.

The caisson, like the submarine, is a species of tin can. If air is pumped into it to maintain an internal pressure equal to that of the water outside, then it is subject to no stresses whatever, and the only problem is to get a man inside it who can work at that pressure.

The submarine, on the other hand, works with internal pressure no greater than that of the atmosphere at sea level. Thus the hull takes the full load of a water weight that increases about 45 pounds to the square inch every hundred feet down. Until this war began the maximum depth at which any submarine could maneuver in safety was considered to be about 200 feet. Hulls have been strengthened enormously, what with new steel alloys, welding, and greater over-all tonnage. Ships can be taken several hundred feet beyond the old safety mark and still come back. But no submarine skipper, Jap, German, British or Yank, is going down in that drowned stratosphere unless he has to. For the laws of foot poundage are never suspended. A modern submarine would be under a pressure of, say, 200,000 tons at 300 feet—half a million tons at 600 feet. How much farther down than that it might operate, nobody at the moment seems willing to say; but there must inevitably come the level at which the sea will win and crush it like a pillbox in the hand of a giant.

We get back to the old theory that men trapped in a submarine could always escape by being blown out of the torpedo tube. And that, too, unfortunately is one of the routine things that never happens in the submarine service.

If the ship comes to grief at a depth of, say, 150 feet, it is possible to get the men out through the escape hatch whence, with the aid of a line and Momsen lungs, they should be able to make a slow, painful but successful ascent to the surface. . . . At depths below 200 feet the pressures—— Well, anyway, you don't get men out of submarines by shooting them through the torpedo tubes.

There have been other weird ideas about the submarines, of course, not all of them ours. Japanese broadcasters in January 1942 used to commiserate with us on the fact that our submarines were unable to operate at long distances from home. I recall the pretty prayer of "Tokyo Rose," as well timed as her more sentimental comments usually were:

"The American pirate submarines have learned how Japan protects her coasts. . . . No longer do they dare to approach this side of the ocean, and we give thanks to Heaven that our land is once more free from this barbaric menace. . . ."

That was the night Lew Parks sank his big one off Japan.

The folklore of the unknown is always the most luxuriant—a thought which leads one to offer excuses for Tokyo Rose, so seldom right, so generally wrong at the wrong time. . . . I seem to remember when the great powers hastily side-stepped a clash with Mussolini in the Mediterranean because of his submarine fleet which, day by day, gained new importance conversationally. And more recently I recall the estimates of Japan's strength at sea—academic arguments at a time when the peace commission was in the United States—all of which emphasized the power of her submarine fleet. The menace of that fleet had sent shivers down the Pacific coast all the way from Dutch Harbor to San Diego. . . . In Juneau a hotel manager spoke feelingly of the time when starvation must threaten the town because of Jap submarine activity along the sea lanes to Seattle. . . . In Sitka a harried doctor recalled stories of subs with six-inch deck guns and airplane hangars, and he figured despairingly that the town might last five minutes in a bombardment against which there would be no defense. . . .

So we may add a sort of postscript to this study in popular delusions:

The things you know best about submarines aren't so . . . and

The things you know for certain that they are going to happen never do happen.

7

THE THINGS THAT DID HAPPEN

In a cartoon widely circulated some months ago a popeyed fisherman stared at a Japanese submarine taken in his net. Most of the submariners in the United States laughed heartily at this except Lieutenant Commander George Porter. He thought the artist had worked on poor information.

There is nothing apocryphal in the story he told me about the U. S. submarine that almost (not quite) got hauled in by the Japanese fishing fleet off Honshu Island, but surely it sounds as if it should be. This boat came up one evening for a breath of air and found itself in a tangle of fish net and strung with a festoon of glass floats, a situation for which no advice had been provided in the book of tactics. The submariners, like the game-fish they were, cut through the net, after which they shot up the sampans to which it was attached.

No less worth including in a book of seagoing folklore is the adventure of a friend of Captain Porter who was voyaging in the same waters. His sound man had reported mysterious screw noises and the skipper was proceeding warily with his periscope barely out of the water. Something happened to the trim; the boat leaped upward three feet. So did the periscope. The captain found himself looking right past the teeth of a screaming woman on the deck of a sampan. Her unheard yell had spread her face all across the periscope scale.

Quartermaster Richard F. Breckenridge stood alone in the conning tower of a diving submarine, the way to the control room shut off below him and the Pacific rolling in on him as he fought back the sea to close the hatch. He lived—which is probably the most remarkable thing about it all. A cook aboard Captain Robert Rice's

47

submarine was just putting a cake in the oven when the boat, knocked out of trim by a depth charge, took an up angle of ten degrees and stayed in that position for two hours. The cake came out of the oven with its topside at a ten-degree slant and the cook announced it as angle-food cake.

Captain Rice took with him on one trip to Japan a machinist who, unable to believe anything that he couldn't see, had got a notion that the submarines never really went anywhere—that they fought, if at all, at no great distance from their docks—that their actual function was the guarding of home ports. He was, as might be supposed, an unimaginative soul. He knew all the jobs aboard the boat and did them with the precision of an automaton. His ideas about what the boat was doing when he turned his valves or pulled his levers with the neat timing of an expert might have been interesting if he had ever put them into words. But he spoke little save to express doubts about where he had been and where he was going.

One day Captain Rice came off the end of Honshu opposite an inlet beyond which a grove of mulberry trees wandered away through white mists. In the background Fujiyama, the sacred mountain, raised its white cone to meet the rising sun. The captain, who is a lover of beauty, looked around for somebody to share this majestic sight and discovered the skeptical machinist almost at his side. He called him and turned over the periscope.

The machinist took one look and gasped.

"Oh, my God!" he said in a reverent tone. After which he wandered dazedly on his way to the engine room.

And there are stories of the *Perch*, long since reported overdue and presumed to be lost, that indicate the destinies that guide the submarines. She fired a torpedo once in a surface attack and watched the white wake veer suddenly from a straight course and trace a circular curve toward starboard. Powerless to do anything about it, without enough time to dive, the men on the bridge watched the scurrying fish complete an arc astern, come up on the port side and streak toward them. The captain was starting to call out the order to abandon ship when the torpedo blew up of its own accord in midflight!

Again the *Perch*, trying to get through a badly charted strait in the Great Barrier Reef off Australia, ran into a tidal whirlpool. In spite of anything that anybody could do she went steadily down. At a depth that seemed more than her hull would ever stand she leveled off and cruised in a circle like a carriage on a merry-go-round. In desperation the captain blew all ballast, and still she wouldn't rise until the notion seized her, at which time she came up like a helicopter. On the surface she kept heading ninety degrees off her course with the rudder at hard left and barely responded to the full-speed thrust of her engines. With a leeway of only a few feet between her and the rocks she came through the strait sideways without touching a thing.

It's history now how Captain (Lieutenant Commander) Thomas Burton Klakring, Jr., pushed his submarine in so close to the coast of Japan that he was able to see a horse race—history also how he tried to move the boat to a position from which he could see the finish line. No contriver of submarine apocrypha has ever thought up a better situation than that.

Captain Lew Parks' boat took a prisoner on one patrol. A ship had been sunk and out of the night close by a squeaky voice in broken English called for help. The captain veered about, slowed down and picked up a small, half-drowned Japanese who had been clinging to a crate.

"So glad," he said. "Me speak good Inglis. Me bellboy Imperial Hotel Tokyo. Me be good. Go along you."

"Okay," said Captain Parks. "Glad you were able to make it. That suits me fine."

They came eventually to Pearl Harbor and into their slip. Ashore they saw an armored car and a detachment of marines waiting to take off the prisoner. A guard came aboard and eventually found him. He was lined up on the deck with the crew!

Finally there is the report of Captain Bell's boat, which blew up a lone freighter one fine morning off Formosa. The submarine made the approach undetected and got so close that the captain could see everything that was happening on her deck. Somebody was tinkering with the forward donkey engine. Three men were taking the sun at the rail near by. The captain was conversing pleasantly with somebody unseen on the other side of the bridge. Walking out toward the stern was a mess boy with a bucket of garbage. For some reason the captain was fascinated by the sun glinting from the bucket. The boy got the bucket elevated over the stern rail just as the torpedo hit. He dived over with the garbage.

These and other chronicles of battle below will sound no more fantastic to a reader unacquainted with submarines than they did to me when first I heard them. But so far as is possible they have been checked against official records and rechecked in the conversations of submariners thousands of miles apart. I mention this merely as a precaution lest they be classed as seafaring yarns such as came out of the New Bedford whaling days. Most of them are not only stranger than fiction but stranger than truth and I have felt in compiling them that I am actually writing this book for the White Queen, who found it easy to believe all manner of impossible things.

8

THE WOLF PACKS

EARLY in this war I learned something of how submarines operate through listening to men who had met the growing wolf packs of the Germans.

There was one evening on the way from Glasgow to Lagos, Nigeria, on my way to the Libyan war in December 1940, when the German submarine wolf packs in the Atlantic seemed much more of a tangible menace than they are ever likely to seem again. In the shrieking chill of a tempest off the Cape Verde Islands one of them closed in on us and sank five ships in as many hours, and, of course, we cursed the submarines then as riders in merchant ships have always cursed them since the day somebody first made them work. We saw nothing of them, heard nothing of the havoc they were wreaking except the victims' carefully coded calls for help that was never going to be sent. We discovered no sign of their presence in these perilous waters save the crash of our bows as we ran over something later presumed to be a 750-ton U-boat, all unaware of it, as fortunately it was probably unaware of us. It is surprising to discover that the British merchant skippers even then knew most of the tricks that the U-boat commanders have since made standard practice.

It is no military secret at this writing (1943) that Germany is now relying, as in the earlier World War, on the submarine as the only weapon with which she can hope to break down the tremendous war effort of the United States. . . . No secret either that she has used the weapon with audacity, efficiency and success.

Yet one feels a little let down to find out that this is so. For we should have known about it. There is nothing particularly new in the wolf-pack strategy—nor does it presuppose any unusual ingenuity on the part of the current commander of the Nazi naval forces. It is just the logical method of operation when you have a lot of submarines and the best thought on this subject is now agreed that the Nazis have a lot of them. If we continue to smash up factories from now until the end of the war they probably will still have a lot of them.

The principal use of the submarine since its inception has been as an offensive instrument against enemy shipping—merchant or naval—and the very nature of its mission has imposed upon it certain definite restrictions. To destroy shipping it has to be where the shipping is. It must have some cover and means for escape. Thus, if it is forced to work alone, it must loiter about harbor entrances or in straits through which ships have to move. And without going any farther into the subject than Japanese communiqués, it would seem that much of our submarine performance in the Pacific has been of that type. In large numbers U-boats may divide the area of ambush and while the basic principles of tactics remain the same, the work is simplified and the danger to the individual considerably lessened.

That night off the Cape Verde Islands, when the ship had righted herself after her crash in the dark and the captain of the old *Seaforth* had come down out of the wet to resume his Christmas dinner, he expatiated at some length on this elemental strategy of the U-boats. What he said was amplified from time to time by the chief steward, then considered an authority on such matters inasmuch as he had been aboard the Children's Ship when she was torpedoed off the north end of Ireland a few months previously. That both, presumably, have since been drowned, proving the theories that they held about submarines as far back as two years and a half ago, would seem to give them rating as authorities.

"What you've got to remember," said the captain as he salvaged some food and a bit of crockery from the mélange on the table, "is that any ship traveling the ocean from one point to another is pretty generally confined to a definite lane. What I mean is that there is always the shortest distance between those two points and unless cases are exceptional the ship's course will be pretty close to the shortest distance.

"You can see the reason for that. Suppose that you knew the

submarines were lying along that lane and that you could fox them by traveling a route twice as long. Well, in the long run what would you have accomplished? You wouldn't have foiled the submarines at all. You would have set up a condition in which you would need twice as many ships to carry the same amount of cargo between those two points in the same time. In other words you would have helped the subs put half your effective shipping out of business without their having fired a single shot at you. Well, then, as long as you're running cargo you can expect to follow a pretty well-defined lane, and you can bet your socks that Heinie knows what it is just as well as you do. And some place along that lane he'll be waiting for you.

"If he's got only one or two boats, he'll do his waiting at the ends where the shipping has to converge to get into the ports. If he has more, he can work anywhere along the line where it suits him best. Maybe you're not coming right down the middle of the great-circle course. Maybe you're a few miles off of it. But you're not going to be forty or fifty miles off of it. So if he's got ten or twenty U-boats to spread out at a rendezvous point, he can have them pretty well scattered and cover a devil of a lot of territory and still be in front of you and ready to do business when you come along. . . ." Somebody said that Y-guns would beat the Germans this time as they had before. The captain snorted and produced some startling figures:

"Von Tirpitz announced his unrestricted submarine warfare in February 1917," he pointed out; "at that time he had a fleet of 110 U-boats. In February they sank 469,000 tons of Allied shipping, in March 524,000 tons, in April 852,000 tons. Only one ship out of every four of ours that sailed during those three months ever came back. And all during that time we weren't smashing up U-boats any faster than the blighters could build new ones. In May they got 550,000 tons, which was just about enough to put us back on our heels. But by that time we'd begun to do a little better with them—that's where your depth charges and Y-guns came in. Pretty soon we were blowing up about two U-boats a week, or so the story went, but, taking all those figures as official and true, you still have a headache when you try to find out why they really slowed down. We sank about sixty-five or six submarines during the year and that means that when the score was totted up they must still have had somewhere around eighty. And they went right on making them. I seem to recall having read somewhere that they had fifty or sixty on the ways when the war ended. Figures furnished by the Germans which you have to take for what they're worth say that during the whole war we sank 178 of their U-boats.

"They credit depth charges and surface shots from patrol ships with fifty-three of the total; mines with twenty; ramming by destroyers or other faster vessels with nineteen; decoy ships—such as Q-boats—with fourteen; nets and similar underwater entanglements with six; aircraft, including the blimps, with five; diving accidents, etc., nine. One of the interesting things about these figures is that the second biggest batch of the lost U-boats got sunk somewhere without a trace and nobody ever knew what happened to them—there were thirty-three of those. And another surprise is that nineteen U-boats were popped off by our submarines. A batch of nineteen ties our subs for third place in the total kill and yet, even now, you'll hear people saying that you can't fight a submarine with a submarine.

"Well, anyway," said the captain, "something stopped 'em in the last war—I'll grant you that. Admiral Jellicoe—or maybe it was the Yank. Admiral Sims—said that if Jerry could have kept fifty U-boats in action along the transatlantic lanes in 1918, Old England's goose would have been cooked. And knowing the way they work and the way we worked then, and listening every blinking night to reports that sound like they were left over from 1917, you just naturally wonder why they couldn't. . . . They had a hundred and eleven of those things when they started the knockdown, drag-out that February, and I'll drink a gallon of palm oil if they didn't have more than that when they inveigled us into signing the Armistice. . . . Now why . . . ?"

There seemed to be a couple of reasons. The counterattack of the Allies may have been ineffective but it was better than none. The U-boats were kept down so that it took two to smash a target that one could have dealt with before. The North Sea mine barrage that the Yank Navy laid forced them to sneak out through the Channel and we made things tougher for them in the Channel.

"Undoubtedly a lot of their boats were damaged in brushes with patrol boats where none had been even bothered in the beginning. So an increasing number had to go home to dry dock for repairs—and considering that a third of their battle force of submarines had to be in dry dock for overhaul anyway, it seems possible that they were considerably short of enough subs to keep fifty in constant action. . . ."

The chief engineer explained this:

"You can take a crate like this one—standard 7,000-ton hull, standard twelve-knot engines—" he said, "and you can run her half a year before you have to start repairing her on the fly. You take a submarine and when she's been out a few weeks she's got to come in for a week's overhaul. . . . I'm not talking about rest and recreation for the crew, that's something else. . . . But she's got to have her engines looked after and her electrical system, and she's got to be examined for leaks and what have you. And if she stays out for a couple of months the amount of repair she needs is going to increase disproportionately. Keep her going long enough and there'll hardly be any sense in bringing her back at all. Subs aren't ships. They're watches."

And that provoked an argument that seemed pertinent to the present situation. "All of that sounds foolish," the captain said. "Looking at it every way I can, I seem to see that the submarines are still the same submarines we had in the last mess except that they're faster and maybe more comfortable for the blighters inside 'em—which is nothing I'm going to hoist any flags about—and they've got better torpedoes. They do just the same things they did in the last war and they do them just the same way. A Heinie never bothers to think a new thought when an old one will do. Well, considering all that, why aren't we putting these fellahs down like we did in 1918, or why aren't we keeping 'em all in dry dock, like you're talking about?"

And even today the chief's answer sounds good. "It's the long hauls," he said. "They're spread out too thin."

"Humph!" said the captain. "If it's thin for us it ought to be thin for them too, oughtn't it?"

"Not necessarily," said the engineer. "A cat with a hundred mouseholes to choose from doesn't necessarily have to watch all of them at once. That's not an exact parallel but you get what I mean." And the captain, who was nobody's fool, nodded agreement.

In the old war, these men recalled, shipping wasn't so bad—even in the bad months of 1917. We didn't have to worry about much in the Mediterranean. You were pretty safe off the coast of France, and once you got south of the Cape Verde Islands you had nothing to worry about except surface raiders all the way to Capetown or Freemantle. . . .

About that time Sparks came in with another message. Another ship of our convoy, or rather of the convoy from which we had detached ourselves to make a run for it alone, had just taken a torpedo out in the wet black a few miles beyond the horizon. There was no question of our attempting to rescue the survivors, as there might have been in that other war that the captain had been talking about, no question of our doing anything but sticking to our erratic course. The men who had not been already blown to bits by the torpedo would undoubtedly die within the next few minutes in the tempest. But we would do nothing about it and the sailors clinging to wreckage in that churning sea would expect nothing of us. Our captain must not bring his ship into an ambush whatever the bait. He must drive on until his own brand of trouble should overtake him and then nobody would do anything for him either.

It is not entirely odd that a vivid picture of that night and the strange table talk of the captain and steward and chief engineer should come back again on a sunny spring day in Mare Island Navy Yard. For on that terrible Christmas in 1940 when one spoke of submarines he meant only one thing—German U-boats. Here, at a submarine officers' mess with some of the brightest young men in the U. S. Navy about me, I had begun to feel with gratitude and pride that when one spoke of submarines one meant only American submarines. And when somebody casually mentioned a report on current sinkings in the Atlantic, memory revived quickly.

Years had gone by. The old ship and her unfrightened crew had survived that night only to be listed sunk a few nights later. But the U-boats were still out there, it seemed. And the scourge that had seemed limitless then had spread far out into the Atlantic.

"Nobody's going to stop them by dropping bombs somewhere near the concrete shelters in Bordeaux and Saint-Nazaire," said somebody across the table. And for a moment it seemed that the chief engineer had only just finished talking.

"The trouble is we're making . . . longer hauls now than we used to before they put this war on. . . . We're spreading our shipping out pretty thin, nowadays. . . ."

And the captain, too, might have been taking a part in this shoptalk of the technicians.

"Come to think about it, shipping wasn't so bad in those days. Once you got past Gibraltar it was duck soup going the rest of the way to China. . . ."

Into this came the dispassionate voice of one of the U. S. submarine skippers sounding like a belated but credible prophet:

"The Heinies are good," he said. "But I don't think they're as good as we've been letting them think they are. Maybe we ought to let some submariners loose for a while to go after them. After all we know all the tricks. . . ."

So some more of that wild night came back and not the least vivid of it the memory of the captain sitting on the side of my bunk with a cup of hot coffee and a sandwich in his hand after he had come down from the bridge at dawn.

"I still believe," he had said, "that the way to win over these goddam subs is to outguess 'em. Do you want to know how they work? Well, I'll tell you."

9

HOW TO RUN A U-BOAT

THERE came after a while the chief engineer and the steward who had been torpedoed aboard the Children's Ship in that gay informality which the constant menace of the U-boats enforced in all ships in those days. And between them they set forth the Doctrine and Practice of U-Boat Operation in a fashion that I have not seen improved upon to this day.

"The principal weapon of the U-boat is its secrecy of movement," the captain said. "If you get a glimpse of it, you've got a chance. If you get one shot at it you generally put it off the surface because a fellah inside an eggshell doesn't want to risk breaking any eggs to make an omelet.

"The German submarine comes fairly well armed aside from torpedoes. It generally has one or two guns of seventy-seven millimeters or larger caliber. Such guns as that are a menace to ships like this. They might make a fatal hole in us at a range of as much as four miles. Also they have a couple of machine guns for use in infighting. But it's my experience that they don't want to do much infighting."

"Only sometimes they do," said the engineer officer. "And when they do they're a blighted nuisance."

"They do," admitted the captain. "Occasionally. After all they don't carry so many torpedoes. Even to a Nazi who can write government chits for any kind of labor, gun shells cost less than torpedoes. So, now and then, you can expect them to stand off and take a sock at you. Mostly they do it at night when they present a silhouette that you can hardly see. When the night is dark enough they are likely to make a lot of trouble. I've known them to sink a cargo carrier and stay on the surface to watch it go down.

Things like that are what burn me up. If they knock me off I'd just as soon they wouldn't be too cocky about it. . . ."

"They're cocky only when they have a right to be," murmured the engineer officer. "They'll never risk a gun fight unless they figure all the odds are on their side in advance."

"Well, anyway," said the captain, "even when they don't break out the deck guns you still have enough to worry about. They carry torpedoes, which are the worst things that could hit you.

"When they hit, of course, it doesn't make any difference to you which one is which. One fish in the engine room of a ship like this will generally finish her. Two are about enough for any unarmored merchant ship. On the other hand, tankers and other ships that have a lot of compartments have been hit by two torpedoes and have come home under their own power."

It didn't sound so sagacious then as it does now in retrospect. Now it looks to me like the epitome of all submarine wisdom. The submarine is deadly but it is also the most vulnerable craft afloat and its limitations must be constantly in the mind of the man who directs its tactics.

The detection devices of submarines—ours as well as theirs—were undiscussed mysteries in those days. But the captain and the chief had definite ideas even on such abstruse subjects. They didn't think the Nazis were doing much shooting by sound despite improvement in echo-ranging since the last war.

"They've done a lot, too, about cutting down their own noise," said the captain. "Nowadays a U-boat proceeding at two to three knots under water is very difficult to pick up. Of course it takes her a long time to get anywhere at a speed like that, but if she can get a couple of hundred yards away from a danger spot in a depth-charge attack, that's fair enough.

"In spite of what we have read about what happened in the last war, a depth charge has to come close to a submarine to rip the hull. The charge merely increases sea pressure to a point where the hull won't stand it and after an explosion has spread through fifteen or twenty feet of sea water there isn't much of the original pressure left. We used to think that whenever we dropped an ash can over the side we busted up all the U-boats in our part of the ocean. Now we know we didn't kill anything but a lot of innocent fish. There's been a lot of eyewash written on that subject."

"And on many another subject connected with the U-boats," mentioned the engineer. "I recall how we were always on the lookout for 'Mother Ships' and 'Floating Bases' in the Southwest Atlantic. . . ."

I was interested because it seemed at the time that the U-boats were never going to be able to bother our Atlantic coast shipping much without some such help. So I asked for a few particulars.

"The first particular," said the engineer, "is that these things are just about the most important seacraft that were ever invented. Any one of these new ocean-going U-boats goes out of its home base with enough fuel aboard to carry it around the world. If it weren't for a few closed alleys such as the Suez Canal I'd say some of them were actually traveling that far. They carry enough other supplies to last them for two or three months—for an indefinite period if they choose to go on short rations. So it seems to me that a submarine operating a couple of thousand miles from home won't need any 'Floating Base' or any arrangement with fifth-column fishermen to get what she needs to stay in business.

"As I see it, about the only thing that would send a U-boat home would be that she needed ammunition. Of course it would be possible to send out an ammunition carrier to fill her up again but in the meantime the crew would have had about all it could take for the trip. Even the Germans have learned by this time that you can't keep a crew out forever and have it function well enough to run a submarine.

"If they were operating some place a few thousand miles from a base they might have to weigh the advantages of coming in to refit and rest the crew. But these boys haven't any such problem. They have a surface speed of eighteen knots or better. So they could leave an ambush point like this one out here and go home and be back here waiting for us by the time we finished our South African run. I've quit looking for 'Mother Ships.'"

"In the first war we used to think that submarines ran around after us submerged," said the captain. "That's one bugaboo we don't have to worry about now. They just aren't running anywhere submerged unless it's making the approach for an attack. And they have to be pretty close in before they dare to try that.

About the best that the new German subs can do submerged is eight knots and they don't carry batteries enough to keep that up for more than a couple of hours.

"At two knots one of them might keep moving for two days— about a hundred miles. But so far as I can make out there's seldom much advantage in doing that except to get out of waters that are swimming with patrol ships. The latest U-boats carry enough oxygen and carbon-dioxide absorbent to stay down for nearly sixty hours. But they can do that only if they spend some of the time resting on the bottom."

"In other words," said the chief, "your U-boat has to obey some of the natural laws. What goes down must eventually come up. For one thing the boat is pretty certain to come up at night to charge batteries and compress air and ventilate, and it's very seldom she comes up very far from the place where she submerged."

"There's been a lot of misinformation going around about how long a German sub has to stay up to get a charge in her batteries —another lot of stuff we learned in the last war. As a matter of fact, in the packs she's on the surface as long as she can stay there, watching convoys from the edge of the horizon and signaling to other subs up ahead or pointing out cripples and slow boats to those behind. Generally she keeps her batteries at full charge in those maneuvers and as a result when you're lucky enough to see her go under she's in a position to give you the horse laugh. If by some unusual turn of luck she has to come up with a flat can it would take her six hours to get a full charge. On the other hand she can take on a half-charge—which is generally plenty to get by on—in a couple of hours."

"All of these rules are flexible, of course," the captain pointed out, "because as long as convoys and escort ships vary their courses and traveling arrangements, the U-boat commanders have to vary their plans of attack. The surface attack—which as the chief says is getting more and more common at night—is a dangerous business for a submarine that goes to work on a convoy in daylight. There have been cases of a surface attack in the daytime, just as there are plenty of cases of attacks with deck guns. But usually the U-boat that hits you by day comes in submerged and fires her torpedoes submerged.

"That's a blessing, naturally, because it limits the field from which you may normally expect a tin fish to come. The speed of the sub in her approach is cut down by more than half and she has to proceed very cautiously, sticking up the periscope for only a few seconds at a time. As a result she has to come in from a position to one side and well forward. The faster you're moving the farther forward she has to be in order to fire a fish at all. Her skipper has to know not only where you are at this second but where you are likely to be a couple of minutes from now and his calculations have to be pretty sharp no matter how accurate his preliminary observations may be. That is why the zigzag course is still the best device we have worked out for foxing him.

"The night attack is something else again . . . as we saw to-night. Convoys have to travel at the speed of the slowest ship and there aren't any very fast ones. In wartime any ship that can carry a cargo is a ship, no matter what kind of a scow she might be in times of peace. So five-knot convoys are no exceptions. A U-boat with a speed of eighteen knots or better is faster than any but the largest and most modern merchantmen and if she can use her speed undetected she has a tremendous advantage. In spite of a lot of superstition on the subject she is a good, seaworthy surface ship and a night like this with a dark, rainy sky and a rolling sea, she is likely to have things pretty much her own way.

"Tonight, for instance, these blighters lay scattered all over the area through which they knew we were going to pass. No lookout on earth could have seen one of them or any dozen of them. It was so dark up topside that I couldn't see the forward winches. But it wasn't so dark that a lookout on the deck of a U-boat couldn't have made out the mass of a lot of ships against the horizon. Maybe a stack threw sparks. Maybe somebody showed a light. . . . Things like that are always happening. Anyway we know that some lookout spotted those ships and the wolf pack came roaring in.

"In a mess like that even one submarine could have done plenty of damage before anybody could figure out exactly where he was. With a dozen or twenty or even fifty boats taking over the job in relays it's no wonder they got five ships. The wonder is that they didn't get the entire convoy.

"On the surface they don't have to maneuver into any spot and wait there for you. They can carry the shot right to you. They can run almost alongside you if it's dark or over the horizon if it's light to a spot well ahead of you. Or they can bore in from an angle somewhat astern. They can angle around until they get you silhouetted against shore lights or a bright spot in the sky, all the time putting the darkest areas behind them. When they finally get you where they want you they toss the fish. And generally the first thing you know about her being in the neighborhood is when the fish goes off and you're hunting around in the water for something to hang onto while you kick at the sharks."

The engineer nodded.

"They've worked out some rules about that," he said, "although when you get around to remembering them it's generally too late.

"You're not likely to see the U-boat herself even in these surface attacks because there's always the chance that in heeling over you may be able to get off a shot from your deck guns and pay her off. It has happened. So she'll most likely dive."

The chief steward, who had come in with more coffee, remained to mention that they were "a very nasty business, these U-boats."

"On the Children's Ship we never knew what hit us," he said. "One minute I was in my bunk and the next minute I was in the water and there I stayed. . . . Plenty of the people on the bridge saw the torpedo track so they didn't have any doubts that it was a U-boat got us. But I don't think anybody really saw the boat herself. There was a lot of talk afterward that she'd come up with a set of dummy sails rigged up and one lad said she had a dummy funnel that had a smoke bomb in it so's she looked like a tug or something. But I think maybe the boys had been reading too many magazine articles.

"We knew the U-boats had been working up there. They'd attacked a couple of ships before we came through and we'd had a good watch out for them. But it's pretty hard to pick out a spot on the water a couple of miles away in a rolling sea. . . . And then they came in a little after four o'clock in the morning—it was just after the watch had changed and the lookout's eyes weren't used to the dark. That's another trick they have.

"But I still don't guess it would have done us much good if we'd seen the periscope a week in advance or if the Nazis had sent us a letter about it. I'm beginning to believe there just ain't much a merchant ship can do about a submarine except man the lifeboats and pray."

"You may call all this palaver just boring," said the captain sadly. "But when you're running up and down this part of the ocean you don't get a chance to think about much else. The Admiralty or somebody is getting out a manual with all sorts of stuff in it about what to do when the U-boat arrives—how to recognize them, how they work, and all that. It'll just go to prove what I'm telling you, that there aren't any very new tricks in the Nazi bag. It's only that we seem to have forgotten what we used to do about the old ones. I guess maybe the steward is right, after all. The only weapon we've got on our side is prayer—and we'll probably need a lot of that."

CREW'S MESS

Meals are generally served in three sittings in the after battery compartment, which at other times is used as a recreation center.

"BUDDHA'S BELLY"

The prominent ends of the torpedo tubes loaded with "fish" 21 inches in diame-

10

KEEP 'EM DOWN

THE LAST I saw of the captain was in Lagos where his ship lay in dry dock for repairs to the damaged bow and, thus constantly reminded of the U-boat menace, he talked of little else. From morning till night his haphazard gun crews got no rest from position drill and loading and aiming drill and blackboard drill. And whenever they were on the point of collapse under the blistering African sun he herded them together in the dining saloon for lectures on the habits of U-boats and the tricks by which a wisely handled ship with good gunners and a few ash cans could fight them off.

His ship, at twelve knots, was faster than most of the cargo carriers that traveled with the convoys, so generally he voyaged alone and he kept hammering into the crew that they had better make a virtue of this necessity. He had an idea that with no destroyer commander's orders to bother him he might be able to work out more elaborate plans for maneuver. At any rate, he said, he wouldn't have to sit and take it boxed in between a couple of five-knotters like a duck at anchor.

"Keep 'em down," was the burden of his harangue. "Maybe we can't hit 'em but if they're down they can't hit us—not if they're far enough down—and that seems to me to be the most important point in all this business.

"When they're below the surface they'll be doing about two or three knots and we can run away from them. On top they can run rings around us. . . . So you see what I mean. . . ."

How much of a chance he got to test out his idea will never be known because he was reported sunk on his homebound trip. But however fantastic he may have sounded in the crowded saloon of a totally unarmored, indifferently armed freighter, subsequent study of his subject shows that he had quite a fund of common sense. You needed to go no farther than the Lagos docks to find verification of that. There was a civilian in the harbor master's office, a man whose arthritis had only recently taken him out of the submarine service, and in the last war and early in this he had seen practical test of all the theory that had been table talk on our ship since Christmas Eve.

"The Old Man probably will make it if he can get the gunners and ash-can dumpers to get out the shots fast enough," he said. "Everybody knows it's a hard job to get a direct hit on a submarine after she dives. In the artillery they'll tell you it's hard enough to hit something you can see, let alone something you can't see. But a submarine at best isn't much more than an eggshell on a larger scale. And no submarine sailor in the world likes to hear dynamite going off in his neighborhood.

"One hit, even from a three-inch gun, on the surface will put any U-boat in Hitler's navy out of action for keeps and a couple of good twenty-millimeter slugs at the bottom of the conning tower would cause a lot of serious damage. The U-boat skippers learned all that in the last war when they were always risking gun fights with Q-boats. It always did look to us like a silly technique for them to stay up where they were at such a disadvantage. I can explain it only with the guess that they were trying to save torpedoes. Nowadays they're bold enough but they're not foolhardy. So when you shoot at them they dive and when they dive with ash cans following them they're in trouble.

"We got a lot of U-boats early in this war because they had to operate in narrow straits and shallow water where we could get at them. When they started to build this new fleet they got ready for deep-water patrols, they got away from the shores and out into the Atlantic, and the boats they sent were a whole lot sturdier and more efficient and harder to catch and harder to destroy. They invented a technique of diving deep to avoid the depth charges and their hulls are very strong. But don't get the idea trouble doesn't follow them even at that.

"The pressure on a submerged object is 4½ pounds to the square inch for every 10 feet of depth. At 300 feet, which is test depth for most of their submarines, the pressure will be 1,350 pounds to the square inch and at such a depth weak spots may show themselves and even under normal conditions there are likely to be leaks. With the added pressure of a depth charge water is likely to come through valves, glands and pipes through the pressure hull, hatches may buckle, gaskets may fail—and all of these things do happen often enough to keep the U-boat commanders worried no matter how successful they may be in their general operations.

"Even before I left the service we had learned of several instances in which a leak caused by a depth charge at a considerable distance put the boat in such a condition that she eventually sank. . . . That is to say, we were certain of what had happened in one case where they succeeded in surfacing for a minute or two and getting some of the crew off. We could suspect it reasonably in other cases.

"We know of numerous other instances where a leak such as that of a buckled hatch could not be kept under by the pumps and the boat had to come topside and surrender or be sunk. And there are lots of reports on actions in which the outer tanks of the U-boat were smashed, causing such fuel losses that she had to withdraw. In such cases her troubles were generally only beginning, because the oil streaks trailing behind her through the water kept the escort ships informed about where she was headed and how fast. Diving planes get jammed by heavy explosions, making it impossible to handle the boat, driving her up to the surface or down to dangerous depths. In almost any severe depth-charge barrage the blasts may leave the hull intact but cause great damage to the electrical installations. Periscope lenses are frequently damaged and while all the ocean-going U-boats carry auxiliary periscopes such accidents have frequently been severe enough to send a boat back to her base. All in all the ash-can slingers may not be 100-percent efficient and, looking at the list of sinkings each month, a lot of surface skippers may have good reason for believing that they're no good at all. But I believe that they justify every shilling spent on them . . . without them things would probably be a lot worse."

I mentioned that I couldn't see how little boats could have lived at all in such seas as those we had come through on our way down from Glasgow and he smiled at me with the tolerance that all submarine people show toward laymen who keep on repeating ancient foolishness.

"They are probably the most seaworthy craft ever devised," he said, "and rough water doesn't bother them as it does other ships, such as destroyers. Of course in extremely heavy seas the sub may be hard to manage on the surface and have to dive or abandon her approach. But even in the worst storms if she finds herself in a favorable position to do it she may come in at right angles to the direction of the sea and do a fairly good job of it. I judge that is what happened up there off the Cape Verde Islands.

"Surface motion except in hurricanes doesn't go very deep and sometimes U-boats are able to maneuver almost normally at periscope depth or maintain an ambush at lower levels, rising to periscope depth for occasional sights or to fire torpedoes. All U-boats have very good sound-detection devices. They can pick up screw noises and are entirely too damned accurate in direction.

"The worst weather for a U-boat is what the old surface skippers used to think best—a calm sea with a long swell running. In conditions like that it is virtually impossible for a submarine to creep up on you unseen. A U-boat is more likely to get under and stay there in weather like that than in a storm. In broken water with whitecaps nobody on earth could pick up a periscope feather and if you did, what of it? With a gale blowing a surface ship is certain to have a tougher time shooting than the U-boat is. On a calm sea even a bad gun crew can hope for a little bit of luck sometimes. . . ."

So in the main it appears that the captain had logic on his side in planning schemes for "keeping 'em under." Whatever happened to him was probably illogical—a thought that would be more comforting were it not for the fact that the illogical and unpredictable seem to be cropping up with such increasing frequency as the U-boats' secret weapons.

With the Mediterranean fleet in 1941 nobody seemed to give much thought to the U-boats. The Italians had started the war with one of the biggest fleets in the world but apparently, like their tanks and their army, they were saving them for something.

Outside *Mare Nostrum* and beyond the range of the land-based bombers skippers were a little more conscious of their menace but they were doing nothing at all in the Red Sea or off the ports of India. Beside Reuter's news-bulletin board in the steaming hotel at Port Sudan hung a few mimeographed sheets outlining principles of German and Italian submarine tactics for the use of itinerant merchant-ship captains but I doubt if anybody ever bothered to look at them save me.

From my point of view they were interesting just as the bulletins were interesting, as information from a strange and fantastic world. For by that time Hitler's new submersible fleet was coming down the ways in quantity and the Admiralty was beginning to be reticent about figures on shipping losses. With the memory of the Cape Verde Islands raid still fresh and poignant, I had been wondering a lot about U-boats and their methods and the men who operated them—much as I have been wondering ever since.

In Port Sudan I learned that the Germans were beginning to slip into the Mediterranean to help out the Italians, most of them, apparently, staying close to bases off North Africa or the boot of Italy. Mine layers were still at work and still were looked upon as one of the most serious menaces of the submarine war. It was mentioned that these boats generally operated in shallow water until they had placed forty-eight eggs by methods not yet revealed. When they had finished this work they were still likely to make a torpedo attack before going home.

One item which it seemed to me had been insufficiently stressed mentioned that ordinary ocean-going submarines had been used as well as the big mine layers for distributing the magnetic mines, Hitler's "secret weapon" from which he had looked for such important results. These charges were generally small and could be thrown out by compressed air from the torpedo tubes as many as three to a tube. Thus a 740-ton U-boat could carry eighteen of them in her tubes and about twenty more as spares. The Germans seem to have been quite clever about this business, sowing their mines at regular intervals or in groups. And the U-boats were persistent even after the widespread use of degaussers on merchant ships had taken the sting out of such devices. On some occasions they were known to have followed mine sweepers through important channels putting down new ones to replace those just swept up.

The big mine layers were generally believed to specialize in moored mines in parts of the North Sea and the Atlantic in depths of from 50 to 500 feet. Such charges, it was said, are dropped into place from inside the boat but the mechanics of the job had not yet been analyzed.

There was one bit of divergence between the Port Sudan estimate of German operating efficiency and those of our chief engineer at Lagos. The chief had figured that one-third of the commissioned strength of the U-boats would be in port at any given time for overhaul and resupply, etc. The Cassandra of the bulletin board thought that two-thirds would probably be at their bases most of the time, apparently basing the estimate on the need for resting the crews and training substitutes. You got what comfort you might out of that as you read an adjoining bulletin to the effect that Hitler was planning to turn out four or five U-boats a week and that he already had more than three hundred in service.

The compilers of the warning didn't seem to think that it made much difference what type of submarine Germany turned out inasmuch as even the trainers would have operating fields where they might turn out to be a sizable menace. It was pointed out, for instance, that they could cover the Baltic quite effectively, leaving the larger ships to plague the Atlantic convoys as they later did.

"All German submarines can be said to be in use against shipping," the notice said, "mainly on the ocean routes. Ocean-going U-boats usually leave and return via the North Sea, proceeding north of the Faeroes and occasionally calling at a Norwegian port. Recently, however, they have established bases in the Bay of Biscay from which they can cover the whole of the North Atlantic down to the Equator regularly, and on extended patrols have been known to operate as far south as the Cape of Good Hope. With bases in the Bay of Biscay there is no necessity for their returning to Germany at all."

There followed a little more elaboration on the captain's theory of the U-boats' system of attack:

"When attacking unescorted ships in open waters, a U-boat will probably try to reach a position well ahead, unseen and on the surface. From this point she will gauge her target's mean course. She will then dive fine on the bow, choosing her position from the point of view of light and the sea. She will attack from an angle of roughly ninety degrees from the target's course, firing one or more torpedoes at a range of 1,000 yards or less.

"When a convoy has an escort that method would be risky. It is unlikely that an attack would be made on a single ship with an efficient escort unless she were known to be of great value; but a convoy so escorted would probably be shadowed, the U-boat proceeding hull down on the horizon. She would then choose her line of attack so as to avoid the escort as much as possible and would dive at high speed on a closing course.

"It takes an appreciable time for a 750-ton U-boat to maneuver under water. Submerged at three knots it may take between five and eight minutes to run through 180 degrees.

"The amount of periscope that will be shown in an approach for attack varies with the weather. In rough water much of it has to be lifted to permit the operator to see over the waves, often as much as two feet and a half. As range decreases less periscope is required and at the end of an approach only about six inches may be above the water.

"In the early stages of the approach a U-boat generally sticks up the periscope once every five minutes for only a few seconds at a time. Near firing position she will raise it every four or five minutes and for not more than two seconds at a time."

And there followed this discouraging bit:

"A periscope as a rule cannot be picked up at more than 2,000 yards even with good glasses." It seemed almost useless to read farther through the dry detachment of the news about how U-boats could receive wireless messages immediately upon surfacing over two jumping wires that run the length of the boat, how she could possibly communicate with other submarines through sound devices submerged, how she could lie without moving for an appreciable time between two layers of water of different densities, how fast she might be expected to complete her dive. . . . But there was something a little less removed from the realities of life in a paragraph or two for the guidance of coroner's juries on the escort vessels:

"Oil on the surface is not any proof that a U-boat has been destroyed unless it is accompanied by air bubbles or continues for a considerable length of time," this notice read. "German submarines are fitted with an arrangement for ejecting oil fuel and use this to mislead or delay their pursuers. Oil on the surface sometimes indicates that a U-boat is submerged or lying on the bottom with internal fuel tanks leaking. A depth charge causes appreciable discoloration of the water and this may sometimes be taken for an oil leak. Oil and bubbles frequently indicate the wreck of a sunken surface ship."

At this point the writer apparently had exhausted most of his information about how you find evidence that you've sunk a U-boat.

"The only certain way to verify the destruction," he concluded naïvely, "is to identify wreckage known to have been inside the boat or to pick up some of the crew."

It is not difficult at all now to recall how those unread messages of warning hung there beneath a lot of fishing-club trophies, their frayed sheets languidly stirred by the hardly noticeable fans. I remember how an R.A.F. flight lieutenant, last man of a task force of twenty-five, watched me copying them and if I heard his voice only distantly then I was to hear it more loudly a couple of years later: "Don't see why we have to worry anything about the U-boats," he said. "Beastly things. They fall to pieces under the water and they kill men forty or fifty at a time. How they get men to serve in those things I never could figure out. . . ."

And I remember also a bulletin that was pinned to the board the next morning.

The *Robin Moore*, an American freighter with the U. S. flag painted on her sides, had been torpedoed somewhere near Capetown. News had just been released of the sinking of an Egyptian ship destroyed by a U-boat on her homeward voyage. Looking back at it I should say that both the aviator and I had small talent for interpreting portents.

11

THE MAKING OF A CREW

A few months before the collapse of France I asked Commander Hillencotter, one of our naval attachés in Paris, what was to prevent the Germans from turning out submarines like model-T Fords on an assembly line. His answer is still good despite the recent ravages of German U-boat packs in the Atlantic.

"If they set their minds to it, nothing," he said. "The Heinies are smart factory men and when they concentrate on producing anything, from airplanes to rowboats, they'll roll 'em out. Right now their shipyards are laying down one sub a week, and they may possibly produce four or five, or more. But don't let that upset you too much. They can't produce the crews.

"Submarine crews aren't like those of any other ship. Every man aboard has to know not only how to do his own job perfectly but when to do it. He moves in split-second timing with everybody else in the boat. The crew has to function not part of the time but all of the time, like a Rockne backfield. And when it doesn't, we have a *Squalus* or a *Thetis* or a *Phenix*. It takes years to develop that sort of perfection and I don't think Hitler is going to have the time."

At that moment, January 1940, the German subs had been taking a discouraging beating. Of the sixty boats with which they had entered the war, twenty were in dry dock or unable for other reasons to leave their home bases at Wilhelmshaven; thirty-five were reported on excellent authority to have been sunk. Commander Hillencotter's comment had in it a combined warning and a solace, neither of which seemed to be worth more than an academic interest until the world upheaval began to be felt in Iowa and Mississippi and New Mexico. Then we began to wonder if

73

the Nazi drillmasters had been training children for years in rhythmic valve-turning and lever-pushing exercises as they had been training them in other strange arts. Of a sudden the U-boats were running up and down our coasts virtually unchecked, strewing the Florida beaches with wreckage and smashing up ships within sight of New York Harbor. The mass production of submarines certainly had come, as Commander Hillencotter had said it might. And, you realized with a shock, there seemed to be no lack of skillful and willing hands to run them.

Here was another submarine puzzle steadily increasing in importance, and when I got to the New London submarine base I put it before Commander Lew Parks, then aide to Admiral Freeland Daubin.

"Hillencotter was right," he said. "The Germans reached the elastic limit of their crew expansion a long time ago. They have kept on building submarines and in one way or another they have manned them. But you can take it as an opinion based on experience that our chief weapon against the German submarine menace in the Atlantic is going to be the personnel of the German submarine. From now on the more boats they try to put in commission, the worse they'll be handled. And that is not wishful thinking. It's a matter of mathematics.

"As against that, German submariners don't need so much training as ours as long as they hunt in packs. They attack mostly on the surface at night and they never have to go very far. U-boats strung out along the sea lanes tip one another off about approaching targets, and all any of them have to do is lie there in ambush and wait." Commander Parks ought to know. He established a lot of rules for this business.

"It takes a long time to train a good submarine captain to make an approach submerged. He sticks up his periscope for a five-second look every five minutes. And in that little time he has to size up his target—the number of ships in an enemy convoy, for example, their direction and speed, their position with reference to one another and with reference to himself, their bearing off his bow. They may be zigzagging and if so he has to figure their mean course. Finally when he fires a torpedo he has to make a calculation based on bearing, and range, the target speed, the speed of the submarine, and he has to determine not where the enemy ship is at the moment of firing but where it is going to be when the torpedo comes up to it.

"In addition to that, the picture the captain sees through the periscope is in segments—jigsaw pieces that he has to put together in his mind. It is never the same twice as he looks at it. When he is twisting, the target is also twisting. And while he is figuring all these details of the target's course and speed and his own course and speed, and the constantly changing relative positions, he has to make his run in, and keep from broaching all the times he's doing it.

"As a matter of routine, he has to know not only his own job but that of every man on the boat from grease monkey to navigator. He is not alone in that. Every officer aboard has to know how to do everything that is to be done by anybody in the enlisted or commissioned personnel.

"The men undergo a training just as rigorous. Every sailor has to know every other sailor's duties, and by the time he is graduated from a school such as the one we have here, he does. Submerging nowadays, when every dive is what we used to call a 'crash dive'—a dive under the power of the Diesels—requires precise timing in closing hull openings one after another in the correct order. The men have to be taught to do those jobs more or less automatically. They have to know all the tricks of emergency operation and repair. It is only when they do these things as a sort of second nature and in teamwork with everybody else that they can be called a first-class crew. Such a routine as that is not learned overnight nor out of books.

"The chief petty officers aboard a submarine are selected for unusual skill at all jobs and outstanding skill at some of them—such as Diesel operation. They are always men of long and varied experience. Men of the submarine service are paid on a scale fifty percent above the base pay aboard surface ships for men of their rating. In addition to that they get ten percent bonus for sea duty, and considering what is required of them they are worth it."

Aboard a submarine once she is at sea the captain is probably the most independent officer in any of the services. And, inasmuch as he is the sole director of battle, the sole judge of tactics and policy, and generally the only man who actually sees what is going on in an engagement he gets a loyalty and respect from his crew entirely at a variance from their free and easy discipline.

The executive officer as on the surface ships is second in command and his battle station is generally beside the captain.

The diving officer is normally the chief engineer. However, any officer aboard is able to dive the ship and the job in an emergency falls automatically to the officer of the deck.

All of the men in the crew have double jobs. A yeoman may stand a quartermaster's watch. The pharmacist's mate generally runs the laundry, such as it is. On Lieutenant Commander Robert Rice's boat he did both those things, wrote up the daily log and was also chief sound man. Captain Rice discussing this versatility observed, "I don't know when he got his housework done."

Machinists may have stations at the diving-plane controls or serve with the gun crews. The mess boys also have battle posts and are part of the intricate ballet that does the valve closing when the klaxon sounds.

The cook may likewise be a torpedo man or hold one of the controls at the air manifold because, like everybody else, he knows every job on the ship. However, most of the time, in hell or high water, he cooks. He may have other talents but he has been selected chiefly because he is a good cook. The food in the underwater navy is the best in any armed service in the world and the skippers have no patience with can-opener chefs.

The radioman gets out a little newspaper every day—and the title of his publication is seldom the same any two days in a row. The news has less variety.

Routine work is not tedious although a certain amount of daily housecleaning is necessary to keep the boat habitable and clean. Button polishing, however, is a skill left ashore. Because each man has his special job to do there are no bos'ns chasing the men around on a submarine. There is a lot of complicated machinery to be kept oiled. Electrical equipment has to be kept dry. And that takes up quite a lot of the time between battles.

Mostly the men sleep on long voyages—but quite a lot of the time they read. At the end of each patrol the entire ship's library of 150 current books is traded for another one.

Captain Rice said of this life of boredom that the men take to it more kindly now than they did before we got into the war.

"Before the war," he observed, "the close quarters of the submarines produced all sorts of squabbles. But Pearl Harbor brought a change.

"Nowadays the men seem to be conscious of the important issue of winning the war. They overlook minor faults in one another just as you get to overlook them in a wife. They refuse to let themselves be annoyed by trivia. . . ."

Maybe it's the reaction of the men who are constantly sharing dangers. It doesn't seem to matter so much that Joe Doaks has an irritating laugh or that John Doe said the Giants were bushleaguers that day when the clunks started to bust. Anyway there is peace most of the time in the submarines for all the war that is going on outside.

"The men of the submarines have always had a hard job without much glory. In peacetimes they were the hardest-worked crews in the Navy. At sea we were doing our maneuvers just as the other ships did. In port we were always tearing down engines or refitting or something. Other ships got holidays—the pig boats, no.

"In war they are a little better off because everybody realizes that they have to be rested periodically in decent surroundings. But they are fighting the toughest kind of war. They have learned a lot, and the boats have been coming back from the hot corners until today our submarine service is actually the safest military service in the world. But it isn't pleasant to be depth-charged. To function normally when the bombs are coming down requires guts of the highest order.

"Depth-bombing is like being in a darkened auditorium where one man has a gun. . . . Every time you take a step he shoots. You are certain of that but you never know where the next shot is coming from. . . . That's really how it is.

"Our operations are proving that we still have well-trained crews. As a corollary, the Germans are having their troubles. We may not have sunk enough of them to discommode their submarine-war plan in the Atlantic, but we have bagged more than would have been possible if all their boats were manned by the same sort of crews we have. They get into trouble when they work submerged. They broach and betray themselves regularly. And on several occasions not only their crews but their officers have shown that they lack something in discipline.

"For example, take the instance of the U-boat that came up and surrendered when it was being bombed by a British airplane. There was no way to explain that except that the men aboard were green and afraid of bombs.

"Don't make any mistake about it, the Germans know a lot about submarines. In the last war they made a terrific weapon out of them. They hammed it because they drove their crews too hard. And you'd figure they probably learned a lesson. Submarine crews have to be good to start with, and they have to be rested. In the army the fighting is done in spurts, with lulls between. In the air force the men have to fight only about five minutes at a time, every now and then. In the submarines a man is sealed up with his job sometimes for months at a stretch. So they have to be given some time in port when they come in. Which means that if the Nazis are to maintain fifty boats in the Atlantic with efficient crews, they will probably have to man 150. Despite the bombing of bases and factories I should think that the crew problem is still Hitler's biggest headache. . . ."

Admiral Daubin agreed with this.

Submarines in sufficient numbers can make themselves very nearly unbeatable—he said—but when I say a sufficient number I don't mean just boats . . . I mean boats properly manned. German submarines came very close to winning the last war with all the mistakes the high command made. And they would have won it, too, if Tirpitz had got more crews trained and more boats in commission before he started his unrestricted warfare. Those U-boats destroyed 15,000,000 tons of British shipping, which doesn't need a label to be recognized as a terrific economic loss. But, in spite of all the propaganda that was put out during the war and later when naval-restriction agreements were being debated, the record shows that only 15,000 lives were lost on our side as a result of this destruction.

Fifteen thousand lives represent a serious casualty list it is true— a shocking and horrible list—but one must remember that the communiqués of 1915-1916 which shuddered at the menace of the U-boat and called the civilized world to war over such outrages as the sinking of the *Lusitania* were recording other casualty lists with greater objectivity: "Our troops advanced half a mile today in the Amiens sector. Our losses were 25,000. . . ." "Two hundred thousand Russians have been destroyed in the Masurian Lakes region by von Mackensen's latest coup." "French casualties in the Verdun area are reckoned at a quarter-million as of August 15. . . ."

Today it is a bit trite to say that history is repeating itself. As a matter of fact history is still proceeding logically from the point where we ceased to keep track of it in 1918. The submarine is still with us and is still the most dangerous and unpredictable weapon of the war—but with this exception: it is just as effective this time on one side as it is on the other. Looking only at such figures as have been released in Navy communiqués, we find it evident that U. S. submarines have been conducting a continuous and unrelenting harassment of Japanese shipping in the Pacific since December 7, 1941. The submarines were able to operate with full efficiency from the very first, which is not surprising inasmuch as you can't have a submarine that isn't a hundred-percent efficient at all times. They were at their jobs an hour after the blast at Pearl Harbor, and they have been working on a schedule like that of a suburban bus line ever since. They are constantly whittling at Hirohito's supply lines to the far island bases and Indo-China and New Guinea and the East Indies. With a personnel of only a few thousand men afloat, submerged and ashore, they have accounted for more Japanese tonnage than all the other arms of the service put together. And if nothing were to stand in the way of their increased use it seems likely that they could dispose of most of the Japanese threat to the rest of Asia unassisted.

But in the meantime the policy of war seems to have other objectives. Priorities for war materials are given in order of the importance, and the function, of the thing for which the materials are to be used. And submarine construction is far down on the list.

Up ahead of the submarines are corvettes and cruisers and blimps and cargo carriers and convoy artillery and all the thousand

and one things that have become necessary for assuring that vital war materials shall get past the wolf pack of German U-boats which in a year of battle has defied extinction. What this amounts to is that our submarines cannot expand their program of destruction because the German submarines have already expanded theirs.

It is an interesting if not pleasant thought that in the circumstances about one-half of our war effort—our daily work and sacrifice, our dazzling taxes—may be totted up not against the might of Hitler's arms but against a handful of Diesel-powered iron pipes with which he has cluttered the Atlantic sea lanes.

The submarine, to put it more definitely, is with us just as it was in 1917. And we can't make it go away or erase it from our lives merely by refusing to look at it. And the experts can have the job of figuring out how we are going to throttle Hitler's submarine fleet without at the same time throttling our own.

He looked at me then quizzically.

"As for the crews and what it takes to make them, you'll never be able to believe what we tell you until you see for yourself," he said. "You had better put on your dungarees, my friend, and go out and learn how a submarine is run."

So I went.

12

INSIDE THE BARREL

No LANDLUBBER, no matter how active his imagination—no matter how extensive his theoretical information—can ever be prepared for what hits him squarely in the eyes the first time he drops through the hatch of a submarine.

I picked my way cautiously through the chill of a dark morning over the slats of falsework that make up the more or less familiar outlines of a deck. I let myself through a watertight door into the conning tower, conscious all the while of dampness that was just as I had expected it to be and the slight hint of mildew—or perhaps iodine—in the cold dead air, plus an elusive but easily identifiable smell of fish.

The conning tower, you feel with some disappointment, is no great surprise. It is an iron room about ten feet by twelve with a rack of pilot books and a wheel at one end, numerous sounding gear, navigational and fire-control indicators about the walls. It might be part of the equipment of any cruiser save for a couple of polished steel pipes about ten inches in diameter that run through it from ceiling to deck like pillars—the periscope tubes. And these, as the boat lies in her berth, seem no more novel or significant than the old scissors telescopes of the artillery which they somehow resemble.

So, deceived by familiar things all about you as you come aboard, you are in no proper frame of mind to slide down a steel ladder and find yourself in a world as remote from reality as Mars.

The first thing that amazes you is the dazzling brilliance of it all. Somehow I had imagined that the inside of a submarine—a ship without ports, with no eye to the outside save the periscope—must be dimly lit and rusty and dank and grim. I had envisioned the routine of it as something like life at the bottom of a well or in one of the more crowded corners of the Paris sewer. I had fore-seen, probably as a result of looking at sundry moving pictures, that it would be a puzzle of tubing and wire and control wheels, but I had felt I would become aware of these things largely through a sense of touch. And then my feet hit the deck at the bottom of the ladder and my eyes blinked in the flood of a hundred lamps and I saw something like a hospital operating room in which somebody had mislaid the equipment of a comic-strip rocket ship.

The bulkheads curving overhead were white, the brasswork shining. And there was no smell to the place save for the clean engine-room attars of oil and brass polish and a whiff of coffee from somewhere forward.

The boat I went out on first was a trainer of ancient vintage but, I was to learn, very little different save in size from the big new ones that we were sending out into the Pacific—very little different for that matter from the big new ones that the Germans have been sending into the Atlantic. From the point of view of a neophyte in search of knowledge it had points over the modern boats in which I sailed later, in that you could see all of it from engine room to forward torpedo compartment through a succession of open doors as you stood at the foot of the conning-tower ladder.

As in all submarines this chamber under the conning tower is the control room. On the port side of it, behind the ladder, are the depth gauges and the apparatus that works the diving planes—fins fore and aft that determine the angle of descent and ascent like the hands and feet of a human diver. Forward of the gauges is an indicator board with which submarine-disaster investigations have made the general public more or less familiar—the "Christmas tree." This is nothing but a bank of red and green lights, one red and one green for every vent and valve in the ship—every opening through the hull. When a valve is open its indicator light shows red. The lights save for a couple of ballast-tank indicators must all be green when the ship dives.

The forward bulkhead is cluttered up with engine and motor controls and speed indicators and sounding gear. Along the star-board side of the room range the electrical meters and fuse boards and the compressed-air manifolds and pump controls by which ballast may be shifted from one tank to another or blown out into the sea. A gyro compass and electrical steering lever are just behind the engine-control boards. Aft of the conning-tower ladder is the periscope, and behind that along the bulkhead are a desk and some odds and ends of radio equipment.

I didn't find all this out immediately. It took a couple of hours of concentration and a lot of patient explanation from some experienced officer to make me see anything but a chaos of gauges and meters and cables and leads as purposeless and untraceable as if they had been tossed there by an eaves swallow with plumbing experience. Eventually when I learned to look at certain assortments of levers and gauges *en banc*—thirty or forty of them at a time—I began to see that after all this weird mechanism is a necessarily complicated means to produce fundamentally simple results.

Experts say that the submarine has undergone no radical changes since 1905, and that seems to be conservative. In principle it does not seem to have changed to any great degree since the storage battery and the Diesel engine gave it motive power and the periscope gave it eyes.

You have a cylindrical hull pointed at the ends and flanked by ballast tanks. Water may be admitted from the sea to any of these tanks, or pumped from one tank to another for purposes of balance, or blown into the sea by compressed air. You have diving planes, or fins, at the bow and stern of the boat, and by changing the angle of these you determine the slant of the boat as she descends or surfaces. You have oil-consuming Diesel engines to drive the ship on the surface, battery-fed electric motors to drive her submerged. You have a periscope, a telescopic device that rides up and down in a well through the hull. You have a set of deck guns that can be fired on the surface, and a set of torpedoes that can be shot through torpedo tubes fore and aft with compressed air when submerged. Every submarine in the world very likely has all of these contrivances and none has anything of much importance besides.

Contrary to a belief general among landsmen, the submarine does not submerge as a bottle does when you shove it below the surface and let it fill with water. When "rigged for diving" it is in what the trade knows as a "state of neutral buoyancy," which roughly means that it rides just about awash on the surface, so balanced that a few pounds more weight would send her under, a few pounds less bring her superstructure well up out of the water. In this condition various tanks have been loaded with the weight which the trim of the boat requires. The bow buoyancy tank (which in modern boats is in the space between the inner and outer hull just forward of the control room) and Number One and Number Two main-ballast tanks (also in the space between the hulls and near the middle of the ship) are principal agents in the descent.

All of these tanks have two openings. One large one, the Kingston valve, is on the bottom leading to the sea. A second is an air vent on the top. When rigged for diving the Kingston valves of the main-ballast tanks and bow buoyancy are opened. They are then in the condition of a teacup inverted in a pan of water which remains dry because the air inside it prevents the water from coming in. The opening of the vents on top of the tanks will allow the air to escape and the sea to rush in. The process of proceeding with the bottoms of the tanks open thus becomes known as "riding the vents."

There are numerous holes in the hull that have to be closed before it is safe to dive—the hatches for instance and the conning-tower door. In addition to that, the radio antenna operates through a valve, and there are eight or ten pipes of varying diameter which pierce the hull for engine exhaust, waste discharge, ventilation exhaust, etc. The principal holes are one very nearly a yard wide which supplies air to the engines—"Engine induction," they call it—and another labeled "Hull induction," which is about twenty inches in diameter and feeds the ventilation system. Electrically and hydraulically operated valves close off these holes at the touch of a button in the control room but each has somewhere in the line behind it a manually operated "flapper" valve just as insurance in case—as happened in the tragic dive of the *Squalus*—something should jam.

When the klaxon sounds the diving alarm the holes are closed, but not in any haphazard order. Engine induction is left to the last or until word is passed that the Diesels have stopped. Otherwise, turning over with everything else closed up, they might suck their air from whatever source available and create a vacuum in the ship. The bridge is cleared. The men who have been on duty above tumble down the ladders and dog the hatches. The vents are opened on the required tanks. The planes are set for the angle of dive. The electric motors are switched on and the boat starts down.

Literally she is driven down by motors and fins, with the increasing weight on the ballast tanks giving more and more aid to the descent. At a depth ordered by the captain she is leveled off and placed on an even keel by the shifting of water in trim tanks. Motor speed is reduced to just enough to keep her level. And all of this happens in literally a matter of seconds. And that is where complicated machinery is of minor importance and the efficiency of the crew is everything.

When you have seen a dive—even a training-boat dive—you have seen a co-ordination of human effort such as no ballet has ever duplicated. I called to mind Commander Hillencotter's remark about the Rockne backfield and I found the comparison in error only through conservatism. . . . These boys have to be a little faster, a little more sharply timed, a little more aware of what everybody roundabout is doing, than any team that ever played for Knute Rockne or anybody else.

They move to their stations with a deceptive lack of effort. Save in the rain of men through the conning-tower hatch you are not aware of any great bursts of speed. But when you have seen every station manned ten seconds after the first clamor of the alarm you can assure yourself that it wasn't through any accident and that it couldn't have been done if there had been any wasted movement whatever.

You look at this performance and then you go away and sit down somewhere slightly dizzy. Outwardly you have looked at the most nondescript mob ever assembled in the hold of a ship— lads in dungarees or skivvies or college sweaters moving about with no semblance of military order, with no semblance of any kind of order. They converse with their officers as equals—even argue with them. No two of them ever seem to be doing anything for the good of the ship at any one time. They are lolling on the deck of the torpedo room or raiding the icebox in the galley aft of the radio shack. To anybody who ever looked at a Navy muster they must seem the worst-disciplined lot who ever put to sea.

Yet if they are to stay alive, they must have the most precise discipline required of any sailors in the U. S. service—the inflexible discipline of the moving cam and the mutually moving roller—the unvarying discipline of the levers in the escapement of a watch. You know, even if you know nothing about submarines, that they must have that. And in astonishment after you have seen them work you know that somehow they do have it. You can't detect it in action. You can't overlook its presence in the results. And the more you look at it the more you respect the judgment of the commander in Paris who told you what it was going to be like.

"Every man has to be able to do his job in all circumstances in the same unvarying fraction of a second," he had said. "If he doesn't do it he dies and so, very likely, does everybody else. There can never be any such thing as a seventy-five-percent-efficient submarine. . . . Not for very long."

You begin to wonder how the Germans are making out.

13

"TAKE HER DOWN!"

So WE went under.

The order "Rig for dive" had come from the bridge through the loudspeaker system and what happened then had been like the lap dissolve in a moving picture or the mingling of two separate events in a dream. Every man within sight—and I could see half the crew of this abbreviated tub from the foot of the ladder—had turned casually from what he was doing to do something else. The mess boy, carrying two cups of coffee into the coop known grandiosely as the wardroom, had casually hung both cups on the forefinger of his right hand, reached up for one of the copper wheels in what a landlubber would call the ceiling, and had closed one of the vents before the order had ceased to echo. He hadn't spilled a drop from either of the cups but his skill went for nothing. The officers who had been waiting to drink the coffee were already on their way to the chaos of the control room. The technician was putting on the headphones of the sound apparatus in the bow torpedo room. The black gang was pouring aft into the motor room. The cook was hanging to another bronze wheel above his galley.

There is always some tension about a dive order that you can't detect or define—less tension, perhaps, than consciousness of mutual dependence. Perhaps in training each gob gave it expression to himself: "If I muff my play, you'll muff yours. You muff yours, and curtains for everybody." And the idea lingers long after anybody has bothered to put it into words. The sense that something important is going on clings to this maneuver no matter how often it is done. For, as the captain explained it, any man's mistake is as good as the next man's and on a submarine no mistake is unimportant.

The conning tower had been shut before we got into the control room. The captain had come down from the bridge and returned to the so-called wardroom to pick up some of the abandoned coffee. The executive officer who was to take over the ship stood near the glistening shaft of the periscope.

The control room in ships of the "O" class is about ten feet square and littered with the same amount of mysterious impedimenta that you'll find in the larger types. This one was like an election headquarters at six o'clock after the closing of the polls, jammed with as many people as could find standing room and thick with the atmosphere of melodrama.

"A pipe fitter's nightmare," somebody had called this cabinet of Dr. Caligari. And as you watched the men taking their corners at valves and switches you felt a despairing sense of your own ignorance, plus something of a fear that no collection of human beings could ever make so abstruse a puzzle as all this work out right. . . .

"Rigged for diving," the diving officer reported.

The officer of the deck answered: "Clear the bridge." The chief of the boat at his post in the control room sounded the dive alarm on the klaxon. The people on the bridge started to pop through the conning tower and down the ladder. The last man down was the quartermaster who secured the latch. By that time the boat was already on her way down, the water breaking about the foot of the conning tower.

"Pressure in the boat, sir," reported the diving officer. The officer of the deck answered, "Very well."

"Secure the air," said the diving officer.

All this ritual has a simple explanation. The diving officer sets one hand of the barometer at atmospheric pressure as the boat dives. With all hull openings reported closed he releases compressed air and watches the barometer. If the boat is tight the needle shows increased pressure. If the needle doesn't move there is a leak. . . .

You became conscious of an unusual approach to silence. There was a throb of motors in the air, accompanied by occasional squeaks and strains—unaccountable sounds, but all casual conversation had ceased. All through the boat men were concerned with nothing but their immediate jobs, their attention fixed on myriads of brass wheels, their ears lifted for the next command.

The Christmas tree had been green for some seconds now. The first phase of the dive had been accomplished in good order.

"Take her to thirty-six feet," ordered the skipper pro tem.

"Thirty-six feet," repeated the diving officer.

The diving officer, during all this ticklish operation, was standing between the two big brass wheels that give manual control to bow and stern planes in an emergency. Alongside him a couple of enlisted men worked things like elevator handles that controlled machine operation of these fins. Over each handle was a level indicator and above the indicators hung two big clocks around which long white hands crawled to show the depth of water in feet between the keel and the stormy surface of the Atlantic. Every few seconds the diving officer tapped these gauges to make sure they weren't sticking. The men at the handles glanced up quickly whenever he did it. But mostly their eyes were kept fixed on the little white bubbles in the little red tubes that showed how the boat was maintaining its angle of dive. Presently the hands of both gauges rested at thirty-six. The diving officer called, "All ahead normal . . ."

All this had taken a little more than sixty seconds from the time when I had set down my coffee cup on the wardroom table and moved in to watch the drama of the control room!

The diving officer had taken charge of the speed of the boat from the moment when the Diesels stopped and the motors took over and would remain in charge until he reported his final trim. (The boat is in trim when she is virtually at neutral buoyancy, and will hang suspended where she is leveled off, with no help from the propellers.)

While the boat was diving the hands on the ammeters above the motor control stood at 1,500, and the engineer officer reported speed by mentioning that we were "drawing fifteen hundred a side." In this operation the batteries were in series, the speed high and the drain terrific. At the command "All ahead normal," the men at the rheostats cut down the amperage to 600 a side. Later, when control had been established, they shifted the battery connections to parallel and proceeded at "50 amps a side" which means a speed of about two knots.

"Pump from forward trim to sea through manifold," ordered the diving offcer. "Report when you have fifteen hundred in forward trim."

Like acolytes at a Solemn High Mass, the serious-faced young men went through their various rites—the bubble watchers, the wheel spinners, the lever pushers, the handle turners.

"Fifteen hundred in forward trim," sang out a man in the corner who had been looking at some gauge that none of the rest of us could see.

"Very well," said the diving officer. The ship was on even keel, moving forward at two knots. The dive was finished. I tried, with some difficulty, to analyze the experience.

Here we were, at periscope depth and leveled off—down among the dead men with nothing to remind us of our presence in the weird half-world of the deep save the continuing unreality of the vehicle in which we had come. I looked around and wondered if Death itself would someday turn out to be as complete an upset of forecasts and philosophies as this had been. Death would be only a little more permanent separation from the old routine—certainly no greater one—than this journey from the land world to the region of the fishes. Yet except for the momentary thrill of watching the diving crew in their formless ballet, and the momentary chill when one of the men on the plane controls let the bubble go skittering and the captain cautioned, "Don't let it get away from you!" there had been no hint of adventure in this trip, no sense of danger or accomplishment. We had seen nothing. We had felt little. This, insofar as the norms of a man's life are concerned, had been a voyage between home and somewhere in interstellar space. But there had been less novelty about it than I had once noted crawling down through an air lock into the pressure-filled boiler rooms of the old *Swayback Maru.*

The executive let me look through the periscope and I got a hazy glimpse of the world above, a world filled with whitecaps and snow. We were still moving at two knots but totally without any feeling of motion. Even through the periscope—the window through which as through the door of a tomb we looked back into the blustery open spaces from which we had come—there were few signs that we were going anywhere.

Over in the distance on the rim of the horizon was a gray point of land with a white storm wreathing it, and a little closer at hand a ship plunged onward through the roaring channel. And as I looked at it all my old feeling about the unearthliness of this service came back to me. I felt like a detached spirit looking on his one-time associates from Olympian heights—or rather from Stygian depths. I felt like a spy from another planet. Less poetically, I felt as if I were looking through somebody's keyhole.

I gave the periscope back to the executive. The business of living in two worlds at the same time was too much of a strain. I went up to the forward torpedo room where eight or ten youngsters stood about a chief petty officer learning how you fire a torpedo. They weren't going to fire any torpedo this time—the spit of land I had seen in the crystal ball of the periscope was still ours, and the ship rolling about up there in the blizzardy channel was also ours. The torpedoes with their war heads lay locked in their cradles. But the technique of loosing them could still be demonstrated—harmlessly. . . .

"You open the outer door. . . . You bleed air in through this valve. That gives you so many pounds of pressure in this chamber. The air can't get past this chamber till you push this lever. . . ."

Over the loudspeakers came the voice of the skipper in the control room: "Stand by to fire Number Two. . . ."

The torpedo crew stood alert, facing a bank of two-foot circular disks which, but for their polished brass rims and white enameled surfaces, might have been fire doors in a boiler room. Beyond these circles, of course, lay the torpedo tubes with outer caps that could be opened or shut from this compartment.

"Fire Number Two!"

The chief pushed the lever so that the pent-up air went out to meet the sea, pushing a column of water ahead of it. There was a hiss like that of the compressed air in a cruiser's guns, then an indescribable rush as the water came back into the tube.

"Close all doors," ordered the chief. "Open this valve. . . ."

Shadowboxing all of this, part of the mumbo jumbo of this fanciful existence under the sea—a shade ludicrous, it seemed, but not too ludicrous. It was only a matter of geography that the ship out there was not an enemy ship, that the water slug which the boys had just put back into the ocean had not been a war-headed torpedo.

I went aft again and heard the engineer officer explaining some facts of life to some of the crew in training. He outlined the phenomenon of the air cushion that keeps the sea out of the main-ballast tanks when the Kingstons are open and the vents closed, and he pointed out the overhead "B" vent control where some one man must shut off the escaping air on signal or let the ship plunge to dangerous depths. . . . And he went into the matter of "trimming."

"If the ship is heavy over all after reaching depth," he explained, "trimming is begun by pumping water from the regulator tank [a small tank amidships] to the sea. If it is still heavy after the water has been blown out of the regulator, the technique is to pump from the auxiliary tank to the sea—the 'auxiliary' or 'safety' tank being something like the permanent water ballast in a surface ship. It is filled up as the voyage goes on, to compensate for decrease in weight due to firing of torpedoes, consumption of supplies. . . .

"If there is undue heaviness forward or aft, water can be pumped out of the forward or after trim tanks which carry 2,000 gallons."

There was nothing much in this watery discussion for anybody taking his first dive in a submarine. But I did get something out of it: The best way to run a submarine, it appears, is to use as little compressed air as possible. Then you'll have it when you need it.

We surfaced three or four times. Once I was at the periscope and had the uncanny sensation of seeing our bow suddenly bubble up out of the the water, and then the black deck come after it with a swirling froth breaking off of it. This was easily the outstanding trick of the day—juju like the old Town Hall Concourse of Magic in which the magician dissociated himself from his own shadow. We came out of the water like a leaping salmon, and the executive officer murmured something warmly about plane angles. And we dived again—and again. The quiet young men changed places at the controls, and we stayed for a few more hours in this Never-Never Land.

In the wardroom, as is customary in wardrooms the world over, we talked of everything save the commonplaces of life in front of our eyes—the rubber situation, recent raids on Berlin, the economic condition of the South, sharecropping and, of course, the Civil War. One always gets to the Civil War in Navy conversations. You couldn't help it with so many of Dixie's sons in ships on the sea or under it. And any one of them can tell you what size collar General Lee wore and what delayed Longstreet at the battle of Gettysburg. . . . Just the same, when I heard Pickett charging across Minister George Waller's living room in Luxembourg three years ago I didn't think that the echoes were ever going to overtake me on the bottom of an ocean.

The engineer officer and the executive had recently come back from the Pacific. The engineer officer had spent some time with a submarine on patrol off Japan—a journey on which they took a large bag of ships. He had seen a ship, torpedoed from short range, blow up in twenty seconds, with a blast that had almost sunk the submarine. He had helped the ship crawl along the bottom while depth charges came down and Japanese destroyers roared back and forth overhead like vagrant express trains. He had been part of an attack from which, thanks to tide and bad weather, there was only one narrow way out. And like everybody else on his boat he had discounted his chances for survival when Jap destroyers chased them into shallow waters.

They had seen doom in preparation for them. Through the periscope they had watched, for a fraction of a second, the planes that were to hunt them down. . . .

Ashore, the story would have been stirring enough—a yarn like one of Verne's accounts of adventure on Mars. Here, in a submerged submarine, it was a simple recital of everyday life, a narrative as nearly routine to those in the submarine service as a report of latitude and longitude in the ship's log. Submariners expect submarines to sink ships, just as they expect them to sit down in lightless waters like those we were in at the moment. All at once I began to grasp a great truth about the reticence of the Silent

Service. It isn't shyness that keeps its members from reciting its magnificent saga—it's just that heroes of sagas probably don't realize their importance.

We cut off this conversation to have another look at the silent watch in the control room. We'd been under a couple of hours, but many of the men were smoking. Back in the engine compartment you could see the blue haze of Diesel exhaust lingering still, despite blowers, despite the long idleness of the engines. But the air seemed as sweet as when we had come in. Cigarettes were glowing, matches were still lighting and you could still see through the atmosphere as far as the other side of the room.

The second dive was straightening out.

"All ahead normal. . . ."

"Blow regulator to 500. . . ."

"Regulator 500, sir."

"What's the reading on the forward trim?"

"Nine thousand, sir."

And from the executive:

"Fire Four!"

"Secure the tube!"

"Secure Number Four."

Still the routine of the diving officer goes on. Always his eyes are on the depth gauges. Always he's tapping them with nervous fingers. . . .

And afterwhile we come up.

You know when the ship has reached the surface because of the shake she gives. And in quick order come the diving officer's commands:

"Low pressure pump on main drain. Close Number One Kingston. Open Number One drain."

"Number One Kingston closed, sir."

"Close Number Two Kingston. . . ."

And the voice of the executive cuts into the dialogue:

"Down periscope!"

"Number Two closed, sir. . . ."

"Open Number Two drain. Open hatch. Ready on engines."

There is a hiss of air as the hatch opens. Bells ring in the engine room. The ammeters stand at zero.

"Rig in bow planes. Put stern planes on ten rise!"

The throb of the Diesels shakes the hull again, and an icy draft sweeps down to them across the deck.

"Stern planes at zero," orders the diving officer.

Somebody comes down the ladder tracking a bit of slush.

You can get out on the slippery iron deck now and look once more at the world you were born in. You do it.

14

THE NEW SUBS

ONE zero day I crawled along over a string of snow-covered box-cars to the New London Navy dock to watch Captain Ralph D. Lynch try out one of the new submarines. The trip had a significant beginning. A yellow quarantine flag was flying over the gate. A sailor with a suspicious rash had been found aboard a ship recently arrived from South America and an armed guard stood at the turnstile. But he stood with his rifle at the port for only a moment. When I told him that I was going aboard the submarine he stepped aside.

"That's different," he said. And I crunched through the frost to the gangway trying to figure out his meaning. He may have felt that germs would stay away from submarines, or perhaps that men condemned to the submarines wouldn't worry about the germs. In either case I saw this lad as I myself had been a year ago in Honolulu when the seagoing pipes were a forbidding mystery whose men were beyond all human regulation or understanding. Out of the depths of my recent experience with the O-boats and S-boats I was able to smile at him. For just a moment, as I tried to keep my footing on the streak of ice that was the gangplank, I assured myself that the other-world atmosphere of the submarines would never fog my consciousness again. When I came down the ladder into the gleaming whiteness of the control room I wasn't so certain.

The new fleet of submarines that began to come down the ways in quantities in the spring of 1943 are still in theory John Holland's old *Plunger* with Simon Lake's double hull. But in appearance and convenience they are as far ahead of, say, the 1940 models as a

A NEW SUB GOES TO SEA

Most of the recent additions to the U. S. underwater fleet are of this type.

Lieutenant Commander (*Captain*) Ralph D. Lynch and the author on the deck of one of the new U. S. submarines.

streamlined train is ahead of a mixed freight. Living with the trainers in the cozy intimacy of a short hull where you can see everything at once, you get to think that no new arrangement of submarine contrivances is going to arouse a moment's notice. You have just about memorized the control panels and know roughly where the principal valves are. You are no longer mystified by the activities of the huddles in odd spots of the ship when the dive alarm sounds. When anybody mentions a submarine you have a clear picture of it—the same old control room with its big brass wheels under the depth gauges on the port side, steering apparatus and motor control ahead, Christmas tree in the forward port corner . . . and a length of brilliantly lighted ship stretching on and on through the bulkhead doors to the brass shields of the torpedo tubes, like the image of a room repeated endlessly in mirrors.

Then, having convinced yourself that submarines are forever the same, you go aboard one of the new ones and find out how wrong you were.

The new fleet submarines are not so big as two or three that were in commission before December 7, but they are bigger than most—more than 300 feet long, with a surface displacement of 1,500 tons or better. Outside they look like their prototypes, small and dirty. Inside they are a revelation of functional beauty. The control room—with much of its rat's-nest of pipe straightened out and enameled if not concealed, its lighting rearranged and its trim glistening with stainless steel—looks like a highly polished station on a supersubway. The rest of the ship, particularly the forward battery room—the officers' country—appears to have been designed by George M. Pullman, Joseph Urban, the John Doe who worked out the folding gadgets for automobile trailers, and perhaps—just a touch—by Buck Rogers, A.D. 2000.

All through the ship goes this motif of silvery paneling in satin-finish stainless steel. There is bright modernity about the galley, crew's mess and living quarters aft of the control room. Bunk arrangements are still crowded, even in the officers' section where two men sleep, wash, keep their clothes and do odds and ends of paper work in a cubicle narrower than a Pullman roomette. But the accommodations such as they are are better, and the canned-sardine effect of the bunk room is missing. The officers' berths are permanent uppers and lowers. The men's berths fold up out of the way when not in use, with the result that there are wide areas of open floor space never before seen in a sub.

There is air conditioning in these new ships—a system that already has made living possible for months in tropical waters, wringing the moisture out of the air as well as cooling it. And with the economy required of everything that a submarine uses, this device condenses the moisture—from sweating pipes, the humidity of the original air supply and exhalations from human lungs—and delivers somewhere around 150 gallons of wash water a day, better than two gallons per man.

The air conditioning was tried out in some of the old S-boats solely with the idea of keeping the crew alive long enough to fight in them. But it was found to pay unexpected dividends. The men who were kept in condition to work had less work to do. The removal of surplus moisture from the dank atmosphere stopped the nearly continuous short-circuiting of electrical cables which up to now had been almost wringing wet. The wash water was pure lagniappe inasmuch as bathing on the S-boats had been confined to one scrub on the way out and one on the way in—the inbound bath depending of course on how much of the ship's machinery was still working after patrol.

As a sort of companion piece to the air conditioning, the new ships are fitted with sun lamps. A pharmacist's mate demonstrated one for me.

"Steadily the idea gets around that they're going to make us like other people," he said a bit sadly. "It used to be that you could tell a submariner easy. He kept walking doubled up and shaking his head every three or four steps because he'd learned how to dodge things. He had a face like paste and couldn't eat anything that wasn't flavored with burned Diesel oil. Then they began giving us chow you could really eat—strawberries and beefsteak and other sissy stuff like that. And they gave us vitamin pills to keep us from having rickets, and now this sun lamp to give us drugstore-cowboy complexions. . . .

"Well, maybe there's something in it. We don't any of us see the sun for weeks at a time. Seventy-five percent of us never get up through the hatch from the time we start on patrol until we get back. And anything that keeps the guys standing on their feet is all right with me. Whether it comes in a lamp or a bottle."

The yeoman's office in these new ships is clearly the work of the automobile-trailer designer. Everything in it folds up but the typewriter. The whole compartment is hardly larger than a telephone booth, but once desk and filing cabinet and typewriter stand and mimeograph have been arranged in proper order everything fits into it, including the yeoman.

The wardroom is another masterpiece of Pullman artistry. It is the size of a Pullman drawing room, with a sideboard at either end and a "transom" or bench than can be converted into two berths. A table is permanently fixed in the middle of the compartment, but it can be made smaller simply by lifting pieces off of it and hanging them somewhere in the service pantry adjoining. Fully assembled, the table will accommodate eight for dinner—the usual complement of officers.

One of the sideboards is used for the storage of linen, silverware, china, etc. The other contains the library and charts and records. A cupboard at one end of the library shelves contains a phonograph, whose output can be "piped" throughout the ship over the loudspeaker system.

The engineer officer who showed me around the first of these ships I had ever seen was Lieutenant Frank Lynch, formerly of the Pacific patrol, formerly of the battleships. He is about six feet two tall and proportionately broad, and when he spoke of the subs it was not to complain of their crowding but to breathe prayers of thankfulness for having found a naval ship he could move about in!

"Maybe the subs are crowded," he conceded. "Maybe we do live pretty close together. But I can show you plenty of surface ships where sleeping quarters aren't any more commodious. Some people come to the submarines for one reason and some for another. But there wasn't anything heroic or even mercenary about my move. It was just that I got tired of walking stooped over all the time as I had to do when I was on the battleships."

The tall colored boy who had just brought in a cup of coffee joined in the conversation, as mess boys are likely to do in the sub service.

"That's how come I know all about submarines," he said. "For just same reason you-all talkin' about. Me, I got six feet maybe couple inches, an' they put me on one them O-boats. An' I go around that O-boat couple weeks and then I know where every valve on that boat is. I find 'em all with my haid. . . . Yessir. Jes' like you say. . . ."

"Well," said Lieutenant Lynch, "there's plenty of it here. We haven't sacrificed anything. We've got everything aboard that any other ship has. We've got plenty of power and fuel storage and supply space. But a lot of gadgets have been redesigned and compressed. The galley on this is the most efficient thing I've ever seen, and it's not so big as a railroad dining-car kitchen. It will supply sixty men with three full meals and a lot of snacks every day—with homemade pie and cake and pudding for dessert—without straining the cook.

"Our cold storage is something to look at. And we use every cubic inch of it. Our meat, for instance, is the very choicest—we have the best ration in the Navy. But it comes to us pressed in square packages for economical stowage in the icers. Some thought has gone into every little thing like that. We stow a lot of grocery stuff between the ribs of the pressure hull, and get more space for sleeping quarters."

This ship had been launched only a few days before and, as is customary in the Navy, the repair crews were already taking her apart.

"The world changes," said Lieutenant Lynch. "And we sat out there in the Pacific and watched it change. We learned about a few things that needed fixing and we're fixing 'em in this boat right now."

You could see your face anywhere in the white-enameled walls of the engine room but already the chief machinist's mate was dissatisfied with it.

"There are spots in it," he said with the same critical attitude he might have shown in buying an icebox for his home. "Wouldn't you think on a six-and-a-half-million-dollar job they could at least get a one-armed paperhanger to paint the engine room? I'm going over to the paint shop tomorrow and borrow a can of enamel and touch this place up myself. . . ."

Parts of an engine lay scattered along the catwalk between the banks of Diesels. Mechanics were sweating below in the harsh light of an unshaded globe on an extension cord. Squeezed in between the engine parts, a brace of lads lay on their backs polishing a strip of metal that couldn't be reached otherwise.

"What the hell is this?" inquired the communications officer.

One of the boys grinned.

"I'm just remembering the last sewer pipe I was in," he said. "God! I hope we can keep this one clean!"

"An idea that has its points," the lieutenant admitted.

The engineer pointed proudly to his system of change-over switches, and spoke technically of the improved transmission. Submarines were getting away rapidly from the bugs that brought their principal hard luck in the early depth-charge attacks.

"We have a couple of lighting systems now so that we aren't blinded when one goes out of order," he said. "We have one system spring-mounted so that the bulb filaments won't break. But even if everything should go out at once, things are arranged around here so that an experienced man can work it in the dark.

"Depth charges don't do us so much minor damage as they did at first because we have learned how to rig for them. The main danger from them now is that they may throw something out of line. When that happens, of course, you're there until you get it fixed, and repair facilities when you're submerged off Japan consist of a couple of hammers, a monkey wrench and luck. . . . And yet some of the boys have had just that sort of trouble out there. On occasion they've just about remade an engine room in twenty-four hours, finished their patches and come in on their own power. . . ."

He paused and took another proud look around the gleaming room.

"That's it," he said. "Everything fits. . . . Look at those little lockers between the ribs in each compartment. Every one has a can of beans in it and something else for each man. Those are emergency rations for use if the compartment should have to be sealed off. The can of beans is just about enough to last him for the rest of his life unless outside rescue comes down. . . . Everything cut to measure. Now take the Momsen lung—the oxygen lung that we use for fighting fires and gas and for escapes from

sunken boats—that's made to fit, too. Some men have been rejected
from the submarine service because their teeth were the wrong
shape to fit the bite of the lung—interesting, isn't it? . . ."

We went back to the wardroom and had a luncheon of steak,
baked potatoes, lima beans, ice cream and coffee. I was disposed
to talk of the steak, which was the only one of its kind I had seen
for a long time. But as usual in wardrooms the conversation was
beyond direction. One young ensign with a fund to spend for
magazine subscriptions was deeply concerned about expressions of
choice he had received from the crew. There had been a fair vote
for moving-picture fan magazines, with a brace of factual murder
magazines running a close second, and a technical photography
journal in the running.

"I'm not sure that's a good cross section of taste," said the ensign, "because we've already got a couple of subscriptions to avi-
ation magazines. All of them want to read about airplanes. Why
do you suppose that is?"

" 'The desire of the moth for the star,' " quoted somebody—I
thought it was the captain. But nobody seemed to notice.

"It's a close choice," said the young officer for my benefit,
"because we can't take much reading matter. The men have a
fairly catholic taste. They don't want all picture magazines. Some
of them like the informative sort, but they want to get the information as painlessly as possible. After they're out awhile they'll read
anything they can get and like it. I read one Australian magazine
seven times on my last patrol out of there. And it wasn't a very
good magazine to begin with. . . ."

A lieutenant explained the system of library exchange. Each
ship takes out a hundred books on a patrol, and trades them with
another ship for a hundred different ones on her return.

"Merit hasn't such a popularity as it might otherwise deserve,"
said the lieutenant. "The long books are most popular because they
last. *Les Misérables* lasted me a couple of trips, and I'd already read
it two or three times."

After that, the talk ranged over every topic, from North Africa
to the squabble over who was to get the tolls from the new bridge
over the Thames River. And as the conversation flowed from one
side of the table to the other I made a new discovery about the

submarines. These lads who had been living in barrels for more than a year, alone in the far reaches of a war that they could see only from the bottom side, were not only the most highly literate men I had met in the Navy but the best informed. When they talked of the North African business they talked of places and people whom they called by their right names. They seemed to have heard of every minor general who ever fought under Rommel. Most of them could draw accurate maps of the Tunisian front and mark them with notes on the differences and difficulties of terrain. They seemed to know all about Spanish Morocco and Spain. And I met few who weren't able to tell what general was where on the Russian front and what he was doing at last report.

The point of this seems to be that these lads not only read what they read intelligently but they remember everything. Information may be a long time getting to them but they assimilate it quickly and thoroughly. And while you know that they could not be submarine officers without such mental acquisitiveness and judgment, their uncanny talent startles you none the less. Once more you realize the minor part our ingenious mechanisms are playing in this war. Once more you wonder how the Germans are managing to turn out men like these on their assembly line.

15

KEEP 'EM RUNNING

THE submarines went out and the submarines stayed out. Some of them have come home on one groaning engine at three or four knots, some still smoking from battery explosions and underwater fires, some with bridges shot away and tanks leaking and much of their complicated innards askew, some of them long overdue. But nothing save permanent sinking has ever stopped one of them.

When I'd listened to the eerie recitals of how some of the old boats almost fell apart in the depth-charging and how much trouble some of the new ones accumulated in sheer ill luck, I began to wonder if all the medals were going to the right addresses. It takes a lot to sink an enemy ship but it sometimes takes just as much to keep your own afloat.

Repair work on the fly was one of the most important factors in keeping ships going until long after the fall of Bataan. Most of them were homeless for weeks after Manila was closed to them. Until months afterward they were never very close to such facilities as repair shops and dry docks. Spare-parts depots were something unheard of.

It was the monkey-wrench mechanics who took over the submarine fleet then—lads who could make watertight patches out of canvas soaked in paint, cable insulation out of rags and tar, new insides for gauges out of clock parts and bits of tin. They fixed things under water and under fire with the weirdest collection of ersatz that ever went into a ship. But the makeshifts they contrived seem always to have worked and to have lasted as long under stress as the things they replaced.

Even without the assistance of Japanese bombs, the submarine is subject to plenty of wear and tear. German writers after the last war said that a third of the Kaiser's effective U-boat strength was out of action continuously for overhaul of matériel and the resting of crews. There may be some quarrel with that, inasmuch as the fatigue of the men was one of the principal factors in the collapse of Germany's underwater campaign. But the estimate of time out for repair seems somehow reasonable.

In our own service the technique of repair improved as rapidly as the technique in fighting. An overhaul that once took two or three months now is finished in two or three weeks. "And it's a real overhaul," one of the chiefs told me. "We tear down the engines and jerk all the fish, and when we put her back together again, she's ready to run.

"It used to be that the engineer officer of a submarine never got any rest in port. He lived with the ship to make sure that the overhaul crew didn't get things balled up. But that isn't necessary any more. We've been training good mechanics as fast as we've been turning out good submarine men—faster."

But complete overhaul means docking facilities and shops and spare parts and tools. And the captains of the homeless submarines at sea after Manila fell were never certain that they were going to see a dock again nor very hopeful. Mechanical failure became a bugbear to more than one of them. Yet not one boat failed to come to port because of breakages that the crews weren't able to patch up. Captain Eugene McKinney had a sundered plane shaft. Captain Hiram Cassedy had a fire. One of the smaller boats burned out a motor-control panel. Captain Moon Chapple had a battery explosion. Any number of boats had engine troubles and mysterious electrical disturbances and jammed planes and leaks.

Aboard ships without air-conditioning apparatus—and quite a lot of them had none in the beginning—the continual sweating of the ship in tropical waters rotted insulation, shorted power wires and grew verdigris where it would do the most damage to instruments. What that meant to leg-weary electricians is something that nobody can appreciate who has not seen the mat of cables with which a submarine is lined. To a layman it would seem impossible that a short circuit in a cable could be traced—that the cable itself could be traced—in less than a couple of days. And yet, despite the seriousness of some of these accidents, the trouble spots were generally located and repairs completed in a matter of minutes.

There were dangerous leaks in some of the boats—such as the old red submarine that got away from the attack on Cavite Harbor. And I for one will never be able to explain the black magic with which the crews met such difficulties as that. The point is that they did. They patched up hulls to stand deep-sea pressures. They brought ships to port with bridges shot away and gaping holes in the tanks. And, all in all, they made the worries that had been important in peacetime service seem very remote and incomprehensible.

Always went with them the supreme danger that some one man would forget to do his assigned job in the fraction of a second allotted to him. Even such crews as these, which were turning out to be the best in the world, were not proof against the numbing processes of repeated shock. . . . Once, it is a matter of record, a chief, suddenly called out of his bunk after a couple of sleepless days, let the ship get under without closing the engine induction— the same sort of trouble that had sunk the *Squalus*. In this instance some other automaton had shut the flapper between the main valve and the sea, and the flapper had held, though the leakage was something to worry about until the chief's battered reflexes finally functioned and the induction light showed green on the Christmas tree. Another time a lad left the conning-tower voice tube open with somewhat similar results. There were cases of late timing in the closing of hatches. . . . Not many of these incidents in something over a million dives, but always a possibility of them —and whenever they did occur the repair crews had their work cut out for them.

After listening to tale after tale of how submarines, among the most complicated mechanisms on earth, had been patched, made to work and virtually salvaged with a little ingenuity and a great deal of baling wire, it seemed to me that here must be one outstanding reason why our boats had been doing so much better than other underwater fleets, such as, say, the Japs'. I seemed to hear the commandant at New London repeating what had sounded less like information than a slogan of the service: "Every man aboard can do every other man's job. Every officer is trained to do the work of every other officer and every enlisted man in the boat." And slowly I came to realize that this must be true. These men were not only quick-brained and dependable as stop watches in their life-and-death routine among the valves and vents and controls but they had skill in their hands as well. What is more important they had adaptability and that native ingenuity too often overlooked among our military assets.

"They took us for a long hard ride up there off Luzon," said the chief. "There wasn't any question of going into a base and fixing things up because we didn't have any base—not for quite a time. I began to think maybe we'd stay out forever, if the sheet iron and the monkey wrenches held out.

"But it was a good practical school. We learned most of the things that can go wrong with submarines and we worked out a lot of short cuts for dealing with them. Nothing like that worried us much after the first month. I guess you might say we were veterans by then . . . all of us."

16

CONCERNING THE PLUMBING

It HAS been said often by the submariners themselves that any man with an alert mind and ordinary mechanical gifts can be taught to dive and maintain the boat but that one really needs an engineering degree to work the controls of "the head," the *cabinet d'aisance*, or as it is somewhat generally called ashore, the bathroom. Like all generalities this one isn't entirely true but it's not so untrue either. No other device or collection of devices aboard the boats provides so effective an illustration of the complexity of even the familiar things of life when one gets below the surface.

Ashore you give little thought to conveniences that have become as common as window glass and electric doorbells in most communities. If you do, you are not impressed by their ingenuity, because gravity sewage systems take care of the chief problem that their installation presents, and gravity is something that nobody has been much excited about since Newton discovered it. Designers of surface ships, with high superstructures and waste tanks and pumps that can be worked at any time, had no trouble making adaptations of such devices as they are found on land. So the difficulties that stem from such ordinary matters in the life under water greet the layman as a distinct surprise.

The trouble, one hardly needs to be told, comes from the varying pressures outside the boat as she dives. Water can be expelled only under greater pressures—and there you are.

How the engineers have met this problem is best illustrated in the book of rules which every submariner memorizes as an infantryman learns his general orders.

1—See that the bowl flapper discharge valve "A" is closed.

2—See that Gate Valve "C" in discharge pipe line is open.

3—See that Valve "D" in water-supply line is open.

4—Open Valve "E" next to bowl to admit necessary water.

5—Close Valve "D."

6—Close Valve "E."

7—After use, pull Lever "A."

8—Release Lever "A."

9—(For air expulsion) Open Valve "G" in air-supply line.

10—Rock Valve "F" lever outboard to charge measuring tank ten pounds above sea pressure. Determined by comparison gauges.

11—Open Valve "B."

12—Rock valve lever inboard to blow overboard.

13—Close Valve "B."

14—Close Valve "C."

15—Close Valve "G."

16—(For pump expulsion) Open Valve "B."

17—Pump waste receiver with hand pump.

18—Close Valve "B."

19—Close Valve "C."

It is difficult for a landsman to follow this schedule in exact order or to envision what catastrophes may result if he doesn't. The earlier operations are simple enough, once one is able to identify the valves and levers and to find them in a reasonable time among others in their nest of pipe. The adjustment of the air pressure and closing of valve "A" are more important jobs. Once the pressure is up and the air released, the associated valves in the drain line had better be open or a geyser of water is blown back into the boat and over the person of the operator—which is too much of an old story aboard the submarines to be interesting to the skippers.

Sometimes, for serious purposes—such as giving the "comeuppance" to stuffy visitors—these eruptions may be prearranged, despite the resulting inconvenience of wet decks. It seems, for instance, that at one time there was a sort of malicious good fellowship between the naval aviators at a Florida field and the sub-

mariners whose base was in the same neighborhood. The pilots
generously offered to take submarine officers for rides, and then
stunted with them just to show their skill perhaps, or maybe to
see just how airsick a submarine officer could get. The submarine
officers retaliated by making some instruction plates special but
erroneous for display in the "head" on days when they invited the
air pilots for return visits. The submariners after a year and a half
of war are still well pleased with the results.

Naturally a whole folklore has arisen about these retiring rooms
and their ingenious mechanisms. Elsewhere is the story of the young
ensign who got hit in the eye by a valve handle during the Battle
of Midway. And there is a considerable book of anecdotes about
the distinguished personages who were taken off Corregidor with
no previous knowledge of such matters. There are some apocrypha, such as the legend of a captain who was transferred from an
old trainer with no conveniences to a new boat that had equipment
much like the present models. As this story is told, he was in
trouble for many long hours, because he knew that if he ever
started to ask questions he would have no peace forever after. In
this emergency he showed sound judgment. He figured that somewhere aboard the boat would be a set of specifications and blueprints similar to the descriptive books in the glove boxes of auto-
mobiles. At a crucial moment he found what he was looking for
and—with an armload of instructions—he retired.

There is another legend, more simple, more likely true, and
better loved by the submariners, of a brass hat who was being
taken from Pearl Harbor to the Philippines. On his departure the
chief of staff warned him of the indoor perils that were likely to
beset him out under the deep.

"I shall try to be a good submariner," he said. And the chief of
staff gravely answered him:

"When you learn the routine of this important tactical operation, you may consider yourself at least half qualified."

From somewhere the other side of Wake a radio message came
back a few days later. There was little in it about hot nights submerged, or rough seas on the surface, or the constant dangers
that Japanese destroyers and airplane patrols had brought to the

area . . . little in fact save a reassuring word from the traveling brass hat:

"I am now half qualified."

Just how the Germans have dealt with the problem may not be known until the end of the war. But there is some evidence that in the last one they had succeeded in preventing unforeseen geysers. They put one more tank into their system—a reservoir that maintained a vacuum in the drainage arrangement below Valve "A."

Commander Jack Crenshaw, first lieutenant aboard the late USS *Northampton*, once told me of a visit he had paid to Hamburg in 1919. He was ensign aboard a destroyer, the first U. S. naval vessel to enter the port after the Armistice, and he was assigned to go ashore and escort the German admiral on his official visit.

The Germans were pleased and had run out the red carpet and hung up the bunting. But when young Mr. Crenshaw stepped ashore the admiral wasn't there. In his place was a captain who spoke good English and had a reassuring message.

"The admiral has been delayed," he said. "He went aboard one of our submarines fifteen minutes ago for an inspection, and he ought to be back shortly." So they conversed on a variety of subjects for another fifteen minutes. Then the captain showed signs of concern.

"We'd better go and see where he is," he said. "So many things may have happened to him on a submarine. . . ."

They went aboard the boat and they found the admiral where apparently the captain had expected to find him. And he blessed their opportune arrival. He had pulled the wrong lever and produced a vacuum of twenty-five pounds to the square inch, and he couldn't get off the seat.

17

GREMLINS IN DIVING SUITS

You may have heard about the Gremlins, the little people of the air that make trouble for tired plane pilots. Their weird doings have been mentioned in dispatches and analyzed in long magazine articles and widely discussed wherever aviators are gathered together. They make planes heavy in the wrong places and bring the ice and foul up the spark plugs and get in the way of machine-gun and cannon sights and do odd things to the oil pumps, and any number of pilots have seen them and sometimes talked to them. In appearance they are something like the Irish leprechaun whose habits they seem to copy slavishly. They have a sort of combination hatred and contempt for the human race, particularly for the men who try to make engines work outside their natural element. And good is not in them.

They are mentioned here not because anybody is likely to have overlooked them in the current literature of the war but to indicate why a search for them in the submarine service appeared to be justified. It didn't seem likely that such interesting characters would ever be content to bother the airplanes when such a fine field as the so-called pig boats was theirs for the asking. Even without Gremlins the submarines had contrived to collect a lot of mysterious troubles. If some species of leprechauns hadn't yet taken over the work already half done for them by the gauge-makers, then something was wrong with the leprechauns. The answer, as might have been expected, is that the Gremlins, or a reasonable facsimile thereof, have been in the submarines for a number of years.

Lieutenant Robert Madison, submarine engineer officer, is their historian at the moment. He denies that he is their discoverer, for he says the Navy divers have known them since the invention of modern diving apparatus. They had been in the hair of the under-water men for at least a couple of decades before the imaginative lads of the R.A.F. ever heard of them. Lieutenant Madison told us all about it in an office in New London where he was inter-viewing part of the crew assigned to a submarine just commis-sioned.

"Of course the Navy doesn't call them Gremlins," he explained. "In the diving service, and in the submarine service insofar as it has had contact with the diving service, they are called Ganomies. The word, I take it, was originally spelled g-n-o-m-e-s. But Grem-lins or Ganomies, they are unquestionably the same breed of polter-geist.

"Captain J. L. DeTar, an old diver, first introduced me to the Ganomies. When he took over the ship I was on he found that these strange creatures were rattling gear in the superstructure. They used to do things to the bow planes. . . ."

One of the sailors nodded approval and smiled as if he had just seen the answer to a puzzle.

"I've often wondered what did things to the bow planes," he said. "Lots of mysterious things happen to bow planes."

"The Ganomies," repeated Lieutenant Madison with assurance. "They are the most mysterious thing that can happen to any-thing. Captain DeTar told us all about them when he heard these rattles and everybody in the boat got interested. We were going out to fight the Japs on their home grounds, and we'd heard that they were pretty tough, but it seemed to everybody that the Gano-mies probably were tougher and they certainly were closer at hand. We started to make Ganomie traps out of matchboxes and pins. Everybody in the boat was working out some idea for the things and some of them were really ingenious. But we never caught any Ganomies. They're just too slick.

"We even made decoy Ganomies out of paper. But that didn't do any good either.

"Quartermaster MacDonald put in a lot of time making match-stick Ganomies, and he'd drop them through the conning-tower hatch into the control room on little parachutes. They were very realistic. Many of us thought after we'd been without sleep for a couple of days in a bombing that they were the real thing. But the regular Ganomies weren't deceived. They were still working their regular beats when we went up to the Battle of Midway and so far as I can discover they're on the job still.

"One day up around Midway we probably got a couple of them although we've had no official recognition of the capture. Captain DeTar came into the wardroom with his hands cupped together and asked us to guess what he had. We were slow in guessing so he told us. It was a Ganomie lure. He took it to a locker and made the gesture of tossing it inside and locking the lid. We'd seen that he didn't have anything in his hands, although by that time we were goofy enough to look and make sure.

" 'What kind of a lure?' somebody asked him.

" 'The very best,' he said. 'A female Ganomie.'

"After that we dropped the Ganomie hunt for a while and let nature take its course. But there was always something to remind us of them. During the Battle of Midway a reserve ensign went into the head and did something wrong, which is so easy to do in those places aboard a submarine even when you're not worrying about any battles. The handle came back and hit him in the eye.

"When the tumult and the shouting of the battle had died, the captain called the crew together. With great solemnity he handed the ensign a large aluminum medal embossed with a fine representation of a submarine outhouse. With it came a citation engrossed in all the formality and pomp of correct naval usage for such occasions. It stated that the recipient was being honored because he was the only man aboard who had been wounded at the Battle of Midway and that, in token of his heroism, he would be called 'Pump-Handle' from thence forward. It was further stated that if the officer so desired, a copy of the citation would be attached to his file in Washington."

That, of course, was not the end of the Ganomies, for they are a persistent and ubiquitous lot.

"We were lying off a Japanese port," said Lieutenant Madison, "and we hadn't been doing much business. After a couple of days we fired a torpedo at a ship that looked like a very fine setup, but the Ganomies or something carried the torpedo under her. Then,

I guess, they went out and found some Japanese-speaking Ganomies and called their attention to what had happened. Anyway the next day we slapped one at a freighter and I think we hit her. But the Japs were there waiting for us to come back. Destroyers were lying where we couldn't see them and they came out in a hurry and chased us. We'd dive and wait till the propeller noises got dim and then we'd surface and try to make a run out of there. But they'd see us or the Ganomies would signal to them or something and we'd be in for it again.

"They forced us down and we stayed there an hour and a half. Then there was nothing much doing. At that time the captain was on the bridge and nothing was in sight except for a dark mass on our quarter. Then the skipper suddenly found himself looking up into a light that was squarely over his head. A destroyer was right on top of him. The destroyer tried to ram, but the Ganomies apparently were working on him, too, so he missed. The skipper yelled to take her down and we did.

"The ship angled under me and I went down the ladder after she'd started her dive. And believe me that boat went down. We were pulling so much a side that the ammeter needle was up against the stop. I had a guy sitting on the circuit breaker and we were roaring.

"Up in the conning tower the skipper was screaming like an Indian, 'Damn it, Bob, take her down! Take her down!'

"He was talking to me because I was diving officer. We'd been heading down about ten seconds although I suppose it seemed longer than that to him. . . .

" 'Damn it, let's get this thing down!'

"I don't know yet whether or not our diving time was right. Maybe the boy with the stop watch made a mistake. We were really headed for the bottom.

"We leveled off and lay quiet for a while. The skipper was pacing back and forth and mumbling. The Ganomies were all walking in step with him. Every now and then he'd stop and swear and say, 'Dammit! I can't see. What am I doing here?'

"After about five minutes, he answered himself and we went up. He seemed happier then. He was all enthusiasm when he took the periscope in his hands and began to walk it around. He'd just got it about dead astern when his hands froze and his elbows shook. He was looking right into the searchlight again.

"He gave some directions and we fired a couple of fish.

"In ten seconds there was a magnificent explosion and the Old Man roared.

" 'That put out the searchlight,' he said.

"We weren't bothered much more that night, by destroyers or Ganomies or anything else. There seems to be something in the idea that the best way to keep from getting depth-charged is to sink the guy who's carrying the depth charges.

"Once when we were coming by an island on patrol, the Japs got an idea of our position. So every day they sent over planes to look for us. Every morning we'd figure where we were and how far from their nearest island base and how long it would take them to reach us. After about three days of that calculation we had their habits pretty well calculated and we never gave them a chance to see us. By that time I was willing to figure that we'd got the Ganomies pretty well on the run. They never really bothered us again, although I have heard that they're doing pretty well in other localities. . . ."

Captain DeTar's submarine was one of a detachment sent up to the Aleutians for a tour of duty that needed no embellishment by Ganomies. It is said by submarine men who have had to live in that area that no Ganomies ever come up there and very few animals save one or two species of subnormal fish. The weather is cold. The boats get cold. The bulkheads sweat. There is never much visibility, above or below. The winds are terrific. The currents between the islands are vicious and unpredictable. The water unaccountably lies in strata of varying density, making diving a constant adventure. And it would seem that very likely the experts are right about the Ganomies. There seems to be no reason why a Ganomie should be wandering around in an area where his work is already done for him.

"Last summer we had one bit of adventure out of the ordinary up there," Lieutenant Madison recalled. "We went up to one of the islands to do a little passenger carrying. We had to pick up a lot of Aleut scouts. The skipper called them 'Zoot Aleuts with the Droop Snoots.' These scouts were an odd mixture—Aleuts, Eskimos, Northwest trappers and odds and ends. I had thought before I went up there that the days of Daniel Boone were gone. But they weren't.

"All of them had beautiful rifles. The reason for that is, of course, that they live by their rifles. But the rifles were the only thing beautiful about them. They came aboard, filthy, ragged, stinky—the oddest lot that ever stepped into a submarine.

"An Army colonel had them in charge. He said that he never let them go into town. People in towns somehow didn't like them and when they persisted in showing up in more or less civilized communities there were always fights. So he kept them in the woods where they seemed to have a pretty rough time of it. A month before we got there they had shot a deer and they'd been living on venison until it ran out. They were getting down to the last of the larder when we came in. Then they caught some salmon and smoked it.

"They brought their own provisions aboard: a little packet of rice, some tea and two smoked salmon apiece. They all had packs. I hefted them and the lightest weighed ninety pounds. That didn't seem to worry them any. They probably were used to lugging ninety-pound packs.

"We were to land them on an island where some construction work was going on, and that presented a problem because we didn't have any boat. They said to think nothing of it. They just went ashore that night before we started and made their own boat— wood frame and canvas covering that they could knock down. And it was really a good boat. It would carry twelve people.

"The trip wasn't very long but they didn't seem to like it. They didn't say much till we came to the landing place. Then they said good-by enthusiastically. One of them explained to me how they felt as they started out for that Godforsaken wilderness: 'I don't see how you can stand the life in one of these things,' he said. 'We are brave men, I think. But we are not so brave as that. We value our lives. . . .

"We waved good-by to them. Then we aired out the boat and sat down to a meal that would have been good in any restaurant in the United States, and we thought of the Zoot Aleuts on their nice cool rock with all their tasty viands of smoked salmon and pemmican. . . . It's all in the point of view. . . ."

Captain DeTar's submarine, however, doesn't seem to have been too much better off than the Zoot Aleuts during the next weeks of his patrol. He wasn't sitting on a cool rock, perhaps, but his navigator was always worried lest he might be at almost any time. The navigator was as cold as anybody else in the boat and just as damp from the condensation that continually rolled down the bulkheads. But he forgot such things in the greater worry of unpredictable currents and uncharted reefs.

"We sat up there for more than a month," said Madison. "Nothing happened. We couldn't see anything most of the time but the bow of the boat. We couldn't hear anything but the lapping of the water against our sides.

"Then one night when I was on watch, I saw a phosphorescent streak coming toward me. I called 'Sub! Call the bridge!' and the QM pulled the plug. The boat was on her way down as I went through the hatch. And we leveled off and heard his engines passing over us—very close. . . . He ran. And we weren't sorry."

Which leads one to wonder about the Ganomies. They may be working in enemy submarines as well as ours.

PART TWO

THE BOATS

18

THE UNHAUNTED GHOST SHIP

ONE man in the control room had been there that other time—an older man than most of the kids at the valves and levers. He looked about him with placid eyes missing nothing—the Christmas-tree lights, the angle on the bow-plane indicator, the gauges and handles and gadgets. Back through the ship, men were standing with their hands extended to wheels among the tapestry of pipe above them. . . . Some of them he could see. Instinctively he pictured the others. . . . All was well, as it had seemed that other day. . . . Just the same sort of day, too, perhaps. Only that morning you didn't know how close you were to the end of everything. And today you knew. You certainly knew.

A couple of bombs cracked somewhere aft. They sounded close. But probably they'd have sounded close if they'd been a couple of miles away. You couldn't be sure about bombs. . . . Well, anyway, this was it. . . . No fooling this time. The Japs were over. Clouds of Japs. And if you managed to live through this business you wouldn't be thinking much about ancient history tomorrow. Even a couple of years ago would seem a long time back. If the ship came through nobody would be remembering May 23, 1939, or pretending not to be looking back at the watertight door to the engine room every time she dived. . . .

Everything just the same, except a lot of new faces. Funny, he hadn't thought of Preble for years—Harold C. Preble, the naval architect—but at a time like this it looked as if Preble ought to be here—one foot on the bottom rung of the ladder, his stop watch in his hand. . . . The engines were roaring now, sure enough. The ship was swinging forward with her screws finally taking a bite.

Then from above: "Sound the alarm!" The klaxon squawked. No change in that, either.

The diving officer was getting down to business. . . . Only it wasn't Doyle this time.

"Open all main-ballast Kingstons!"

"Open vents on bow buoyancy!"

"Open vents Number One Main Ballast. . . . Number Two Main Ballast. . . . Safety tanks!"

"Bow planes at hard dive!"

The skipper was coming through the conning-tower hatch from the bridge.

"All ahead emergency!" ordered Doyle. . . . Only it wasn't Doyle. It was this other officer. . . . The diving officer looked up to report to the conning tower: "All engines stopped and valves closed, sir."

"Close hull and engine inductions!"

"Green board, sir. . . ." As the diving officer looked at the Christmas tree, "Pressure in the boat, sir."

A hollow-sounding "Very well," from the conning tower and the diving officer's command: "Secure the air!"

Over the bow and stern plane apparatus two men watched the fluttery bubbles. Crouched above them, the diving officer watched the bubbles on the level indicator and also the depth gauges. The hands of the gauges came rapidly around. Two blasts echoed far astern and that made you realize right enough that this wasn't May 23, 1939, but December 9, 1941. . . . You'd have realized it anyway when they got to depth and straightened her out. She just hung there flat as if she could stay there always.

Somebody muttered: "This ought to be deep enough to fox the s.o.b.s." And that's all there was to it. The USS *Sailfish* was well out of the raid on Manila Bay. The USS *Sailfish*, née *Squalus*, had just completed her most momentous dive since that other day . . . that day off Portsmouth. . . .

The *Sailfish*, which like many another great lady put tragedy behind her with a change of name, was lifted out of the unnumbered class of anonymous submarines in a citation by President Roosevelt which startled the working Navy and indicated that to some extent the President was a little startled himself. The civilian world, which had once been more interested in the *Squalus* than in any other submarine afloat, and had seen in her unexplainable dive and heroic rescue all that is suicidal and magnificent about the service, had forgotten her . . . or, remembering briefly, wondered what had become of her. With a new world war approaching a climax, only a few experts paid attention when she went down the ways for the second time in Portsmouth, New Hampshire, in April 1940, less than a year after her foundering. Afterward only the submariners themselves were aware of her, and their interest was purely professional. Afloat or in dry dock, or possibly on the top of some scrap pile ready for shipment to Japan, she was a craft that existed in shocked memory rather than reality . . . a ghost ship whose actual crew must always be the twenty-seven men who died in her.

The President's commentary on her performance to anyone who heard it come over the radio one dark day in mid-Pacific is unforgettable.

"You may remember the tragic sinking of the submarine *Squalus* off the New England coast in the summer of 1939. Some of the crew were lost but others were saved by the speed and efficiency of the rescue crews. The *Squalus* itself was tediously raised from the bottom of the ocean.

"Eventually she sailed again under a new name, the USS *Sailfish*. Today she is a potent and effective unit of our submarine fleet.

"The *Sailfish* has covered many thousands of miles in operations in the far western Pacific.

"She has sunk a Japanese destroyer.

"She has torpedoed a Japanese cruiser.

"She has made two torpedo hits on a Japanese aircraft carrier.

"Three of the enlisted men of our Navy who went down with the *Squalus* in 1939 are today serving on the same ship, the *Sailfish*, in this war.

"It is heartening to know that the *Squalus*, once given up as lost, rose from the depths to fight for our country in time of peril. . . ."

The story of the *Squalus* has been too well told in Nat Barrows' book *Blow All Ballast* to need more than a brief recapitulation here. The *Squalus* went out for some test dives off Portsmouth with a veteran crew and one of the most brilliant captains in the service. With the precision customary in such maneuvers she was rigged for diving. The executive officer automatically gave the orders checking all main-ballast Kingstons or flood valves through which the sea would come pouring in when the air vents on top of the tanks should be opened. He tested main-ballast vents partly to ease pressure, partly to make sure they were working. The stern planes were rigged out, which is to say they were unfolded from their compartments in the side of the ship until they stood at right angles to the hull, great iron fins like shortened airplane wings. He tested their movement with automatic and hand control and noted from the angle indicator at the side of the control room that they were in perfect order. One after another he received reports from the numerous compartments that each little job of closing valves and testing equipment had been completed. And he watched the Christmas-tree indicator board to verify each report as one after another the red lights turned to green.

He reported to the bridge that except for bow planes, main-engine exhaust valves, engine and hull inductions, radio-antenna trunk and conning-tower hatch, the ship had been rigged for diving. On order, the bow planes were set in place and tested as the stern planes had been. The radio operator hauled down his antenna and locked the trunk in the valve through which it entered the ship through the hull.

The alarm sounded. The Kingstons and vents were opened. The bow planes were set at hard dive. A machinist's mate in front of the hydraulic manifold heard reports that the engines had been stopped, heard his own orders to close hull and engine inductions. On the board he saw the lights for the exhaust valves turn green and he threw over the single lever that controlled both the inductions. Another pair of lights turned green.

Everything was in order as it had been on eighteen previous dives and the executive so reported as the bows went under. The diving officer reported pressure in the boat which should have indicated that there were no leaks. The *Squalus* slid down to her projected depth of sixty-three feet and started to level off. . . .

Everything was in order except, as they found out some time later, both inductions, two holes thirty-one inches and twenty-one inches in diameter, were still open to the sea and not only that, the inboard flapper valves, set behind them as a precaution against any failure of the hydraulically operated valves in the hull, were also open. The board still showed green as the captain noted when he walked over to the periscope to give orders for a submerged run. About that time somebody sang out that a tide of water was rising in the engine room. It was impossible but there it was.

The *Squalus* began to go down by the stern at an angle of about thirty-five degrees and men slid across the control-room deck or held themselves upright by clinging to valves and gauges. Seven men fought their way up out of the engine-room flood through the after battery room with the water following them. The bulkhead-door guard was swinging the door to against a pressure that almost succeeded in throwing him back. He got the door closed—and that was the end of the twenty-seven men in the after compartments but it was also the salvation of the thirty-three who remained forward. The *Squalus* went on, to rest in two hundred and forty feet of water.

So far the story of the *Squalus* resembled that of other submarine disasters. It differed only in that thirty-three men were to come out of the trap alive and, for the first time in the history of submarines, give eyewitness accounts of what had happened. Rescue ships came out and divers went down while a skeptical world looked on as it had looked on similar situations—stirred by the dramatic suspense that is engendered by mine disasters, by underground explorers imprisoned in caves, by doomed men in hospitals looking consciously on the approach of death. But this was drama different somehow from all other drama, in that it was filled with the ultimate horror of the unknown—the unknown deep, the unknown monster that was the submarine. Nobody had ever told of the easily imagined torments of slow death by cold and gas and suffocation in submarine disasters. . . . For only dead men had ever come back from them, and only a few of those.

Then, incredibly, the divers found the *Squalus* and the wet, shivering men inside cheered as lead shoes thumped slowly across her deck. A line was attached to her and a McCann diving bell was guided to the forward escape hatch. The flexible skirt of the bell sealed to the submarine by sea pressure, the water in the lower chamber was pumped out. The operator opened the hatch, stuck his head inside, and in one of the most noteworthy greetings since Stanley met Livingstone announced: "Well, here we are, fellows. . . ."

Nat Barrows' account of the series of trips that the diving bell made between the *Squalus* and the rescue ship is one of the finest accounts of peril and heroism at sea ever written, and need not be repeated here. But it may be noted that four such round trips had to be completed before the captain—last man to leave the *Squalus* alive—had been brought to the surface, four trips during which the air in the submarine became less and less breathable and the bite of the cold almost beyond endurance. It may be noted that the fourth trip was probably a more harrowing experience for the nine survivors carried in the bell than the foundering of the ship had been, for at one hundred fifty feet a cable fouled. The bell returned to the deck while divers freed it. The journey was resumed toward the surface but halfway up it was discovered that a vital wire was fraying and threatening momentarily to part, a contingency that would have sent the rescue chamber hurtling up from the deep to crash against the bottom of the rescue tug. They came up anyway and, unaccountably, the line held, and so ended the first drama of the *Squalus*.

The salvaging of the ship, which took three months' time and several miracles of engineering, was the second. A board of inquiry exonerated the captain and ascribed the accident to unexplainable mechanical failures. The *Squalus* was hauled into dry dock in the Portsmouth Navy Yard, her dead buried, her name painted off her bows. And there she stayed for eleven months of reconditioning while the world forgot.

There were no flags waving when she started on her trip to the South Pacific with a few of the old crew left aboard under a skipper who, apparently, didn't believe in ghosts. She led a shy, retiring existence noteworthy even in a service where all ships and the men who sail them are necessarily coy. And so, eventually, she came to a mooring in Manila Bay on the morning of December 9,

1941, awaiting, as her officers may have suspected, the third great drama in her struggle against a hard-working Doom.

"She's a fine ship," said Lieutenant Commander Hiram Cassedy who was her executive officer during that crucial period. "You couldn't see that anything unusual had ever happened to her when I was aboard. She handled well. She dived well. She never again showed any signs of skittishness. . . . And we just never gave a thought to her bad start. After all, in the service men know that submarines are going to be submarines and that things may go wrong with any of them. That's why we get extra pay for operating them. . . ."

As he talked you saw the sense of that, but you couldn't help trying to reconstruct the thoughts of her captain and crew when they sent her down for the first time after she had come out of dry dock in Portsmouth. Ghosts must have been riding with her that day if they never did again. And the men who rode with them will rate in at least one man's estimation as the bravest she ever took aboard even though they got no medals for it.

So the *Sailfish-Squalus*, known through the fleet as the *Squailfish*, escaped the bombs that the Japs brought to Manila and set out on her new way of life. Five days after the start of the war she was in a position to work on the fleets that were pouring in men and supplies against MacArthur, and almost immediately she got her chance. Her captain spotted a convoy in the dusk, drove into it and fired a spread of fish that he hoped might pick off two transports in the middle of the column. The torpedoes missed. The *Sailfish* had no chance to dive before a destroyer was on top of her. Lieutenant Commander R. G. Voge at the periscope may or may not have seen all of the ship's past life swimming before his eyes at the moment, but if he did he paid no attention to the spectacle. He swung the ship about to meet the gravest danger she had ever faced, took a split-second sight at the roaring destroyer and fired two more fish. The destroyer blew up. The *Sailfish* dived.

That, you might say, was the moment of resurrection for the old *Squalus*. The officers and crew looked about her, less in terror of their first ash-can barrage than in critical approval of the ship. She didn't leak. She didn't shake her insides to pieces. She didn't broach. She hung there as other ships have hung in a similar blasting and the men with great complacency sat down to listen.

"The jinx is off," said the cook to the gunnery officer. But he didn't say it out loud. The skipper had never admitted that there might be any jinx.

As the accomplishments of the submarines go, the luck of the *Sailfish* was spotty. She got out of tight places, which considering her history seemed to be luck aplenty. But it was her fate that when other ships found sitting pigeons in groups, where a spread of torpedoes would sink two or three at a time, she was eternally fighting warships. After the destroyer it was a long time before she sank another. But the personnel were satisfied. After all, she won in these encounters, in itself an enviable record for a 219-foot boiler.

When she came out of the depth-charge attack that the sinking of the destroyer brought down on her, she was called back to port, and lay off Manila submerged for five days. Like the other submarines that had been loading when the war came, she was low on supplies. But for weeks she was given no opportunity to get more aboard.

Her next assignment was farther north where the Japanese invasion fleet had begun to operate in force. There the crew hoped for at least a couple of transports, but their area seemed to be outside the main lane of traffic. One evening they discovered a ship on the horizon nearing them at an angle and they made an approach at their best speed.

The captain was only mildly concerned when he noticed destroyers in the offing, because it was to be expected that big ships would not venture into those waters without escort. So he angled until they came within a few thousand yards of him, and only then made his most startling discovery. The ship he had been stalking was a cruiser. What might be behind her toward the black horizon he couldn't see. Submarine men say that a cruiser is about the most difficult of all targets because she will not close in for a fight. With a speed like that of most destroyers, and maneuverability almost as great, she will turn and run as soon as a periscope has been sighted, making short-range torpedo fire impossible, and easily outdistanc-

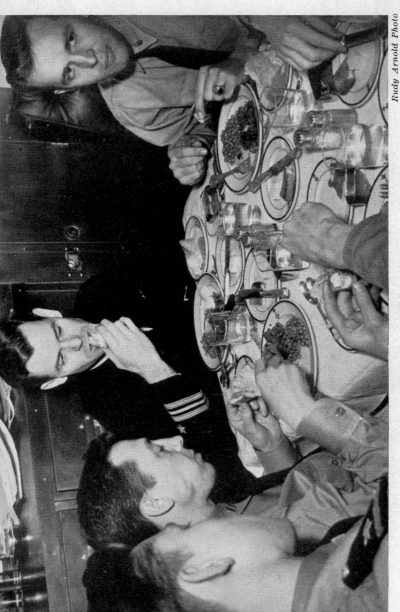

OFFICERS' COUNTRY

Meals, which are the best in the armed services despite their preparation in a galley little larger than a telephone booth, are the same for all the personnel. Officers' meals are served in the wardroom, a corner of which is visible here.

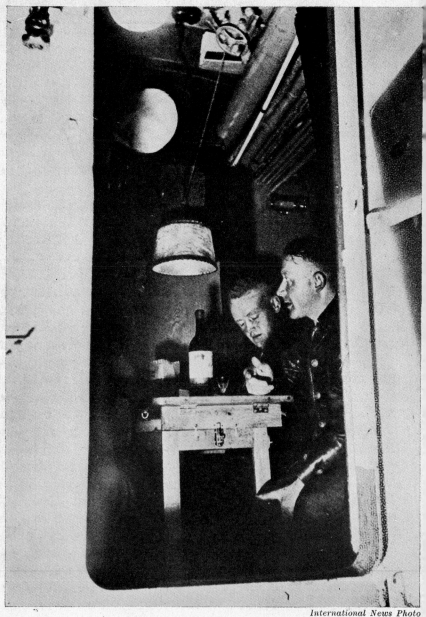

HOW THE OTHER HALF LIVES

Officers' quarters aboard a German U-boat. Comforts are singularly lacking.

ing pursuit. The destroyer, which is primarily an antisubmarine vessel, is likely to be more vulnerable because in normal practice she does come in—she can't be effective unless she does—and in attacking lays herself open to destruction.

Thus, when Captain Voge saw what he had picked up he was not sanguine of much success. It's not on the cards that you can fight a warship every day and hope to live long. On the other hand the cruiser, which undoubtedly would be worth the risk of a bold attack, would get away from him the first instant a sound apparatus picked him up.

He solved the problem by letting one destroyer slip by him. Then, with another bearing down on him, he fired one long shot at the cruiser.

The big ship was already turning around when the torpedo caught up with her so the aim was spoiled. . . . It would have been nice to bury a torpedo in her somewhere forward of the bridge where the skin was likely to be thin. But he could see even as he called the order to dive that no such fine calculation was going to work out. He was just about to feel discouraged about the whole business and damn the Japs for their lack of co-operation when the fish struck. There was a blast the full force of which did not come back to him until his ship was under water. But there was an upshoot of flame from somewhere in the fore part of the cruiser—orange flame that mushroomed outward for perhaps fifty feet. He felt, as he dropped from the bridge into the conning tower and heard the quartermaster dog the hatch, that even with destroyers crashing in on him as they were at the moment he would rather be where he was than on the deck of that ship behind the flame.

He got no credit for a sinking. The destroyers wouldn't allow him any time for observations and the Japanese communiqués were not likely to say anything about it. But his crew, listening to distant explosions beyond the ring of ash cans, was satisfied. It is the consensus of the trade that flaming cruisers seldom last long. They burn brightly for half an hour or three-quarters and then they sink.

That about ended the activities of the ship in Philippine waters. Captain Mumma took over from Captain Voge, who went to another command.

The record wasn't particularly good in the early patrols, Lieutenant Commander Cassedy recalled.

"We went places where we were sent but the ships just weren't there," he said. "And we had a pretty tough time of it. The bases moved from the Philippines to Java but it didn't make much difference to us. We were out well over a month before we saw one of them. Then we were in for only a couple of days and out again.

"Most of the time we were stuck in a strait, and after a few weeks of it we felt pretty useless. We had to stay there because that was our area. On the chart it had looked like a fine trap, but after we got there we couldn't be sure whether it was a good trap for us to catch Japs in or for the Japs to catch us in. There was a narrow neck of water at one end of the strait with land on both sides, and while the cargo ships and transports didn't come through there during our stay, there was no lack of other traffic, mostly cans . . . dozens of cans day and night . . . and they were all looking for us. . . ."

Then one day when the world seemed at its worst they got orders to move and made a break for open water. They reached the edge of their new area one morning just before dawn and saw why they had come. Just ahead of them and coming around a spit of land was what appeared to be a floating island with several cans and some masses that may have been cruisers ranged about its edges.

The lookout called that he had sighted a ship and escort and gave the bearing.

"She's a big ship," he added. "She's a hell of a big ship. . . ."

The captain took a look and made out some further details of the floating island. He was staring squarely at the side of the sort of target for which in those days every submariner said long prayers every day.

"She's a carrier," he said without excitement. "One of those made-over battle cruisers, either the *Kaga* or the *Akagi*, and it doesn't make much difference which. . . . Stand by to fire torpedoes. . . ."

Undetected, the submarine closed in, and the torpedoes spread out fanwise, their wakes sparking with purple phosphorescence as they went—streaks so brilliant that the lookouts aboard the destroyers must have seen them even if the sound detectors hadn't aroused their attention. The cans were already rushing in for the kill when two torpedoes hit the carrier amidships and the submarine once more started for the bottom.

Just what the *Kaga* was doing down there is something only the Japs can tell. But whatever it was, her mission was finished. We know now that she went back to Tokyo and lay in a repair yard for months, returning to service just in time to be sunk in the Battle of Midway.

Her escort, the captain of the *Sailfish* found out, was numerous and well armed, and from the moment the *Kaga* leaned over with the force of two blasts in her thin sides the destroyers had only one mission.

"We've never had a more rugged time than that," Lieutenant Commander Cassedy recalls. "They worked on us hard and we weren't in very good condition to take it. Except for a couple of days in port after the first patrol, we had been out since the beginning of the war. The men were so tired they couldn't stand up. Without ash cans the going would have been tough. But there was nothing we could do about it. It looked as if they might go on forever. We'd get up only a few minutes to charge batteries. Then we'd go down again.

"I remember I went into the wardroom to get a cup of coffee and a young lad we called 'Amby' came in. He'd just been relieved of his watch as diving officer. He sat down with his coffee and listened to the noise for a while, and I couldn't help think how cool he was. You'd have thought the depth charges were Fourth of July fireworks in his home-town baseball park. He didn't say anything for a while but I didn't think anything of that. There isn't much you can think up to make interesting conversation in a spot like that. Then all of a sudden he looked up at me and said:

" 'You know, I'm wondering if maybe I oughtn't to turn in my suit. I don't mind kidding myself but I don't want to be a menace to the lives of everybody around me.' I said, 'What the hell are you talking about?' And he said, 'I don't like to confess it but it's physically impossible for me not to be afraid of these things. I'm scared stiff.' And I laughed at him.

" 'What do you think about the rest of us?' I said. 'Don't you think we're normal? Show me a man aboard who isn't scared stiff. . . .'

"He looked at me again. 'Do you mean to tell me everybody else is afraid too?'

" 'My God!' I said. But he didn't let me finish.

" 'Well then,' he said, 'that makes everything all right. . . .'

"And he went to sleep right where he was sitting. . . .

"I left the old ship after that patrol for a command of my own. I was sorry she hadn't had better luck, but I figured she wouldn't be getting bad breaks forever. . . . And she didn't. She's been doing better ever since."

It seemed futile to ask him what he meant by "better." The standards of the submarine scorekeepers must always be incomprehensible to a landsman. Secretly I agreed with the President of the United States that the officers and men of the old *Squalus* hadn't done badly at all. . . . A destroyer sunk, a heavy cruiser blasted, a first-class carrier sent home out of action . . . not badly at all.

19

THE RED PIRATES OF THE CHINA COAST

ONE evening while we were wandering around the South Pacific with the old *Swayback Maru*, sometime called USS *Salt Lake City*, we picked up an incomprehensible message from Tokyo. It was part of the English broadcast with our favorite, Tokyo Rose, reading the lines, but it seemed to us that she was even less coherent than usual.

The United States had sent a fleet of red submarines to the Chinese coast—this was the burden of her indignant plaint—and these wanton killers were plaguing a lot of peace-loving Japanese merchant skippers who wanted only to be let alone in their job of transporting noncontraband cargoes of troops and munitions toward the Cannibal Islands. These Red Indian pirates of the China coast would one day be punished severely. The "civilized world" —which apparently meant Japan, Italy and Germany—would rise in protest against their violation of Hirohito's rules of warfare. The Western barbarism that had fostered the Red Pirates and sent them out on their murderous mission would surely be destroyed ... and more to that same effect.

We naturally could make no head or tail of this because we knew from looking at them that U. S. submarines were not red but black and that they weren't manned by Indians—not entirely by Indians, at any rate. And if Rose had spoken of "Red" submarines in the sense that they might be Russian ships, well, that didn't make any sense either because Russia thus far had showed no inclination to fight a war in the Pacific.

"It looks as if our submarines were doing some sort of good job out there," said the Engineer Officer. "But I can't make out what the rest of it is about unless Rose is color-blind."

So we let it go at that and not until a couple of months ago did I learn the truth of it.

The denouement was startling. Into one of the offices of the new submarines in the plant of the Electric Boat Company at New London, Connecticut, came as tough-looking a sailor as I had ever looked upon. He was dressed in the nondescript uniform that cold weather brings to the submarine trade. The icy wind had whipped his face blood-raw. His hands were like hams. He walked with a definite swagger. And in his ears were a pair of delicate golden earrings.

"And what," I inquired of Lieutenant Robert Johanson, the press officer, "might this be?"

Lieutenant Johanson shook his head.

"Offhand I couldn't say," he answered. "But I've seen him and others like him before. . . . They all wear earrings. I should say, looking at the mug of this lad, that it's out of no courtesy toward feminine tradition. They must belong to some sort of secret society. I'll ask him."

The brawny youth of the earrings heard the question with a pleasant smile.

"Well, it's a long story," he said. "It means that we're all off the same boat—a boat that patrolled the south end of the China coast. . . . Maybe you remember how the Japanese used to scream about the red pirates of the coast. Well, we're the 'Red Pirates.' . . . I can't tell it to you very good because I get things all mixed up but I can put you in touch with some guys who can. They'll tell you. It's a long story but they're the guys who know all the words. . . ." And, after some preliminaries, we were introduced to Earl Oschner, motor machinist's mate first class, Arthur Killan, electrician second, and Harry Wilson, torpedo man second.

The lads weren't at all reticent, and like all of their kind they seemed perfectly at ease in the company of strangers—even a civilian stranger. They were in no hurry about getting to the history of their weird organization or explaining the supreme incongruity of the earrings. They preferred to talk about shore leaves in Australia, the kindness of the natives there—all submariners seem agreed on that subject—the odd habits of cruiser sailors turned loose among the veterans of the Asiatic fleet. Oschner mentioned among other things that he had once intended to write a book about life in the submarines.

"I never got any farther than the title," he said. "But it was a honey of a title. I was going to call the book *Each Dawn We Dive*. Pretty sharp, don't you think?" And then eventually we got around to the war and the fleet of red submarines that had so annoyed Tokyo Rose. We weren't particularly surprised to learn that the fleet had consisted of one lone ship.

When the war began, they explained, this boat, like so many others that began to make immediate history, was based on Manila. On the morning of December 9 she was lying alongside a tender in Cavite Harbor next to the *Sealion* which was fated never to get away. As the bombing started she slipped her moorings and started to back out, but hadn't got very far before a bomb hit the *Sealion* and blew her up. Fragments struck the moving ship, tore off a part of her bridge and ripped up a lot of her superstructure and punctured her tanks. In spite of this she was able to get back about three miles and submerge. When the strafing was over she somehow crawled back to the surface and got to a repair dock, where the principal holes in her were patched up with what materials happened to lie at hand. She had been in need of a paint job when she first came into the harbor, and thereafter it was long and many a day before she got a chance to improve her looks. With jagged rents in her bridge and much of her superstructure still torn up she went out on patrol, and in a number of fantastic days was battered around until all her black paint came off, leaving her red-lead primer exposed. Thus she became the only red submarine in the navies of the world.

Her activities along the coast of Luzon north of Manila appear to have been just like those of the other ships of the fleet. She harassed the Japanese debarkation port. She was chased and depth-charged. She flirted with death on the reefs. She fired a lot of torpedoes and got a few hits. But, as the graduates of her crew indicated, nobody gives you any kudos for routine like that.

The Japs came to notice her in a few encounters off Indo-China. Particularly they noted her color—which by that time was easy to note. She had become a flaming scarlet that could have been spotted by any airplane pilot even if she had happened to be lying at the bottom of the Tuscarora deep. Apparently more than one Japanese observer saw her, and each saw her in a different place, which gave rise to the pleasant legend that she was not one ship but about a dozen. Survivors of the ships she had sunk started their complaints to Tokyo's so-called "civilized world." The startled Japs in turn aired their novel protest against attacks on transports, tankers, supply ships and other innocent merchantmen. And that might have been the end of it all if the men on the red submarine had not heard the broadcast.

However they did hear it, and were much set up about having been singled out as an important and implacable enemy. As soon as they got shore leave—a considerable time later it turned out to be—they had their ears pierced and fitted with rings in the fashion once approved by the uncolored pirates of the Spanish Main.

A lot of them were still wearing the decorations of their order when they came to the submarine school at New London or joined the crews of freshly launched boats. Another lot who never left their original assignment were the high point of the submarine social season at Mare Island when finally the battered pirate ship came in at last for an overhaul. Wherever you ran into them they were an amazing sight and the object of general attention. But they didn't get into so many fights as you might suspect. Whatever might be the idea of outsiders about earrings as a male decoration, these lads undoubtedly wore their badges with muscular grace. Like the first one we saw in New London, they were all hard specimens, probably the hardest that this essentially hard service has produced. You have to be tough to be a submariner. You have to be tougher to wear earrings before the critical public of a navy yard.

Oschner did most of the talking. He is a stocky, humorous lad of the type one used to see so often in movies of the fleet. "The cops here aren't like those in Australia. They pinched us right away. And we were only having a friendly fight. We didn't know what we were being pinched for." Wilson was the least voluble. He is a well-set-up boy of the good-listener type and apparently feared that somebody, particularly his companions, might think that he was bragging. Killan, a bright youngster with a good sense of news, was an excellent end man for Oschner.

The conversation skated around over most of the Far East

until it was suggested that maybe they had better begin at the beginning, no matter how uneventful that beginning had seemed to them.

"Well," said Oschner, "we were in Manila when one of those ships came in that they gave all the medals to. Nobody gave us any medals. I guess that's because we were too modest to tell anybody where we'd been."

"When Manila got too hot for us to stay there any more—and that was right away—we went on up north to this bay the Japs had taken over, and we monkeyed around there a while, just like the rest of them. Then we moved on down the coast and eventually got to Sourabaya [Java].

"It was a tough trip . . . but there were lots of other tough trips in those days so I guess maybe we haven't any kick. We were kind of short on supplies. We took out enough food to last us normally for three weeks and we were out twice that. We learned how the Jap submarine crews were getting along then. We lived on the same sort of trash they had—rice and such stuff as that. Nobody got fat on that trip.

"There isn't much to tell about the submarine service for those first four months of the war. We were hauling supplies and ammunition to Corregidor and taking people out of places and delivering them to other places. We'd take out twenty or thirty passengers at a time. They'd be sleeping all over the place, on the wardroom table and on the engine-room catwalk and all over the decks. We'd take them down to Australia and dump them and come back and get some more.

"One of the guys we hauled out was taking a lot of records back to the United States. He was certainly glad to get away from the Philippines and the Japs. He told us all about what was wrong with the Army and how he wished he'd gone into the Navy and how the submarine service was the best part of the Navy. And then he got back home and took the pants off us. Everything about the trip was wrong. I remember reading that he was particularly sore at the captain for making him split up his baggage into smaller lots so's it would fit through a hatch. I never could see what the captain ought to have done about it except maybe expand the hatch."

His pals grinned without sympathy.

"It wasn't like any other ferryboat service either," said Oschner. "Every time we'd get out of the harbor the cans would be waiting to run us around. We'd have to submerge with all that mob aboard and turn every valve just the same as if we weren't standing on about three people apiece when we did it. In those days we couldn't maneuver around the way we did afterward. That is, we had to go in and out of places almost on a timetable where nowadays, with only the Japs and no passengers to worry about, we'd be able to pick our own time.

"On one of those trips we had to go under so often and stay down so long each time that our batteries began to get low. That wasn't the worst of it. Our air began to get low, too. We had a nut aboard. He hadn't worried us so much before the start of the war because we conceded that maybe a nut was the only guy who'd want to get into the submarine service in the first place, but he got to be a nuisance when we were all fouled up with soldiers and civilians.

"On one occasion we had to go down several times in a row and the last was too much for him. He knew—we all knew—that if it turned out that we couldn't blow ballast we were going to stay there for keeps and he kept moaning: 'The air's all gone. The batteries are all gone. We'll all be killed this time for sure.'

"The soldiers just didn't know what to make of it. And the rest of us weren't very happy either.

"He got classified later. They gave him shore duty—I guess with a keeper.

"He was quite a guy to have aboard a submarine when he wasn't getting in your way. He furnished a lot of conversation. I remember one day when he came to the chief pharmacist's mate and asked to borrow the microscope. 'I've been working for years on a cure for cancer,' he says. 'And now I think I've finally got it licked.' We all thought that would be fine business, discovering a cure for cancer down there in a submarine, but he turned out to be mistaken. He was anxious to get to be an electrician and he was always getting things connected up backwards. He burned up a radio set by hanging it onto a high-tension line. Probably he kept getting his cancer cure mixed up with his electricity.

"The pharmacist's mate was Wheeler B. Lipes, the guy who performed the first emergency operation in the submarine service. He was a savvy dude all right. He stood a watch, and when the yeoman wasn't there he did yeoman duty too. And he was good at his own work. You ought to see the job he did on cuts and breaks and such simple stuff.

"The night of the operation I was on the bow planes. It was a long watch. The operation took about two hours and forty-five minutes altogether—with the preparations and everything. We didn't want any angle on the boat. She was kept in trim all the time."

"I was asleep when all that was going on," reminisced young Mr. Killan.

"So was I," said Wilson. "I didn't know a thing about it."

"Well, everybody else in the boat knew about it," said Oschner. "About half of them were trying to help with the job and the other half were trying to get up onto the table so they could see better. . . . This guy came out of the ether cursing me. I'd been giving him hell occasionally about the way he handled the planes, and it looked as if he thought I was still giving him hell all the time Lipes was carving on him.

"They thought some of giving Lipes a medal for his job. But just about that time a regular doctor lost an appendix case on one of the surface ships and it would have made him look like a chump to give a pharmacist's mate a medal for showing what an easy job the regular doc had muffed.

"Lipes was a good guy. I remember that in spite of all he had to do he'd give you everything you wanted. He'd come looking for you if you were sick even when he wasn't asked. Mostly we call the pharmacist's mates 'Quack,' just like you call the radioman 'Sparks' and the carpenter 'Chips.' But the pharmacist's mates don't like it. They'd rather be called 'Doc.' I guess I'd be willing to call Lipes 'Doc.' "

The other lads agreed with that.

"Those early days were complicated by a whole lot of things," said Oschner. "We kept getting new batches of men and when we did we'd have to stand four on and four off until we'd get them broken in. Then we'd come back from a patrol and get all but three or four of them transferred and take on a new outfit of boots.

"The paint was always a lot of bother to us. We'd taken a trimming in Cavite Harbor from the airplanes. The hull was full of holes. We'd patched up the important places to make the tanks watertight but we didn't bother with the rest of the damage, and we didn't try to fix up the paint which had never been much good the first time we put to sea.

"We got into a storm off French Indo-China and that cleaned all that was left of the black off of us. When we got into clear water nobody had to use sound gear on us. They could see us no matter where we went.

"The storm was unusual. Generally it's pretty good sailing up there, and when we first came into our area the weather was calm. We went to work right away.

"One evening when we surfaced we saw some ships ahead of us—merchantmen and a can. The can was lying back. I don't know what she was doing and we weren't in position to attack. But pretty soon it began to look like she was the convoy and the merchant ships were the escort. One of them—I think she was a transport—certainly took on the job by trying to ram us. She swung around and came after us hell-bent.

" 'Well,' the captain said, 'what's all this? She's trying to run us down. Make ready the stern tubes.' He seemed surprised about it and so did everybody else. But he wasn't too surprised to know just what he was doing. He spun around, too, as she came down on us, and he shot two fish out of the stern tubes. Her bow came out of the water a mile and she went down in a hurry.

"We used to keep the radio going all the time in there," Oschner continued. "Working the radio didn't tell them anything they didn't know. They'd figured it out pretty well that we were in there. They said they were going to get us and they certainly showed that they meant it.

"We used to listen to all their broadcasts. Even while we were still hanging around Manila after they'd taken the town, we heard them. They used to say a lot of funny things. Once they said that all American sailors could go on liberty in Manila if they would wear white hats and carry no guns. We thought there might be a catch in that. Then another time they said that all sailors would find the clothes they had dropped on the beach waiting for them when they came back.

"I got to hoping they might mean that, because I left a lot of things ashore when I left. My shack was a palace all fitted up with stuff I'd picked up in China. I hated to lose it.

"Well, we stayed out on our Red Pirate patrol, and the Japs kept screaming about us all the time. It was very encouraging. They kept hunting us and spotting us and shooting at us. But it was always the same story. They couldn't hit us. While they were chasing us, we sank several ships—a couple off China and more farther south.

"Lieutenant Commander Farrell got a medal for the job. When we finally came to a base we were feeling pretty proud about everything, but mostly about having annoyed the Japs more than anybody else in the neighborhood.

"When we got in Herman Hettrick got the idea of this pirate business. He is a big, dark guy—looks like a bigger edition of Tyrone Power. He went ashore and got his ears pierced and came back wearing a pair of rings that hung down an inch and a half. They were just like the pictures we used to see in kids' books and we all thought they were swell. Then I decided that if it didn't hurt too much I'd have my ears fixed up too. Lipes did it for us. He froze our ears and stuck needles through them. A couple of guys we held down by force and fixed them up whether they liked it or not. All in all twenty of us got earrings."

"We were going to get little figures made of the fish our ship was named after," said Killan. "But you couldn't get any work like that done in Australia. There just weren't any workmen. Everybody was off doing something for the war. So we got what we could. There wasn't any particular style."

"I made a pair out of baby rings," said Oschner. "And I made a lot of other kinds for other fellows. Some of the guys had loop earrings. But those weren't a success. When they got into fights or tight quarters somebody would make a grab at them and just about pull their ears off. And when a guy makes a pass at you you just can't tell him to wait until you get your earrings off."

"One guy had a heavy pair," said Killan. "They pulled down his ear lobes and made his head look funny."

"It was all in the way of diversion," said Oschner. "And almost anything looks like diversion when you're out on a long patrol. But I've often wondered what the Japs would think if they captured one of us with these things on. . . ."

It was an odd thought. I mulled it over and wondered myself.

20

THE DOMESTIC LIFE OF THE RED PIRATES

LOOKING back on the conversation of the Red Pirates, I am struck by the number of inconsequential things that lingered in their memory apparently more vividly than battles. And the only explanation I can find for it is that any peak that rises out of monotony is a high peak. These lads might ask to consult the records before trying to tell you what day it was when a blast almost upended them, or what sort of ship they sent down on the third day of the second patrol. But they know all the circumstances of how the cook came to break an egg in his own face and who was doing what the night Mike Milligan fell out of his bunk. And yet, make no mistake about it, their ship didn't arouse the ire of the Japanese merely because she was painted red, and their captain didn't get decorated just for his navigation or even for his understanding of a submarine crew's psychology, although, perhaps, he should have received an extra star for it.

"It's hard to find things to do on submarine patrols," said Oschner. "The first weeks generally we used to sleep. Then we'd get tired of sleeping and we'd read everything there was to read until we got tired of reading."

"Then," said Wilson, "you'd go off in a corner and talk to yourself."

"There was a lot of conversation," Oschner recalled. "When everything else had been done we'd have experience meetings. The guys would talk about what they had done on the last shore leave, and they'd mull over the beer they'd drunk and the girls they'd met. And finally we'd all sit down and lay out our plans for the next leave. That would just about take us back to the base. Then we'd go ashore and do something else."

"The officers played cards and chess," said Killan. "The skipper was pretty good at chess."

"He sure was," said Oschner. "Once we got locked up in a narrow channel with a couple of cans crisscrossing us. I was ready to pay off just about then but the captain wasn't a good chess player for nothing. He sneaked us out just by guessing in advance what they were going to do."

"He always got us out," said Killan. "And he always won when he was playing chess."

"Nobody was ever scared when he was running the boat," said Oschner. "We had a lot of confidence in the Old Man. The only damage we ever got was while the boat was in Cavite getting plastered by the airplanes. After that, every other day or so we got depth-charged all over the place and it never bothered us . . . anyway it never bothered him.

"I remember one night when we were catching plenty and Bueb, the quartermaster, began to chatter, 'Who's scared here? Who's scared? You scared, Captain? You scared?' And the captain says, 'No, Bueb, I'm not scared.' And Bueb says, 'Then I ain't scared, Captain. I ain't scared if you ain't scared.' And fifteen guys yelled at the same time, 'For God's sake shut up. . . .'

"You get awful serious about depth charges," said Oschner. "I remember one time . . . we're diving. I know we're diving but just for the moment I'm not paying much attention to it. I've got a nail in my shoe and I go aft to the engine room to fix it. I take off my shoe, put it in a vise and start socking it with a hammer . . . Clunk! Clunk! Then all at once I notice that nobody's making any noise in the boat. It's as still as a cemetery, and right after that I hear everybody in the place howling at once. And one of the officers says, 'Damn it, I'll chain you to a periscope.' It seems to me that the hammering sound is too familiar to them.

"We had a chief electrician's mate who used to get it up his neck every time a depth charge went off, and it made him mad if everybody else didn't get scared when he did. After the blasting was over we used to go back to the mess room and get a cup of coffee and hash things over. This guy came along and asked everybody how he felt while it was going on and everybody said, 'Just fine.' And he got all heated up. He said, 'Well, if you guys weren't scared you just don't live right, that's all. Everybody gets scared.' He read that in a magazine somewhere and he believed it.

"The rest of the chiefs weren't so fussy about it. Ralph Dickerman, the QM, told him that he wasn't scared either. 'But,' he says, 'the two guys I passed on the way to the deck certainly were.'

"Life got to have just the same program every day on those long patrols. Dickerman would be running around kidding the officers asking them if somebody wasn't going to be made chief today.

"The wardroom would have a chess game going, or cards.

"The Old Man would be bawling out somebody for something. I never stayed to find out what.

"The chiefs would be quarreling about the light in their quarters. If the lights were on, somebody would want them turned off. If they were turned off, somebody would want them turned on.

"In the control room you'd find three guys asleep and one watching the diving planes. In the crew's quarters aft you'd find two guys asleep and ten guys talking about nothing—absolutely nothing. They might as well have been asleep too. And when you could get your ears working in all this you'd hear some guy yelling, 'Have I permission to pump the head?'

"And there never was a time when two guys sharing the same bunk weren't arguing which one was going to get the bunk next.

"We used to get a lot of amusement out of the phonograph in the forward torpedo room. We had one record that we used to play over and over again: 'The Last Trip of the Old Ship.' It wasn't much of a tune but it got a lot of attention. The gunner's mate used to curse and swear every time we played it. He would be sound asleep when that thing started and he'd come out of his bunk roaring."

"The records were mostly Australian stuff," said Killan. "We never heard much of the new tunes from home. We got a few records from some of the newer ships when they came out. We traded old ones for 'em and it couldn't help but be a good deal for us.

"They weren't any Beethoven symphonies. . . . Just songs and stuff. Before one patrol the captain bought 'Jingle Bells' and

'Silent Night.' We were going to have a real Christmas. But we played 'em so often that we didn't care much for them by the time Christmas got around."

"There was something wrong with 'Jingle Bells,'" mentioned Oschner. "I learned to play it on my harmonica, and so help me every time I played it we got depth-charged."

"They say the Japs are good critics of music," said Wilson. "I don't know whether it's true or not. But that's what they say."

"We dove one day," Killan recalled. "We stayed down a long time. I don't know just when we went down. You get mixed up on time in submarines. But we were certainly down.

"The Japs were wild. We'd sunk a ship a few days before and they were looking for us.

"We'd been steaming along on the surface that early morning minding our own business when a ship showed up in the dark ahead of us. She was a big ship—a passenger ship or transport. We threw four fish at her. The first one hit and the ship blew up. The second missed. The third exploded prematurely and lifted us right out of the water."

Oschner remembered that one.

"That was a blast!" he said. "The concussion blew another fish out of the tube and that one began to run hot, too. It hit something right ahead of us and it made the loudest noise I ever heard. It knocked the wrenches off the tube doors and smashed a lot of glass."

".I thought sure it was a direct hit," said Killan. "All the circuit breakers went out and we didn't have any power. We just sat there for five minutes looking at the pressure gauge. A couple of the guys began to mumble, 'Why doesn't he take her down?' And I said, 'The Old Man's taking a picture.' They believed it, I guess."

"Two days later we hit a transport," said Wilson. He said it in the same matter-of-fact way that he had mentioned Japanese judgment of harmonica playing. So far as his tone of voice was concerned one might have thought he deemed them both worthy of the same emphasis.

"And maybe that wasn't a neat job," said Oschner. "We'd made an approach on it and a tin can peeled off and chased us. We dove. We came up that night about ten and there was the transport with the can right alongside her. We got both of them with two fish.

"After that we headed south. It looked like the best bet. We knew that the ocean would be swimming with cans and patrol boats up north where we were. We were feeling pretty secure when we surfaced—and there were cans bearing down on us. They were coming fast and they fired at us with their deck guns just as we dove. They worked on us all night long."

"They just kept feeling around," said Killan.

"They went away at daylight because MacArthur came over and bombed us."

"Not personally," said Wilson. "By proxy."

"It wasn't much of a relief to get rid of the cans," said Killan with something of a sigh, and he voiced the favorite axiom of the submarine service. "All submarines look alike to the guys in the planes. . . . We hadn't been able to surface during the night and when we tried it during the day our own planes came over and poured it down on us. So we had to dive again.

"We had to conserve our battery so we turned all power off except what was absolutely necessary. We worked the diving-plane controls by hand and shut down the air conditioner. Boy, it was hot!"

"It was 130 with humidity about 90," mentioned Oschner. "We were working in puddles all day and the following night. It was a tough break because we were going home. We hadn't any more torpedoes."

"We did better the next day," said Killan. "We surfaced about 4:30 in the afternoon and started our engines. Two cans showed up on the horizon and we felt as big as a barn. But they kept moving. We got on for home. . . ."

They sighted a few sampans before they reached their base but they did nothing about it. They didn't figure their deck gun was so good as those the sampans might have concealed.

"You never monkey with sampans," said Wilson sagely. "A lot of them have five-inch guns and torpedo tubes."

Oschner did not seem to have heard this.

"It was just disheartening," he said. "We couldn't cook a thing. Somebody opened up some canned chicken and called it turkey.

But we couldn't kid ourselves. We got to thinking what was going on at home and that didn't make us feel so good either.

"Lots of things going on at home didn't make us feel so good. I remember how it used to make the guys mad to read about the poor aircraft workers on the night shift who couldn't get any time to spend their money. . . ."

"And when the zoot suits came out," said Killan, "that was the absolute limit. The guys talked about zoot suits for days. There was a reward offered by the ship for the first guy who brought one back. And then the ante was raised for the first guy who came back with half of one."

"We went on home after that to get a firsthand look at the zoot suits," said Oschner. "I really mean we went home. We stopped at Pearl Harbor and they met us with a brass band. They played 'Bless 'Em All.' It's an Aussie song and we'd been hearing it for two years. I like to killed some of the musicians but I couldn't get close enough. . . . And then we got home and everybody wanted to talk about the war."

"And everybody wanted to talk about the war!" That is, presumably, everybody but the lads who had just been fighting it. I began to realize why their conversation had seemed so little concerned with things which in the surface fleet we had come to look upon as the facts of life. For a moment or two they might turn you cold: "I thought sure it was a direct hit!" "All the circuit breakers went out and we didn't have any power. We just sat there!" "We came up and there was the transport with a can alongside her. We got both of them with two fish!" But such things somehow began to seem like minor matters in a world full of zoot suits and Aussie songs.

Little by little the amazing picture of those first few months of the war in the submarine was taking shape . . . but it was the magic of their idle chatter that they appeared to be taking no part in its making. They had gone into almost endless detail about the designing of their earrings and the style and utility of the finished product. You gathered that was because you naturally couldn't be expected to know much about earrings. And they let you supply your own scenery as they skipped over such matters as blood and battle—because, apparently, fighting was the business of submarines and to their notion everybody ought to know all about them.

So you got no graphic descriptions of sundering transports, flame rolling eerily into the dark sky, black debris raining down through the deadly glow, thousands of men or bits of men scattered over the churning water. Your imagination had to reconstruct that for you. . . . That, and the uncanny terror of the depth bombs—a mental horror that shocked memory mercifully refuses to resurrect.

Yet somehow you got the feeling of this as vividly as it is given any man who has not experienced it, while they went on with their inventory of minutiae. Making a note of the can they had destroyed here and the cargo ship they had sunk there, and marking the causation of such things as "that ash-can barrage we got right after we put two fish into the tanker," and adding all this to what you had picked out of other double-talk by other submariners, you began to understand what a blight these men had been to the otherwise unharried Japanese. You saw the war suddenly not as a helpless, hopeless, national shame typified by the burning *Arizona* and her sunken sisters in Pearl Harbor but as a scientific slaughter that had rolled up with increasing momentum from the shallow flats of Manila Bay.

On January 2, 1942, less than a month after the opening raid, the Japanese occupied Manila, and the submarines that had been based there were homeless. The short haul had suddenly become the long pull. Where patrols had previously been a matter of days or weeks, and torpedo replenishment no more complicated than a trip of a hundred miles or so, they now had to stay out longer and when their fish were gone they had to journey thousands of miles to get more. They did the scores of odd jobs for which they had never been designed. They had traveled much of the time under orders forbidding them to fight. And yet, before Corregidor fortress finally gave up on May 6, 1942, they had contrived to make life a literal hell for men aboard the enemy transports. They had strewn the beaches with hulks that neither side bothered to mention in the communiqués any more than the submarine crews bother to mention them now. They made a daily routine of heroism such as no other service has produced in this war and they got no medals for it. Thousands of Japanese soldiers were killed in those first ninety days who might now be alive and adding their menace to the Solomons or Australia if a few pig boats had not been there to take over the work of the Asiatic fleet. You felt that you ought to tell the Red Pirates that the onslaught of the submarines off the coast of Luzon would one day be given proper recognition as one of the great adventures in American history. But these men from another world didn't seem to care.

"The people of Australia were swell," said Oschner. "They'd take you into their homes. They didn't have a thing but whatever they had was yours. They'd take you on picnics—and it was some job to take you on a picnic. They had gas rationing out there long before we had it and a stricter ration. But they didn't cry about it and they managed to get along. . . ."

Killan nodded.

"It made us mad to see articles in the papers and magazines about people at home crying over sugar and gas. The Aussies never let out a yelp. I'd keep wondering if maybe they didn't have more guts than we had."

"Of course," admitted Oschner judicially, "maybe it wasn't right for us to criticize the home folks. We ran out of coffee and sugar and milk once for about a month. But generally we didn't have to worry much about chow."

"No," said Killan. "Nobody ever gave us the short end of the rations. When we came out of Cavite we had just what stores we could pick up in a hurry off the dock, but we never let that happen again. We stuffed all the corners with it."

"On that first trip," said Oschner, "it seemed to me that all we had was rice and vitamin pills. I don't know how we managed to get those aboard but it seemed like we had a ton of them. . . . Take a dose of this and think of it as ham and eggs!"

"I never worried about food so much as the heat," mentioned Wilson. And his pals agreed with that.

"I don't think we could have lived at all without the air conditioning," said Oschner. "We had to turn it off a few times to save current when the cans were laying it on us pretty thick, and we nearly died. It wasn't only that you were miserable but you got weak. You couldn't lift a hand to wipe the sweat out of your eyes. The heat made you so dopey that you didn't bother to jump when the bombs went off. Unless they knocked you down you hardly noticed them at all. And if they did knock you down you just stayed there because you couldn't get up.

"You'd go to sleep and it would take somebody a couple of hours to wake you up. . . . And that wasn't all of it. When the air conditioner was turned off you always ran out of wash water pretty quick. The moisture that this gadget took out of the air and condensed was what we used for washing. We used to get from 130 to 150 gallons a day that way—more than two gallons to a man. Without the air conditioner going there were a couple of extra gallons of sweat and steam for each man to wade around through. We couldn't take a bath. We could hardly wash our faces and hands. And it always seemed to me that wet air got foul quicker than dry air."

"That didn't bother us much—the foul air I mean," Killan said. "You got so used to it that when you opened up the hatch the fresh air would make you dizzy. . . . But air that didn't do you any good when you breathed it made the going tough. That's why most of the fellows on a submarine sleep during the day. They use up less oxygen when they're not moving around. That's why we reverse our day and have our breakfast at 6 P.M., our dinner at midnight and our supper in the early morning. It saves using a lot of current for the galley when you're running on batteries. Also it keeps heat out of the boat. When you can't see the sun it don't make much difference to you what time the clock says it is."

"It makes a difference when you come into port though," said Oschner. "We used to run around all night, naturally. And everything would shut up at nine. Finally the Navy took over a hotel at our base and kept it open on our schedule. Habits like that are hard to break when you've been a couple of years picking them up.

"When we got home New London turned out to be a bad town for us. On my very first liberty I was in town with Joe and before an hour had gone by the cops had both of us. We didn't know what they were picking us up for. It was just a little friendly fight.

"In the morning the chief of the boat was in court and told the judge that we were just back from Bataan. And the judge said, 'Well, you're in America now and you'll have to act like Americans.' He talked like he thought we were foreigners.

"There was a lot of foolishness going on around our base all right. A lot of green kids came in there with a cruiser and started to brag about having come all the way across the Pacific alone. A lot of the tin-can sailors who'd been running up and down Macassar Straits with nothing but a prayer for protection got sore about it. They used to say these kids belonged to the A.I.P.— Always In Port—and called their ship the *Reluctant Dragon*.

"One of these kids asked me one time if I'd been on a submarine that got cracked up and I said I was and he asked me how I got off and I told him I'd come up from six hundred feet in an air bubble and he believed it. I didn't notice while I was telling it that a lieutenant from his cruiser was standing right behind him, and when I got through he said it was the most remarkable experience he'd ever heard about and I guess it was. But he didn't tell the kid.

"Then the kid asked me what we did when we'd sunk a ship and there were a lot of people floating around in the water. I said we flooded down and knocked them off with baseball bats to save ammunition. I don't know whether he believed that one or not.

"Looking back on it, I don't remember any time we were right up against death even when the depth charges were coming down. But it certainly was dangerous ashore. Once at our base the Japs blew up a pub right after we'd all gone back to the boat. They blew up another one in Sourabaya just as we were heading for it. I guess you could prove without much trouble that pubs are more dangerous than submarines."

That unaccountably reminded Killan of the war that had hitherto seemed so irrelevant.

"You remember," he said, "that before this war everybody used to say that a submarine might fight a battleship in a pinch but that she never could fight another submarine. Well, I was figuring up the other night just from what I'd heard from other men in the submarines that in the fighting in the Southwest Pacific we sank eleven of theirs—and that's just counting those that were in our own territory. Our submarines got three off one port alone.

"We got one all for ourselves with the old red boiler. He surfaced just about the same time we did but he saw us first and dove. We dove after him and the captain let go a fish. It got him."

"I'll say it got him," said Oschner. "It was like touching off fifty depth charges all at once. It like to blew us out of the water stern first."

"It was a slick job, though," said Killan, "just like spearing fish with dynamite. It taught us not to horse around with Jap submarines because if we could knock them off it stood to reason they could knock us off. Up to that time we'd never thought they were very dangerous."

The lads had a lot to say about the sabotage of the Philippines.

"We heard," said Killan, "and I don't know how true it is, that the Japs landed there with no equipment at all. They dug up arms and ammunition from a cache in the hills after they got ashore. They picked up drums of oil and supplies from the bottom of the bay where they'd been dumped off ships at night."

"And there was plenty of fifth column," said Oschner. "After we came out of Cavite we could see red flares going off around us all night long and after a flare would light up, the shells and bombs would begin to come over. They shot some fifth columnists but I guess they didn't shoot enough.

"It's no fun listening to bombs even if they're not intended for you. . . . I remember we had one kid aboard who'd been wanting to hear a depth charge. We told him naturally he could have our share. But he seemed to think we were kidding. He kept talking about it all the time. And when the things began to bust he went right down on his knees. He was scared limber. Then he jumped up and tried to get somebody to open the engine-room hatch. 'Open it!' he kept yelling. 'How do you get out of here?' We were in maybe one hundred and fifty feet of water at the time and it didn't seem possible. . . ."

"Do you remember," Wilson asked, "the day we fired at half a dozen ships and sank one and we surfaced and one of them turned the light on us?"

"Do I remember!" said Oschner. "I had an eighteen-degree bubble on her and I started to take her down right to the bottom."

"We went down like a rock," Killan recalled. "But we leveled her off in fine shape. We were twenty feet off the bottom then. The fathometer showed that. I certainly remember that dive. I was topside when the alarm came and it looked like everybody on the boat was jamming up that hatch."

"One guy got his leg in the ladder," Wilson said. "And everybody else just walked over him. . . . That was a close call. That freighter was throwing depth charges all over the Pacific."

"We should have got that ship, too," said Killan. "Whenever you miss they certainly pour it onto you. Coming down the ladder that day, I kicked the executive officer in the face and knocked him across the control room. Of course he had no business loitering there."

"Days like that make you think you could possibly stand the life in the surface ships," said Oschner. "But still when I try to remember the really tough going I always get back to the last trip we made to Corregidor. Maybe it just looks tough because we got used to the hammering later. But I don't think so."

"I don't either," said Killan. "It wasn't so much the hell we caught as the feeling that we were so useless." He explained it to me. "After we got battered up north of Manila we went to our new base and got a load of stuff and took it up to Corregidor. It was a wow of a trip with all the Jap navy and a sky full of airplanes lambasting us all the time. But that wasn't the worst of it. After hundreds of miles of that sort of stuff we couldn't land our cargo and had to lug it all the way back a few thousand miles to Australia."

"That was something," recalled Oschner. "We lay around there until I thought we were never coming off the bottom. And when we did come up there'd always be a tin can waiting between us and the dock. It was something to see, though. The guns on Corregidor were going over our heads and the Jap artillery was coming back, and the shorts and the duds were falling alongside us. The sky all around you would turn red in patches until you thought your eyes would pop out with the flash. And you couldn't hear yourself think."

"You could read a newspaper topside in the flash of the guns," said Killan. . . . "Not just one night but every night we were trying to run through the destroyer screen. . . . I've often thought that if we could have got that stuff off, maybe Corregidor might have lasted a few days more. We had a lot of medical supplies and chow aboard. And they needed that as much as they needed antiaircraft shells. Those guys were falling down for lack of food. They couldn't lift their rifles, a lot of them. They all had malaria and there wasn't any medicine left."

"I was on another submarine at that time," said Wilson. "We went out with a load of food but we only got as far as Mindanao when Corregidor fell."

"All the subs out there at that time were carrying loads of shell and quinine and chow," Oschner told me. "That was our main job but mostly it's the same story. The stuff couldn't be landed.

"It was a discouraging sort of beginning, but when we got going we got going. We were the only red submarine operating around Indo-China but you never could tell the Japs that. She was a good old boat, the old red submarine. . . ."

"Boy! She certainly was red," conceded Mr. Killan.

21

THE HEGIRA OF THE S-BOATS

You probably won't find any wordy enthusiasm about it in the patrol reports, but to the men who survived it the 12,000-mile trek of the S-boats from Panama to Australia will always look like the high point of submarine operation in this war. Sometime in the spring of 1942, with the Jap threat against Australia increasing daily, it became evident that our last remaining weapon—withal our most effective weapon—against Hirohito's expansion was the submarine. It was just as apparent that any kind of submarine was better than none. So a squadron of relics that had been attached to the defense of Panama was detached and chased into battle.

That the S-boats which in days of peace were never allowed out of sight of their escort, could have made a 12,000-mile voyage at all is one of those impossible things previously mentioned. That the journey could have been made with only one stop is something that a lot of them may never believe. That they got there at all is a matter that some Jap destroyer-division commanders are probably still debating with the high command.

The S-boats, whatever you may say for their status in the world fleets of their day, were all turned out in the early twenties and all of them are as much relics of World War I as Fokker airplanes and red pants for infantry. They must have been well engineered and well constructed or they would never have reached their patrol areas. But I suspect that what gave them any usefulness at all in this war was the skill and endurance of the men who drove them.

Their route down through Polynesia has not yet been disclosed. But we know that it was 12,000 miles long and we know that there was only one port of call on it—a hastily constructed base somewhere among the myriad islands of the South Pacific where fuel and food could be taken aboard and sweating mechanics with a few spare parts and plenty of baling wire could fit the old crates for their last and most perilous lap. We know that the course must have been circuitous, that it must have run at all times close to the edge of the Japanese advance and at times squarely into it. We know that the boats ran through the quivering heat and breathless calms and roaring seas that succeed one another to beat down human endurance in the tropical storm season. We know that in the last couple of thousand miles of their hegira they were not only in close contact with the Japanese invasion fleets but squarely in the road of destroyer packs hunting for just such voyagers as themselves—a menace which, considering their specifications and the jobs for which they were designed in the twenties, could hardly be overlooked. Concerning that part of their troubles, however, I have never heard any comment. It was what they had come down there to look for, wasn't it? And they found it. Well and good. The principal thing that we know of the expedition is that it finally came into port with all boats intact and the crews still able to stand on their feet. *Deo gratias!*

Much of this story I got from Lieutenant Les Eubanks who served as executive officer aboard one of these aging whales. More of it I got from his crew and the crews of other boats in the squadron as we sat around coffee machines in the submarine factory at New London. And with the temperature outside at seventeen degrees below zero it didn't seem surprising that they had forgotten most of the hardships of their voyage save the heat. They were ecstatic in their talk about the new boats in which they would presently be sailing back to the old neighborhood, but they didn't seem to be much concerned with any such nonessential details as greater fire power, greater maneuverability, greater speed or even greater space to move about in. They were interested mostly in the air conditioning and in the prospect of showing what they could do with a war when they were left with strength enough to stand up to it.

"We got to port all right," Lieutenant Eubanks said. "We didn't have a single mishap. The old boats were pretty well built to begin with and they'd had some overhauling and we didn't drive them beyond what they could stand. But it was tough going all the same.

"Those boats were never intended to make such long trips, so we couldn't carry the supplies we really needed. Rations got to be pretty thin and uninteresting before we finally reached Australia. But by that time we didn't care much. When you're broiling all the time you aren't too much interested in food.

"There weren't any air-conditioning systems in the boats—not until much later. And as you probably know from what you've seen aboard the surface ships there is no place on earth any hotter than that end of the Pacific. In addition to that we had tropical humidity in which wet and dry were just the same thing.

"We had one stop at an island that had never heard about the tourist trade. It was cut off from everything . . . the sort of place where the natives had nothing to do but fish or wait for their meals to fall into their laps off of trees. The beach boys gave us a hand with anything we had to do but they didn't seem to be particularly interested in us. We may have been the first submarines they had ever seen but they had seen whales before. So far as I know nobody ever called at the place and the people who lived there never went visiting anywhere else. It was just the complete end of the world. And yet it was a grand place to be because the air was soft and warm all day and cool at night. Even then we'd got to appreciate how good it felt to lie in a cool, dry bed. We remembered it a long time after we got under way and ran into water like the bottom of Old Faithful geyser."

Inside the boats there was no such thing as evaporation, the lieutenant recalled. A man would sweat—which is to say the water would run off him in three or four streams at a time—and it would run onto the floor and just stay there until he'd be standing in a little puddle all his own. The electrical equipment would get soaked and shorted and then the batteries would boil and bubble and put out smells that they'd never had to contend with before. They kept wondering how long their lungs were going to stand it.

"Everything got wet, of course," he said. "Day and night it was just the same, although when we got to the danger zone and had to submerge for long periods at night we thought the nights were a little worse. You'd think the men would poop out fast in an atmosphere like that. But they stood up to it. They got heat rashes and scratched them and infected them and sores broke out on them and there wasn't much we could do about it. Of course everybody was working as nearly naked as he could get. You couldn't stand the feel of wet clothes on your skin. But as I say, in spite of everything the men kept on going even when the machinery didn't. I marveled at them.

"I got one big surprise when I found how everybody's temper stayed on an even keel in a boiling hell like that. I guess from the start we realized as we'd never realized in peacetimes that we were all in this thing together—all for one and one for all and that sort of thing. You can't get very critical of a guy who may have the job of saving your life in the next couple of minutes.

"Very few people in the Navy at that time had ever heard any shots fired at them. We could probably have done a lot of worrying except for the fact that we had about the biggest job of our lives to do in bringing these crates safe to port."

It sounded to me like something of an understatement.

"When we started off," he said, "we didn't think we'd be running into much Japanese activity for a while—not at any rate until we'd been sent out on patrol looking for it. We'd figured out that the Japs would move north instead of south, and I guess maybe they did intend to do that. But by the time we'd crossed the line we found out how things were going. There were Jap war vessels all over the Southwest Pacific and there weren't any indications where they were ever going to stop. We kept hearing radio reports out of Australia that showed us how people felt down there. They were looking an invasion right in the teeth and the radio commentators made no bones about saying so.

"I don't know whether or not you'd say we were disturbed when we found out how conditions had changed. Maybe we were disturbed for a couple of days. After all we weren't very well equipped to fight all over the South Pacific without any bases. But then we began to hope we'd run into a couple of them and find out what we could do. We were traveling light but we had torpedoes aboard, and we were as ready for a scrap as we were ever going to be. I guess reaction from monotony is probably the explanation for a lot of daring in war.

"However, it wasn't our job to go on the prowl for trouble. We were carrying enough of it right with us with our old engines and creaking hull. We kept our nose to the line and went on south."

Most of the time the weather was good. They might have enjoyed it if they hadn't been drowning in their own sweat. There were always fog banks on the horizon and magnificent sunsets. There were occasional rain patches and a few blows but no real storms.

"There were storms all around us, I guess," the lieutenant said, ". . . we kept running into airless patches and hot calms and such things. But none of them hit us. The sea was generally as flat and monotonous as everything else on the trip.

"When we sailed we'd figured that we were starting out on a great adventure, that in pushing these boats 12,000 miles we were going to do something spectacular and important. And then one day we slipped into a harbor and tied up and it didn't seem that we had done anything at all. The boats had held together and we had brought them up to a dock. . . . Just a boat ride, that's what it was.

"We stayed in port for a while for refitting . . . but not very long. The war was roaring down on top of us. We weren't going to have to travel another 12,000 miles to find trouble. All we had to do was sit down and let it come to us.

"Looking back on it I think our trek down to the Southwest Pacific had an effect that probably wasn't contemplated in the original plans. The Japs knew just as much about crates of this type as we did. In fact they've got a lot of them themselves, and they certainly knew that such ships weren't meant to make voyages halfway around the world. So when we showed up in the zone of operation, they couldn't believe we were there.

"Our first useful work was observation . . . it wasn't until some weeks later that they turned us loose to break up enemy shipping. So we wandered around quite a lot of ports that the Japs had taken over. We naturally had to do all of this pretty quietly but as time went on it was on the cards that we'd run into a lot of Jap ships. We were sighted several times by patrol boats and men-

Rudy Arnold Photo

THE CAPTAIN'S OFFICE

This compact cubbyhole which serves the commanding officer as a stateroom contains a desk and communication equipment, also a berth, lockers, hot and cold running water and a compass.

OUTWARD BOUND

Looking forward from the conning tower of a U. S. submarine in an unusual formation with two other ships, almost awash, leading the parade.

of-war. Once or twice airplanes flew over us. But nothing happened. There never was any doubt in my mind that we'd been seen. I can only figure that they didn't shoot at us because they figured some way or other that we must be a part of their own fleet.

"We didn't have a great deal of objective luck although we did sink three ships while I was with the boat, one of them a big one. But the main thing was that subjectively we had all the luck in the world. We handed it out and we took it and we came back."

22

INSIDE RAID

It was to be expected that the S-boats would get into trouble at the earliest opportunity, how much trouble depending only on how far they might have to go to look for it. And they lived up to expectations as did few other craft in the U. S. Navy. Other, later, submarines brought in longer lists of sunken enemy ships, but none contributed a more fantastic record of battle against bad luck. They had engine failures and control troubles and leaks and fires. They got pocketed repeatedly by the hunting packs of destroyers. They got depth-charged until their cork linings came out and their ancient paint fell off their bulkheads in flakes like broken glass. But somehow they put down their share of Hirohito's shipping. Somehow they contrived to get into guarded ports where no other weapon of the United States could reach. And somehow, as Lieutenant Eubanks pointed out, they came back.

Captain Fiddler—in whose boat Lieutenant Eubanks came down to the Southwest Pacific as executive—was one of the early adventurers into the seemingly impossible. There were no rule books to guide him. Long-haul tactics for S-boats had not yet been devised. So the captain worked out for himself the rule now pretty generally applied to submarine practice: "Get where they are." He got in and he got out, and between his getting in and getting out he established a standard for melodramatic misadventure, courage, resourcefulness—and luck—that few submarines are going to equal in this war or the next. He had a little general help from whatever operations officer worked out his first battle assignment, for he was sent to patrol an area outside what was becoming quite an important Japanese base in the Southwest Pacific. But once he got into his area he was on his own and he doesn't have to share credit for what happened with anybody except the Japs.

"It was pretty solemn when we went out," Lieutenant Eubanks remembered. "There were a lot of people on the dock seeing us off, including the admiral. Everybody was serious and that also includes the admiral. I recall the advice he gave the skipper.

" 'Don't be overanxious,' he said. 'Don't do anything foolish. Bring your boat back . . . .'

"It was pretty good advice as things turned out. But I don't think the skipper was likely to be overanxious. And knowing the kind of boat we were in and the setup we were moving against, I don't think anybody aboard was interested in doing anything foolish. But we were pretty eager by that time. We were loaded for bear and we figured that with a pretty good section of the Japanese fleet to shoot at we ought to get a nice bag. . . ."

They got up to their area which, not to go into too much detail about it, was one of the hottest corners south of Tokyo. They proceeded cautiously and loitered around the outside of the harbor for a couple of days reconnoitering. They saw plenty of Japanese ships which they were in no position to shoot at. And the captain decided that with traffic spreading fanwise about him and a large tract of ocean to maneuver in at high speeds he wasn't going to be able to do much damage in his present spot without relying almost entirely on luck. He sat down in the wardroom over a cup of coffee and discussed his problem with his officers. Some of the officers talked about it with the chiefs and then the men joined in the conference.

"We had a pretty democratic ship," is Lieutenant Eubanks' comment on this somewhat unorthodox procedure. "We listened to what the men had to say."

Possibly such a thing as this will never happen again even in the submarine service but it does not seem too incredible that it should have happened then.

"The men all wanted to go inside even though the captain wasn't sure he'd be able to get out again," Lieutenant Eubanks recalled. "And so did we. That night we started to ease in.

"The pass into the harbor looked pretty narrow and it got

narrower as we entered it. But in the main I thought the idea was all right. To sink ships you've got to be where they are.

"Our luck held out. As we came in, a patrol boat passed us on the way out. But either he didn't see us or he didn't suspect us. So we came on into the harbor."

They decided to move more cautiously then. The captain figured that the whole port was mined. So for a day or two the submarine just lay doggo watching where the shipping went.

It seems to have been a continuously interesting and peaceful interlude. Shipping came in and went out regularly. They stayed submerged, and stuck up the periscope when they got a chance. At night they came up and watched the dense black shadows moving across the reflected stars in the bay. And so they discovered that the captain's supposition about mines had been right. All shipping turned once it came through the entrance into the harbor and proceeded toward the docks. The submarine was resting at the point of the turn. It was fairly obvious after that where the mine fields lay.

In the course of a few hours they had catalogued the more or less permanent ships in the port—heavy cruisers, several large merchant ships, a long string of destroyers and corvettes. The number of ships, however, varied from hour to hour and the captain gave some thought to a plan of attack which might give him the best targets for the single smash that was likely to be allowed him. They would worry about how to get out when the time came.

How the attack might have gone if the captain had completed his plan is a purely academic matter, for when he stuck up his periscope to make a final study of the situation on the evening of the second day he saw a big warship inbound through the slot. She was almost on top of him—so close that she nearly filled the periscope scale. Her course indicated that she hadn't seen the brief feather of the periscope—didn't suspect the presence of a submarine —and she stood out squarely in front of him, a target as big as a barn. He ordered the torpedo crews to stand by and signaled for full speed ahead to close in for the attack.

One feature of this episode is not given much elaboration by the men who were there—the skipper's willingness to sink a big ship in the one channel through which he might hope to get out of the harbor. But anyway that's what he tried to do and most likely would have done had everything gone as he ordered it.

"But right there," Lieutenant Eubanks observes, "our luck ran out. Every electrical connection in the boat was sopping wet and there were any number of undiscovered short circuits. So when the switch was thrown to increase speed, something happened to the control of the first torpedo tube and it fired. The torpedo shot out ahead of time by several seconds and plowed straight across the Jap's bow. We took a dive and got ready to have hell break loose.

"I can't explain what happened. The torpedo had crossed only a couple of yards in front of bow and must have been sighted. But the depth bombs we had been waiting for never came. We could hear the screws of the big ship roaring over us and then away from us toward the docks but there was no other disturbance—none of the clatter of high-speed engines of destroyers or patrol boats. Pretty soon there was complete silence and we came up again. The ship was well on her way through the right-hand channel into port. Maybe the lookout had been asleep. Maybe he couldn't believe his own eyes. Maybe he thought the torpedo was a blackfish. Anyway our luck seemed to be back with us again.

"The Old Man decided to play out his hand then. We moved on into the narrow channel and headed toward the beach."

"For a while everything went all right," said Lieutenant Eubanks. "We spotted a couple of patrol boats before they spotted us and we cut around them without stirring up any fuss. Then we heard a lot of distant engine noises off the bow and we knew we were getting close to the docks.

"There was a racket close by and the captain came up a little for a look-see. Straight ahead was a mass of shadow and red and green lights and suddenly a searchlight. There wasn't any doubt that we'd been discovered. The Japs knew we were there before we came up.

"The captain had just time to make out that the big blob ahead of us was a cruiser and that she was spinning around on a dime, and then we dived.

"The Old Man yelled, 'Rig for depth charges!' But that was one order we didn't need. We knew we were in for it this time.

In a matter of seconds we heard high-speed screws go over us and swing about aft of us . . . then more screws ahead of us and then bombs came down in the first string.

"We hadn't known what depth bombs sounded like before that and I'll say we learned fast. I thought that the first one had blown us apart. Then I discovered—just as everybody else discovers in the submarines—that you never can judge the distance of the first one—only the next ones. If—as happened frequently that night—the second of the string was closer than the first, the shock was about all you could stand. You could get to be an old man in five minutes of that stuff and it went on forever.

"We'll never be in a worse spot the day we die than we were in right at that moment. We were in a narrow channel with mines waiting to pulverize us on either side and we were cut off ahead and astern by the patrol boats and destroyers. We snaked along under the barrage wondering how long the old crate was going to hold together. And then we ran aground. Right at the time we had no way of telling what sort of a spot we were in. Afterward we found out that we had run into the beach and had grounded on a ledge. Not only that but we'd run into fairly shallow water.

"Of course it was asking for trouble to use much power on the motors but the captain, listening to the depth charges crashing around, said that the motor noise probably wouldn't tell the Japs any more about us than they already knew. So we slapped on the juice and tried to back off. It was no go. We'd slide partly off and then the stern would flop down. So we'd start up again trying to get a lift forward.

"Three times we tried this. The third time she shoved her nose into the beach and hung there. The next time we tried to back out we just trembled and stayed where we were. The captain saw there was nothing for it then but to blow everything and we blew. We came up like a shot."

There may be more dramatic moments than this one in the unpublished history of the submarines in this war but certainly there is none that anybody has ever mentioned to me. Other submarines have come leaping to the surface in dangerous spots—in harbors, along the beat of the destroyers, in the full glare of the sun on calm seas. But this one shot up to take its last chance while the depth charges were still shaking it and the screws of the patrol boats still roaring overhead and all the fire power of one of Japan's ports closing in for the kill.

"When we surfaced we hardly dared to breathe," said Lieutenant Eubanks. "Every second we expected a shell to lift us the rest of the way out of the water. Nobody moved. Nobody said a word. Then the skipper opened the hatch and looked out. He found that in spite of everything we were doing well—very well indeed.

"In pushing blindly along the bottom we had shoved our nose into a little inlet where the beach dropped abruptly into deep water. Now we were still in the inlet. It wasn't much of a port—narrow and not much longer than we were. But it masked us from the rest of the harbor and the rest of the harbor was roaring.

"All along the beach on either side of us the Japanese were running up and down. One mob of them seemed to be heading right toward us and so close we could almost spit on them. We shook hands all around, closed the hatch and got out of there.

"We weren't through with the business yet because the patrol boats and destroyers were still ranging around like scorpions. They hadn't anything against us personally because they had every right to believe they'd polished us off in the channel. But they seemed to have the idea that we might have brought friends with us. And what they thought about how many of us were there wasn't going to help us when the depth charges started to come down.

"We were still in a bad pocket. They kept messing around on top of us, and gave us what they had. It was a terrific experience not only because of the blasting but because of the heat. After a while the bombing would quit and you could take steps to find out whether or not you were still alive. But the heat never let up on you. And in that bottled-up air for four or five hours at a stretch your brains parboiled.

"When you got up topside after a session like that and the fresh air came in you couldn't stand it. It seemed to have a stink in it, a putrid, sweet, sickening taint. And however it smelled to you it didn't do you any good because the muggy heat inside the boat was proof against outside drafts.

"We stayed up there till our patrol was done and went in and out of the harbor every time they gave us a chance. But we never got any more good opportunities to make a killing. The Japs were just too conscious of us.

"I don't know whether their sound up there was unusually good or whether we just had the hard luck to put out a lookout's eye with the periscope every time we stuck it up. But they certainly didn't give us any rest. No matter where we went they'd follow us and they kept the ash cans going day and night—not just one or two ash cans but loads of them. It got to be something of a trick to get up at night in that bedlam and stay up long enough to charge batteries but we learned how to do it after a while. We knew where every land gun and every moored mine was in the harbor and we began to feel pretty cocky.

"When we went out of there we were feeling pretty proud at what we had done. After all not many submariners were going to come back to report how they'd saved their necks with odds about a thousand to one against them. The more we thought about it the prouder we got—that is, until we got back to our base.

"There wasn't any reception committee out to meet us when we came up to the dock . . . only a British officer, and he was tactless enough to call attention to the fact that we hadn't any Japanese flags painted on our conning tower.

" 'What!' he said. 'Did you come back without sinking even one Jap ship?'

"We explained that we had had a very narrow escape, and that didn't seem to impress him very much either. I don't recall at the moment why we cared.

"He lifted an eyebrow and said something about some other submarine somewhere, and then we told him where we'd been and how we'd been the first submarine in the area and how we'd gone inside the harbor and with peculiar daring had tried to blast a warship out of the middle of a big Jap fleet. He brightened at that.

" 'Oh, that's where you were!' he said. 'And how did you find the weather?' "

23

ORDINARY TROUBLE

IT IS an axiom of the S-boat service that nothing could possibly happen to them in the same way twice and that their luck seldom turned except for the worse.

The officers who had shaken hands silently in that tense moment when the Japs failed to discover them had come home buoyed up with the belief that nothing else in the way of harrowing adventure could ever disturb them again.

On another patrol, somewhere up in the same region, the submarine dodged a couple of patrol boats with professional skill and made an approach on a cargo carrier that seemed to be riding all alone. The maneuvering was almost finished. The range was about right. In a few seconds the big ship would be in line for a torpedo. And then a destroyer masked by the larger hulk slid around the stern and charged. Simultaneously an airplane came over and dropped a close one. The submarine dived into a new form of hell. A control stuck and the motors raced and it seemed to the men aboard that the boat would be forever getting down. With clunks sounding close aboard they finally got her leveled off and simultaneously began to choke in the fumes of burning paint and rubber. Black smoke was rolling forward through the after battery compartment, and a voice from the middle of the murk was yelling something about a first-class fire in the engine room.

The overload on the motors had burned out a resistance and shorted something else and hot cables had begun to fry off their insulation. In two minutes the smoke inside the engine room was so thick that one could scarcely see through it and the air in the rest of the boat was rapidly getting unbreathable. It was the sort of fire that would give plenty of trouble on the surface and this

169

time everybody knew the submarine wasn't going to be able to surface—such miracles as that of the earlier patrol couldn't be expected to happen twice even to an S-boat.

Overhead the screws of the destroyer were weaving their spiral pattern, and in the churning water the depth charges were going off in varying ranges.

Only one thing could be done at the moment, aside from the work of keeping the boat at her depth and under way through the curtain of dynamite. The watertight doors of the engine room were dogged down and the bulkhead vents closed. That was done before anybody had had any chance to get a close look at the fire or even to guess its cause or extent. Whatever was going on inside that box must be allowed to go on so long as the barrage should continue. What effect it might have eventually on the fate of everybody aboard was something about which at the time, fortunately, nobody had much chance to think.

There was a man at the pump controls in the motor room aft of the engine room, and when the doors were shut he was isolated.

"We kept thinking up jokes to send back to him over the telephone," one of the officers said later. "They kept him amused, or at least he said they did, and they took our minds off the prospect of being blown up any minute. I've tried since to recall some of the bright things we got up but somehow I can't. All I can remember is sitting there waiting for the pay-off and trying to bring back some of the wisecracks I'd read in the funny papers or heard in the movies when I was a kid.

"Even aside from the fire we didn't have anything to be happy about. We still had a light circuit intact but weren't so sure when another short would put us entirely out of business. Everybody was watching all the gauges on the boat at once.

"We got up an acey-deucy game with the captain. . . . That is the engineer officer played acey-deucy with the captain while I prayed. I felt something like a juggler with all sorts of stuff in the air at once—praying and thinking up jokes and trying to forget the smell of burning rubber.

"We were in a nasty fix. Without the motors we couldn't maneuver even at low speed. We couldn't go forward or backward, that is. There were just two directions we could move in, up and down. And right at that moment when it seemed that under the law of averages we could expect nothing else to happen to us, the sound man reported some more high-speed screws.

"When the captain thought it might be dark enough we took a chance on coming up. It was like coming up out of a grave, Lieutenant Eubanks recalled, even though nobody had any idea about what might be waiting up on top. As it turned out, the patrol boats had gone their way and the boat had the sea to itself.

"We got some air into the engine room and opened it up," said the lieutenant. "After a little while the atmosphere was thin enough to see through and we went in. The place was black as the inside of an ensign's collar but much to our surprise everything seemed to be in its right place. The cork lining wasn't smoldering and there weren't any festoons of gooey rubber hanging from the overhead cables. The control panel was completely in cinders but it was cool to the touch. The electricians went over it inch by inch and said that the fire hadn't spread from it anywhere that they could see. The chief said that the resistance had fused and probably would carry current again. And we had a confab about that. We didn't want to start another fire, and we didn't want to wreck what was left of our electrical apparatus by overloads through shorts that we mightn't be able to see. On the other hand we couldn't operate without the motors and the chief was positive that the resistance would hold together. We tried it and it did. Then the chief said that we ought to leave everything just as it was.

" 'I'd fix it,' he said, 'except that taking that panel apart is a complicated business and we'd have hours of work on it—and anyway if a thing runs without fixing why not let it run?'

"That sounded like common sense and the captain agreed. We went on with our patrol. We breathed burned rubber with all the other smells in the boat for the next couple of weeks."

None of the alumni of the old USS *S-fish* who talked with me about this harrowing affair seemed to think it worthy of further comment. They got the fire out. The motor controls worked in their fashion. The patrol continued.

It is reported that the captain, exercising his official prerogatives, did allow himself to look into an unpleasant future before he got back to port. After all it was his ship and his responsibility and it all looked to be his personal hard luck, too.

The boat finished her regular beat and was assigned to a two-day tour of extra duty on what was called an "extended patrol." The captain set her on her new course and came into the wardroom none too cheered.

He mentioned among other things that the boat didn't seem to have much to show for her long journey except another miraculous escape. And he recalled what everybody already knew, that miraculous escapes didn't count much in the score sheets.

It was hardly to be expected that an S-boat could do so well against enemy shipping as some of the new models then beginning to operate in that end of the Pacific. But even so some of the ancient crates had been doing plenty besides running aground and having engine-room fires. The captain mentioned that, too.

On the last day of the patrol he spoke to his executive about it. The boat had surfaced in the early dark and it looked as if everything were finished except to turn around and go home.

"I figured all the returns were in," the executive said later. "And the captain was certainly depressed. He took a good breath of the night air and said, 'Well, I guess this is my last patrol. I don't seem to get results.'

"And just then both of us at the same time saw a blot darker than the rest of the dark bearing down on us. We didn't have to stir out of our tracks. The skipper gave his data and called his order: 'Fire One! Fire Two!' And then he called the control room.

" 'Take her down!' he said. And he told me as we got through the hatch, 'There's no telling. There may be somebody with him.'

"He went over to the periscope and we dived. Then, just as we went under, he let out a shout.

" 'It's a cruiser! Glory be!'

"In a couple of seconds I began to hear a lot of noises more terrifying than the depth charges had ever been. It seemed as if the whole ocean was lifting up off its floor and coming down again . . . a series of blasts coupled by a sort of crackling sound. It sounded as if somebody were dragging a heavy chain over an iron floor and smacking it against a wall.

"At first I couldn't figure out what it was, for each smash brought the boat up short as if we'd run into something solid. I called to the captain that we seemed to be bumping over coral. But I knew from the tone of his voice when he answered that we weren't.

" 'It's just her magazines exploding,' he said. 'She's finished.'

"We went back topside after that, inventoried a lot of wreckage, and headed for the barn. . . ."

24

RENDEZVOUS AT GUADALCANAL

A few of the S-boats were on duty with the Asiatic fleet when the war started. Some of them, like that captained by Lieutenant Commander J. R. Moore during the first year of the war, seem to have been there always—proof of the stamina of the boats themselves or of the stamina of the men who operate them. They were in the turmoil about Manila after the attack on the Philippines, in sundry actions in the Java Sea, in and out of Japanese invasion bases in the Southwest Pacific, on constant duty through the spectacular fighting for Guadalcanal. As you read the evidence you come to the conlusion that they worked harder than submarines of any other type—as was only natural considering their limitations. They got into a wider assortment of difficulties. They acquitted themselves well. And unaccountably they did come back.

Lieutenant Barney Flenniken, who sailed with Captain Moore during that troubled year, admitted his surprise at their record as he awaited a new assignment in New London.

"Considering what they were they did pretty well," he said. "Most of them have been retired from duty on the long patrols and I guess most of us who served in them won't be too much upset about it. But I can tell you one thing: submarining will never seem the same in any other kind of boat. It certainly will get on my nerves to be in one where things aren't falling down all the time.

"We cursed them a good deal in the beginning. They weren't built for long hauls and they were uncomfortable to live in, but when we learned how to patch them up on the run they certainly did take us around.

"We heard the first and last shots in the Battle of the Coral

Sea. The last one we threw at a destroyer—which we sank. The first one was a depth charge that almost sank us.

"We operated quite a lot around Guadalcanal after the Marines came in, and did a little business outside Tulagi Harbor and Rabaul. All in all we came home with a pretty fair bag—and I guess maybe they allowed us all of our claims—although I know that some boats in our class did better.

"The main trouble with running a submarine off Guadalcanal was finding a place to put it. There were so many submarines around there that we used to say they had been assigned not only by areas but by depths as well. The Japs would come in daytimes to sink our ships. We'd come in nighttimes to sink theirs. It was a sort of gentleman's arrangement and saved a lot of confusion. Sometimes, of course, we met unexpectedly and sank each other— or rather we sank the Japanese and they only tried to sink us. We were unavoidably better at that sort of business."

They had storms to contend with. They got into a bad one in the Coral Sea.

"We had about the same run of trouble everybody else had in that affair," he said. "When we got up there heavy seas were running, and I mean heavy. We had a devil of a time keeping the boat under water when we were trying to submerge. On the surface it was all we could do to keep her from taking off.

"In a spot like that you don't get much chance to pick and choose. It's the other fellow who does the picking and choosing and that was the way it was with the destroyer we tangled with. I don't recall many of the details except that we seemed to be minding our own business strictly—not looking for trouble at all— when we came over a hill of water and there was this thing looking at us.

"He'd spotted us—with sound apparatus probably—and he was bearing down. If it hadn't been for the rolling water he'd probably have taken us apart before we knew he was anywhere in the vicinity. But anyway there he was. It was a fantastic performance, something like shooting torpedoes out of the Giant Swing in an amusement park. Everything was rolling—everything that is except the destroyer. We were actually going up and sideways when the captain yelled, 'Fire One!' and then 'Fire Two!' and I'd enter that as the best trapshooting ever done by a submarine. Both those torpedoes hit so close that I thought they were going to upend us completely. There was a blast that caved in my stomach and then Sound said that he couldn't hear screw noises any more. It was good-by destroyer less than two minutes after he'd started gunning for us, and pieces of him were still a menace to navigation when we came up to look at what we'd done.

"We didn't get in on much of the rest of the battle—which was natural enough considering that it seems to have been spread out all over the place, with the after-show at Midway. But we did sneak in close enough to make an approach on a cruiser and get depth-bombed for our trouble. We certainly heard the last shot fired in that battle—maybe the last couple of dozen shots. And I guess we were the last U.S. warship to leave the area. That, of course, was no fault of ours. We couldn't leave until the cans topside decided to let us.

Once they got out of there and had hung things up again they were ordered to wait for returning cripples. It looked like a very fine assignment. From all they'd heard about the battle there should have been plenty of cripples. So they got into a position so close to the shore that they could see the coconuts, and passed a couple of pleasant days watching the patrol boats run up and down between them and the beach.

"They never made a pass at us so we knew we hadn't been spotted," he said.

"Then one day we saw smoke on the horizon—big blotches of smoke—and we got all ready. It looked to us as if the cripples were finally arriving and that the batch approaching us must be on fire. The seas were still heavy and there were misty patches on the water, so this smoke cloud was almost on top of us before we saw the cripples were really destroyers coming for us at thirty knots. The patrol boats had deceived us.

"We were a little contemptuous about destroyers after our affair with the first one, but we were contemptuous of only one at a time. So we pulled the plug and went down to listen to the blasting. That, I suppose, was really our last observation of the Battle of the Coral Sea. We never saw any more destroyers up there and we never saw any cripples either.

"But we got one more lick in some weeks later. One night we ran into the force that had just sunk the *Canberra* and three U. S. cruisers. There were cruisers and a pack of destroyers. We let two destroyers go by, sneaked past a third one and let three fish go at the leading cruiser. She was on the bottom alongside us in eight minutes by the captain's stop watch.

"That didn't quite even up the score for Savo Island but it was a good starter.

"Of course we spent a very bad evening. Every destroyer in the Jap navy seemed to be up there dropping ash cans on us. We had a fight to keep the lights going. The Japs kept clunking them out every time we got a circuit breaker set. Everything loose aboard the boat was rolling as usual and our ears were getting pounded to a pulp.

"We couldn't move any place much because the whole ocean was cluttered up with Japanese destroyers and they must have been feeling pretty vicious about it all. If they hadn't stopped to pick up their survivors we probably would have been up there yet."

Lieutenant Flenniken was willing to concede that the boat had gone through other, tighter, places, but never one more frightening.

"Stuff like that made Christians out of the crew in a hurry," he said. "Everybody aboard the boat that night was praying but the captain, and he was ordering everybody else to pray. I can see him yet turning half around to an officer beside him and saying, 'Pray hard, John. Pray harder!' And it seemed to work. No nonsense about it.

"That was one of the most protracted bombings we got. I'd stack it up against anybody else's in the Southwest Pacific for the record. But it wasn't the worst one.

"That one came while we were trying to locate the place where the Japs were landing supplies. We had had to dodge a lot of destroyers at one port. But after a while the destroyers went away somewhere. Sound reported all clear and we put up the periscope. The captain walked the periscope around and saw a big freighter standing out there in the channel all by herself . . . a sitting pigeon.

"Judging from what happened to it I guess the ship was loaded with munitions. The captain put a couple of fish into it and it took fire and blew up like a Fourth of July spectacle—a magnificent exhibit. The Old Man was so pleased that he invited members of the crew to look at it. There was plenty of opportunity. It took quite a lot of time for some of the burning chunks of that ship to come down. Then we discovered what the catch had been in this business. An airplane bomb just about knocked our periscope off. And that wasn't the last one. There were lots of airplanes."

There were also lots of other complications.

"The captain started to dive," said the lieutenant, "but there was a green engineman at the controls and he couldn't pull the lever to start the motors. The navigator went down and tried to help him pull it over. In the meantime the shocks were weaving the periscope all over the place and the captain was trying to pull it down by the handles. The quartermaster, running his thumb up and down the bulkhead, couldn't find the button that controlled the periscope. And a Filipino mess boy who had just come into the control room with a cup of coffee threw the coffee away and started to lean forward with both hands against the bulkhead trying to push her down.

"Then the control quit being stuck and we went down in a hurry.

"We tried to pull out at a decent level but there was no pulling out. We just kept on going. We didn't know what had happened to us of course except that everything seemed to have gone wrong at once. But we knew we were likely to fetch up on the bottom if something didn't break our way in a couple of seconds.

"The captain started blowing things and the bow planes were set at hard rise. And I just stood there watching the depth gauges wind up. I saw them winding up in my sleep every night after that for a couple of months.

"Well, things got quieted down after a while. All of a sudden I noticed that the gauges were going the other way and that we were leveling off. I'd never have believed it possible. And while I was noticing that, it came to me all of a sudden that the bombs weren't falling any more either. The whole show had lasted only a few seconds.

"Then one of the seamen came up to the captain.

" 'Captain,' he said, 'I wasn't scared. I wasn't scared a bit. I knew nothing was going to happen to us. They say that when you're in real danger all your life passes before your eyes—poof— just like that. And, Captain, I didn't see a goddam thing.'

"The captain looked at him.

" 'Smitty,' he said, 'when I looked at that depth gauge and saw the second hand passing twenty I was just getting out of high school.' "

I told that story one evening in the officers' mess at the submarine barracks, Mare Island, California, and everybody laughed uproariously save a pleasant-faced lieutenant commander sitting opposite me. In a rush of introductions I had missed his name and so could make no possible guess why he of all the table should be taking the matter so seriously. But I didn't need to know his name to be conscious that I had made some social blunder.

"I'm sorry," I said, "if I've said anything out of turn. . . ."

But he didn't seem displeased, only unamused.

"Who told you that story?" he asked.

"Lieutenant Barney Flenniken," I said. "And I thought it was funny. Don't you?"

He smiled then.

"Maybe I do now," he admitted. "But I didn't at the time I was saying that stuff about getting out of high school. . . ."

Captain Moore—"Dinty" Moore, of course, to his comrades— lighted another cigarette and looked back a few months and a couple of thousand miles.

"That day was enough to drive anybody nuts," he said. "We had a little luck with the conning-tower door. It blew open but it shut itself and held water pretty well. But we had everything else in the world to contend with. I don't know whether a plane got us or maybe a hellish explosion of ammunition on the wrecked ship. But it just lifted the whole ocean up off the bottom and we started down like a plumb. I couldn't see the bubble on the indicator and I was just getting ready to blow everything when she came level.

"And apparently Flenniken didn't tell you the pay-off. When

it got safe to come up topside again we did and we put up the periscope. I knew the thing was working because I saw it come up out of he well, and I knew we were at periscope depth because I could read the   gauges and they seemed to be active enough. But when I looked into the eyepieces I couldn't see a thing—not one damned thing.

"So we hoisted the second periscope and had a look around. That one apparently was all right and I could see that we had the place all to ourselves. We surfaced and had a look at the first periscope. So help me we had a Japanese seaman's coat (off somebody on the ship we'd wrecked) wrapped around the top of it.

"It was pretty fine to be looking at daylight again—even on a hot corner like this. I'd been figuring that we were pretty close to the end of a perfect day.

"It was quiet up there. The ammunition ship was all under and there wasn't any sign of airplanes in the sky. There didn't seem to be a sound anywhere in the world except the engine noises and you're so used to them that you never pay any attention to them. . . . They get to be just a part of the general silence.

"Then I heard a couple of chiefs talking down in the control room and naturally I listened. I was curious to find out what men talked about after a ride like that—and don't think every man in that crew didn't know he'd had one. So I tuned in on what was apparently the end of a very earnest conversation:

" 'As for me,' one of the chiefs was saying, 'when this war is over I'm going into the poultry business. . . . And you'd never guess what got me interested. I'd never seen a chicken farm until a guy took me over to this one in Honolulu. They had a slick rooster there that he wanted me to see. It had only one leg and hopped around on that better than most chickens do on two . . . doggonedest thing you ever saw in your life.'

"So everything seemed to be under control and I got a couple of men up to take the Jap's laundry off the periscope. . . ."

25

ASH CANS OFF JAVA

It is the theory of the Navy in war that once a battle is joined you fight it the best way you know how and with what tools you have available. Something of this idea probably was behind the order sending the S-boats into the South Pacific, for it is hardly likely that anybody in the high command had any illusions about them. They went out to their assignments on the hot spots merely as tools that happened to be at hand, and as in the case of the surface ships at Midway and in the Solomons they proved that, given sufficient brains and skill to operate them, any tools can be used for virtually any job. Before the war was three months old nobody stopped to think of S-boats merely as S-boats any more. They were submarines and not such bad submarines either. There came a time, particularly in the Java Sea battles, when the Japs probably thought we didn't have any other kind.

Records of enemy ships sunk show something of the effect of submarines in battle but they don't show all of it. We have learned from our own struggle with the Atlantic wolf packs that the mere presence of submarines along shipping lanes must necessarily cause extensive rearrangement in operating schedules and the assignment of escort vessels. Antisubmarine warfare presupposes a considerable manufacture of antisubmarine weapons, new allotments of raw materials, changes in priorities, changes in recruiting and training schedules. In the case of Jap fleet operations where, it has been repeatedly demonstrated, timetables are more important than resourcefulness, submarine activities undoubtedly retarded the big push to the south and gave Tojo the greatest single worry he was to have until the surface fleets got strong enough to blast him before Guadalcanal. In the Southwest Pacific they will tell you that the submarine saved Australia, which seems to be quite possible. And for nuisance value if for nothing else the S-boats must be given high rating among the submarines.

You listen to the men who were in them and you follow without difficulty the tales of individual risk and accomplishment. But when you try to envision them in the mass—not one submarine at a time, but a fleet of them working as a team at predetermined places on a predetermined schedule—off Luzon, around Borneo, off China, in the Java Sea—you get dizzy. You can excuse the Japs for thinking that they were everywhere. It looks to me as if they really were.

In the thread of narrative of Motor Machinist (2Cl.) Miles Lasater, who seems to have been everywhere anybody could get in an S-boat, you get some vague idea of the extent of their operations, although nobody could be expected to put together a jigsaw picture with only a few of the parts. You know from the records that we had far too few submarines in the Southwest Pacific to fight a war mostly by themselves as they were suddenly called upon to do. But it would seem that with some hope of accuracy you can figure that every important harbor and strait in the path of the Japanese advance was well covered and that the composite accomplishment of the underwater fleet in that spot is merely the accomplishment of any one submarine—Lasater's, Eubanks', Coe's, Moore's—multiplied endlessly.

"We reported to Sourabaya while the going was still hot down there," Lasater said. "Then we got ordered to patrol an invasion port up north. We went into the harbor up there, too. By that time we were used to sliding around on the bottoms of harbors.

"We had information that a lot of cruisers and destroyers were up there, and by this time we was getting cocky. It was fairly dangerous when you look at it, but already we got to figuring that we had the Japs' number and they didn't have ours. And that makes all the difference.

"When we got there we didn't have any trouble seeing what we was in for. Cans were running up and down across the harbor all day and all night. It looked as though maybe they expected us to be coming around. The way they acted it looked like they was getting pretty tired of having us monkeying around inside ports. Where once they used to chase one can after us, now they were putting them out like schools of whales, but by that time we were learning a few things ourselves. The captain said he guessed we could go in and maybe get out again. And we got away with it.

"We didn't waste much time when we got inside. The captain marked him out a destroyer right away. And then he changed his mind. He thought maybe he'd like a cruiser better.

"We got hell, of course. We knew we was going to when we went in. The captain let off his fish at the cruiser and they should have hit. Maybe they did. But we couldn't wait. We took a dive right away and that time we didn't have any hard luck submerging. Some of us thought that was funny because we'd been diving so much endways and almost upside down.

"I was in the engine room when the first ash cans came down. Maybe they didn't come fast but they sounded to me like something out of a sooper-dooper machine gun. At times like that your mind keeps going fast and slow and sometimes when it's going slow those things sound to you like rain on a tin roof.

"I didn't get a chance to count them. I could see the paint chips crisscrossing on the bulkheads when the next couple of explosions twisted them.

"There were maybe a dozen destroyers up on top. A half-dozen more had probably come in to help look for us. While they was looking for us we got out with most of them right on our tail —or anyway that's how it seemed to me. We made several attempts to get back in but they wouldn't let us do our trick twice. They plastered us every time. Of course they knew we'd have to come up once in a while to charge batteries, and I guess they knew we weren't going to quit hanging around there unless they actually blew us up.

"So they'd come looking for us with all hands at battle stations. It was a nice compliment but we didn't wait. We couldn't monkey around with that sort of stuff. They were dumping dynamite into the bay like dredges tossing sand, and pretty soon there wasn't any paint at all left inside and the deck was covered with chips and we were wondering how long the supply of light bulbs was going to hold out. We kept the lights going most of the time but we were in the dark enough to know how it was going to feel when some bomb got close enough to put them out for good.

"We kept annoying them. What I mean is that they had to give all their time to us and we figured it wasn't so bad if we could tie up a dozen destroyers there in that port. But we couldn't do much more than that with them on the hunt for us. We missed some convoys coming in because we couldn't get near them. We consoled ourselves that they were fast convoys that we couldn't have got to anyway.

"Well, we stayed around there keeping a lot of the Japanese navy from doing anything else but dump ash cans on us until our patrol was over. We went back to our base and Captain Munson was assigned to us. He took us up into another hot corner if there ever was one. We got something new there—airplanes. They were shuttling back and forth over us all the time. A lookout had to have three eyes to watch for those babies and the patrol boats and the cans. We didn't do so much there either except keep a lot of destroyers from useful work. But we got a slick job one day. We really went to work on them. . . . They had a radio station up there on one of those islands and we mowed it down with shell fire.

"We made battle surfaces to get on with this job and it was pretty ticklish because the Japs had a lot of stuff around there, and we had no way of telling how close it was. The light down there was always funny. Everybody was seeing things that weren't there. There was a sort of mirage around this scow and she looked just like a Jap destroyer. So we went down. Once we were down the periscope was under the heat wave and Captain Munson saw what we'd been dodging.

"When we came up again and manned the guns all the gun crew were wearing life belts. The business worried the captain. He was afraid that the next one might not turn out to be a mirage. So he told us that if he had to go down suddenly we could swim around and he'd come back and get us, even if he had to drag us out to sea hanging to the periscope. He gave us directions how to jump off the ship on opposite sides and in turn. It sounded to me like it would be a pretty novel performance and I began to feel that it was actually going to happen and I wasn't going to care much if it did. But it didn't come off that way. We made a run out in front of the island and began to bust it up.

"It was tough work. Iron Mike Murdoch who was ahead of me passed out and went down with his nose flat on the deck. We just relayed shells around him for a while until he came to. He had the hardest job. He was taking the shells out of the scuttle when they came up. We were just too silly to think about getting a relief for him.

"But I guess the worst part of it wasn't the actual firing but the wait for adjustment. The men were grousing like hell before we got going. It looked like the gunnery officer was taking too much time to spot the first shots and correct his firing data. And in the meantime them shells got pretty heavy. The loading crew began to get mad.

"They were mumbling all the time, 'Get these damned things shot off and let's get out of here.' Well, nobody blamed them. Them shells was heavy and the day was hot and so was the place we were in. It was all conversation, and when they got around to it they got the guns loaded and fired right like the book says.

"But you just try to juggle seventy-five-pound shells after you've been cooped up twenty-one days in a sewer pipe. Me, I just sat down on the deck holding one of them things like a baby. After we got the range I stood up. My legs and the shell supply gave out at precisely the same second. Timing it, is what I call it.

"We went home after the bombardment to get some more shells and fish. Then we went south again.

"I didn't see much of the next battle—not any more than anybody else did—but I certainly heard it. We was running up and down through the straits, and the destroyers were over us continuously. They were just ferrying depth charges out there from some base to dump on us—two or three shifts of them, it seemed to me. And every once in a while one of our own surface ships would take a crack at us. In that mess nobody could tell who anybody else was and you never got time to hoist recognition signals. Our ships were worse than the Japs because they're better shots. You had to have pretty good ears to detect the difference though. It's hard to figure out if one explosion is better than another when everybody in the world is taking a sock at you at once.

"Well, while all this was going on we decided to move over to an area where the water wasn't so full of ash cans. And when we moved we met up with a sister ship. I don't know her name and I never wanted to meet any of the guys aboard her . . . not just then.

"They heard us coming. I don't suppose they knew who we were but they knew we were an S-boat in trouble. And it wasn't hard for them to guess that the trouble was following us as we came near them. So they scrammed. And as they did, they attracted the attention of the cans, and the cans laid off us and followed them. Boy! I could hardly believe it.

"We cooled down and sat there and listened to the bombs following them and getting farther and farther away from us. So the captain turned around and went back to where we'd come from. It wasn't so far away that we couldn't still hear the plastering the other submarine was getting with bombs that had our address on them. We got a good laugh out of that. It's not that we wished them any hard luck. But then you get tired of having all the hard luck to yourself all the time, and we were certainly relieved when we got a break. I'd hate to wish a lot of depth-charging on any guy but I can't feel sorry for how I felt then. At the time it looked like a sort of fair distribution."

After the battle there was nobody going to be keeping the home fires going for them. So they eased on through some straits to the south. That place has irregular depths and all sorts of vicious currents. Another U. S. sub spotted them and tried to get into firing position. At the crucial moment the attacking skipper recognized an S-boat and moved away.

"Nothing happened to us," Lasater said, "except that we got into a passage that we hadn't intended to take and we hit a nine-knot current going our way.

"I haven't had a ride like that since I was on a roller coaster in Arizona. We had nothing to do with maintaining depth. The currents took care of that. We just went up and down without touching a control. If we did touch the controls it didn't make any difference. Half the time we were moving sideways and down by the stern. But not always. Sometimes we swung around to the other side and backed up.

"We were afraid that the batteries mightn't be able to take it and that we'd have to surface in this mess. But the current kept up in our general direction no matter how much we swung around and we sailed right through. There were cans overhead most of the time but nothing bothered us except the crazy depth gauges and the slant on the decks. I guess the Japs didn't expect any submarines to be monkeying around in a spot like that.

"Afterward we went to port for overhaul. We had a tender in tow. The men on the tender will tell you they had us in tow and maybe they did. With the sea running the way it was it was fifty-fifty.

Some weeks after that with a full load of torpedoes, shells and machine-gun drums they were sent to blow up an ammunition dump and oil-storage tanks with surface fire. The men took the assignment as a compliment on their deck gunnery.

"Well, we got up there and spent a day looking around. Then we went into the harbor and saw a big ship and a small one. Captain Munson naturally wanted the big one. We made a good approach but they saw us and the big one moved off. The little one swung around and hit a swell that saved her. The fish was right in line but the ship lifted up and it went under.

"The destroyers came roaring around. God! The Japs had a lot of those cans in that area. They had us dead to rights because the torpedo wake gave them plenty of data. The first bomb that came down was almost the last we needed. It lifted us up and shook us.

"We weren't done—not yet—although we weren't so sure about it for quite a while. When we finally got a check on the damage we discovered that we could operate all right. We weren't going to be much heavier than we'd always been. So we came on in. The captain was pretty blue about it although I guess maybe he should have been waving his hat just because we were still alive.

"Trouble followed us all the way in—although it wasn't as tough as we might have expected. One night word was passed to man battle stations and rig for depth charges all tubes ready to fire. And we got it again. I don't remember why we got it that time. As near as I could figure out we was just running along there minding our own business.

"Looking back on it I don't see how the old sewer pipe ever got home. She got a twist in the second or third explosion that made her scream. A whole square of paint came off the engine-room bulkhead—the biggest paint chip I ever saw. I used to carry a life-size chart of it around to show people what it looks like when the paint comes off in a bombing attack. I always felt like my hide was coming off the same way.

"Well, like I say, I guess the Japs had been following us and we cursed the accident that had put us in such a spot. But afterwards we figured that we shouldn't have been so upset about it. The Japs had planted a lot of artillery on that beach that we was all set to bombard and we didn't know a thing about it. Boy, they'd have leveled us off even with the bottom!

"We didn't get much action in the Battle of the Coral Sea. We weren't expected to. We were waiting on the edge of things looking for strays. But the strays didn't come our way. Most of them went to the bottom of Tulagi Harbor or burned up on the beach. And nothing got into our periscope except two airplanes that didn't see us. Everybody was disgusted. . . . A whole patrol of nothing! And in addition to that we had a hell of a sea. We were broaching all the time. We might have been duck soup for anybody who was looking for us if he'd been able to plow through that kind of water himself.

"On our next run we got maybe our biggest ship. There wasn't anything spectacular about this job. It seems to me that we had all our hair-raising adventures while we weren't doing anything but trying to save our own hides. We got a good approach on this ship without being detected and slipped a fish into it. It was just simple like that. The only thrill we got out of the whole business was furnished by Allied planes. They were working on the ship, too, and the closer they came to it the closer they came to us. It was just one of those things. They didn't intend to hit us. But there's no conscience in a bomb.

"Our best attack was a couple of days later in the same area. We sank a big cargo ship while all the cans in the world were working on us. It was a sort of combination sound shot—which is what makes it good.

"We'd been taking a bad beating from the cans and patrol boats all day but there was a lot of supply-ship business going on up topside and the captain just stuck around. Every now and then he'd take a look. Sometimes they'd come howling after us and chase us down. Sometimes they wouldn't. This time he got himself only one look. He gave us our bearings and ordered us to fire. We fired two and both of 'em hit.

"We could all hear the explosions. There was several and at first we thought they were pretty horrible. That ship just took a long time to bust up and she must have had a lot of little packages of explosive in her or something because she made a hell of a noise and we got a lot of shocks.

"We could hear a can roaring around. It got there in no time at all. I suppose the other cans happened to be somewheres else just at that minute and this one was too busy picking up survivors to bother about us. We were happy about it. If he'd dropped a dozen shots we'd have been happy. It looked to us like that would be just about a fair break.

"All in all we didn't get many depth charges . . . not so many as some of the other ships got. But they was enough. But whatever the Japs did it seemed to me it was always the ones that they hadn't dropped yet that made the difference. Those you could hear never bothered you—that is, not so much.

"I don't know whether anybody told you about the heat down there. That was the worst trouble we had, the heat. I'm from the hottest town in America and I never knew what heat was till I got down there. I figured if I ever got back to Tucson I'd have to wear my overcoat all summer.

"The worst of it was in the Java Sea. When we came back from one patrol we had a sort of picnic at a swell resort place. Everybody took something from the party as a souvenir and I got a champagne bottle. I took good care of it. I packed it up in socks inside my duffel bag and carted it around while we got attacked sometimes so's most of the light bulbs on the ship were busted. After every blasting I'd take it out just to make sure it was all right and it always was. Finally after about 20,000 miles of that stuff I got it landed in the United States and I carried it just about in my hands all the way home.

"Then I rang the doorbell and when my folks came to the door I plumb forgot all about it and dropped it right there. It busted into a million pieces. . . . Maybe that doesn't seem to you to have much to do with the submarines but it does to me. I guess all my life is going to be different because of the time I put in aboard the S-boats. No matter what I do I'm always going to feel that the minute I quit thinking about what I'm doing or turn my head the wrong way something is going to bust up.

"After we cracked up that cargo ship we hung around there for quite a time but we didn't get a chance to do much. We ran into one crippled but it got us by surprise. We spotted it on a squally night so's it was almost impossible to see. We was in a bad position to begin with and she was still making more knots than we could make. We got just one good look at her, enough to see that she'd been badly hit topside. It was kind of cheering even if we didn't get a chance to go in and polish her off.

"In the last days up there we didn't get much rest, thanks to the cans and all. We was always breaking things and patching 'em up from the day we got down there. You'd go out and bust something and then you'd finish a patrol and come back to port and spend all of a three-day leave fixing it up again. And things seemed to get worse the tireder we got. That's what made that last patrol so tough—dodge the bombs and work and dodge the bombs and work. We were hardly able to stand up all the time and sometimes we was so dopey it was dangerous.

"I told you about the guy that forgot to close the main induction because he was standing on his feet dead asleep. That left a flapper valve between us and the sea but the valve leaked all over the place and scared us half to death. . . . Nothing happened but we got to thinking.

"All in all that old boat was a heap. Seaman (1Cl) Jim Roland was over the motor room chipping paint one day when he noticed a dent. He hit the dent a belt with his chipping hammer and went right through the hull.

"You could hear him squeaking all over the boat: 'Mis-ter Mel-l-hopp! Mister Mel-l-l-hopp! Come here and look at this.'

"Mr. Melhopp—that was Lieutenant Donald Melhopp, the executive—came to look and I guess after that somebody put a new coat of paint over the weak spots. . . . Come to think about it the old crate must have had a lot of luck. . . . All of them old crates must have had a lot of luck."

26

ABANDON SHIP!

THEY didn't always come back. As this is written the Navy Department has announced the loss of six submarines in battle areas, two known to have been sunk, two presumed sunk and two smashed-up in accidents. The two that figured in the accidents were S-boats, and you might wonder just what sort of accident it would take to damage one of these ships so that the crew couldn't fix it up and bring it home. Pursuing that line of inquiry, I talked with Seamen Richard Ahrens and J. S. Jones who had just come back to New London from the Southwest Pacific. They were very frank about it.

"Well," said Ahrens, "it was this way. We hit. We jammed into that reef like we intended to stay there—and we did. It's a military secret how we got there. They didn't tell us about that. But anyway, there we were.

"The way it happened was this: We'd dumped our executive officer in port where there was a hospital because he had something wrong with his insides that the pharmacist's mate couldn't fix—intestinal flu or something. And while we were there unloading him we got orders to go out and find the war. The assistant navigator took over. He found himself a lot of hard luck right away.

"The going was pretty good for the first part of the trip except that it was cloudy a lot of the time and we couldn't get very good star sights. . . . Maybe that may have had something to do with it—I don't know. There wasn't any gadget for making dead reckoning on those old pipes, so I guess the navigator really needed his star sights to know where he was. Even so it mightn't have made any difference. The charts for that end of the world are pretty lousy.

"After a while we got up there where the Japs were monkeying around. We took all-day dives and got ready for trouble. But rigging for trouble was just routine. We'd been doing that for weeks and it didn't mean a thing. There were Japs all around us but in our own area everything was calm and peaceful. It began to look as if we might have to go all the way to Tokyo to get a look at a Jap ship. We'd heard they were taking over some islands around there but the islands weren't any of our business and we kept clear of them. Keeping clear of them we didn't make any landfalls to give the navigator any check on his position and I guess it all added up.

"So on this night I'm telling you about we surfaced and we were jamming air and charging batteries and going ahead. . . . That's what we were doing when we struck.

"As soon as we hit, the chief said, 'Rig for collision,' and we rigged. Then he ordered us to get out of the forward battery room. It seemed to me that it was right under there where we'd hit. There was a terrible stink. They'd thrown a big load on the batteries trying to pull off with the motors, and they probably reversed a couple of cells and burned out some separators. I opened up the place after a while and stuck my head in. Everything seemed all right . . . no water . . . no gas.

"It's funny, looking back at it—all we were thinking about was little things like battery smells. You'd think being aground was the sort of thing that happened to us every day.

"The captain was plenty calm—almost cheerful. He told us to get what stuff we wanted to save and put it in a pillowcase—one pillowcase for each man—and store it in the control room. We ate aboard that day.

"The captain had sent out his position, so we felt that help would be along pretty soon but we still tried to get her off. We kept charging batteries and jamming air.

"After a while the captain saw we weren't going to be able to do much the way we were. So we threw all our chow over and fired all our fish to lighten her. Then we blew everything. But she didn't come off. I guess her bottom was full of holes. She just shook and turned broadside to the reef. We threw our ammunition overboard and some of it blew up alongside and that didn't do

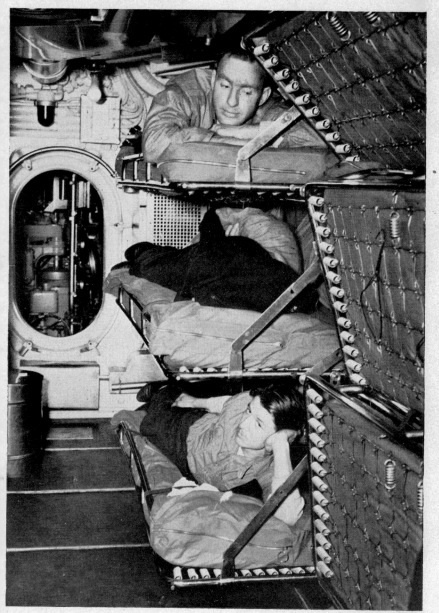

Rudy Arnold Photo

SLEEPING QUARTERS

Bunks three deep, which fold up out of the way when not in use, provide individual sleeping accommodations for every man aboard. There is not much space but the berths are comfortable.

DIVING-PLANE CONTROLS

The man shown is in charge of the stern planes, which he keeps at a required angle as the boat is taken under. The big clock above him is a depth gauge. The horizontal scales are spirit levels showing the pitch of the planes and the angle of the boat from the horizontal.

us any good either. A wind was coming up and she was listing badly. The skipper was afraid she'd go over on her side. We didn't think she'd have far to go.

"While we were lying there, four American bombers passed over. Nobody saw them on account of the haze but they saw us. They turned in a report on us and after a while we got word over the radio that a corvette was coming after us.

"The corvette was due at midnight on the second day but she couldn't make it until daylight of the third. Then we had some palaver.

"It was the original plan to have her pull us off, but her captain said he couldn't get in close enough to do that without running himself aground. He could see where we were and he didn't need any chart to judge where the bottom was. There was some talk of shoving a raft alongside, lashing us to the raft and towing us with it. But they couldn't work that either, for some reason.

"After a while the captain of the corvette said that he'd have all he could do to take the crew off alive without salvaging our old iron. He said he'd run around to the other side of the reef and stand by.

"Well, this reef turned out to be an irregular sort of thing. It had a high backbone a few hundred feet from us—a strip that curved to a little island about three miles away. At low tide it was dry. At high tide it had a couple of feet of water over it. We were aground on part of it but there were forty fathoms of water between us and the high part and a lot of the men couldn't swim.

"While we were considering this we got the order to abandon ship and we went out with just what clothes we stood up in, most of us in tropical shorts. The captain had a lot of new linen stuff in his locker and he told us we could help ourselves to a change of clothes if we wanted to. I got myself a pair of pants. I thought they'd do better than shorts for the long haul. We got the wherry out from under the superstructure but she was busted up. So we inflated our rubber boat.

"We were interested in that. Rubber boats—or for that matter any kind of surface life preservers—were something new in the submarine service. A couple of us took a line ashore and tied it up to one of the fish we'd fired to lighten ship. Most of them had finished up right there on the beach. With the line we made a sort of ferry so that the men could pull themselves over. Only the men who couldn't swim came in the rubber boat. The rest had to swim for it and it was quite a sight. Everybody but the chiefs just thought about saving their lives. The chiefs only wanted to save their hats.

"I guess I don't blame them much. It's impossible to get a chief's hat in Australia or any of those places down there and when you're a chief, a chief's hat naturally means a lot to you."

Mr. Ahrens was quite serious about this. He appreciated the Roman motto about letting the man bear the palm who has won it, although he mightn't have put it exactly that way.

"Paul Spencer, the chief of the boat, missed his somehow after he got ashore," he said. "He kept running up and down looking into every wave for it. Smitty—Chief Yeoman Smith—he saw his floating around and he swam back after it.

"Smitty had a miracle happen to him while he was looking for his hat. He dived under the boat and came up on the other side of it. And when he got ashore he found that his matches and some cards and pictures in his left breast pocket weren't even damp. In the right-hand pocket he had a lot of other stuff. He had his watch in that pocket in a tin box taped up with surgical tape, and his watch and everything else in the pocket was ruined.

"Blum—he's another chief—he saved his hat all right but he nearly drowned doing it. He had to dive pretty deep because the hat had something stored in the band and it was submerging with an eighteen-degree bubble when he caught up with it.

"There weren't enough rubber life jackets to go around, so some of us broke out Momsen lungs. Blum got one of the lungs. When he put it on he broke the straps so when he took his dive it floated up around his face. . . . That's where the hat came off first, I guess, and he noticed it even though he was in a bad spot. He had to hold the lung down with one hand and reach for the hat with the other while he swam around kicking his feet. He got upside down but somebody turned him right side up and he came out with the hat. We all congratulated him.

"When we got where we could put our feet under us we made

a count and found out that we were all right. Everybody had come off. But nobody had saved anything except one guy named Kowalski that we used to think was pretty slow on the uptake. He saved his watch by putting it in the finger of a rubber glove and tying a string around it. And nobody told him how to do it. He thought it all up for himself.

"Our grub was in boxes when we tossed it overboard. It rode in on the surf and the boxes smashed up on the coral. We salvaged quite a lot of it that day and we had pretty good chow. It was a sort of surprise party. The labels had washed off all the cans and when you opened one up you never knew whether you were going to get corned-beef hash or pineapple.

"Then the corvette came in about two miles from us on the side of the reef opposite the submarine. The captain sent in a couple of boats for us but they couldn't take more than half the crew the first trip. We had to wade out about half a mile to meet the boats but even then they were in trouble. They smashed their bottoms on the coral and were leaking like two-dollar raincoats. We bailed all the way to the corvette and when we got aboard they hauled the boats up onto the davits. They tinkered with them all night and in the meantime there was no way to send word to the fellows left on the beach. We got aboard about 7:00 P.M. The rest of the guys stayed on the reef while the tide came up. Jones, there, slept in water up to his hips."

"It was wet," Jones remembered. "And I kept wondering how long it would be before I'd have a shark in bed with me."

"Jones was a sort of pilot when we were abandoning ship," said Ahrens. "He got out of another S-boat that got into trouble before that. He's about the only guy in the Navy who got away from two submarine wrecks. Everybody was looking to him for advice."

"We took pretty good care of ourselves. We weren't so badly off as lots of guys who had to sail around the Pacific in rubber boats and catch fish by hand to keep alive. We passed out about eight gallons of water sealed up in a ten-gallon can. That we floated ashore. We put the confidential charts and papers in an ammunition container. The service records came off in the Old Man's laundry bag. Aside from that we saved a pair of binoculars.

"I guess if we hadn't been spotted by the planes we might have been in a bad position. But we weren't worried about it much. We'd just come through a submarine crack-up without losing a man and we felt pretty good. This island I was telling you about —you could see the top of it three miles away beyond the lagoon— looked as if there might be green vegetation on it. The reef curved over to it and we had figured that unless the corvette got around to a position where she could pick us up we'd wait for low water and swim or wade to the island. We'd have made it, too. . . . Then they took me off in the first load and I didn't have to worry about that any more. . . ."

They broke up the submarine in leaving. Jones told about that. And singularly he described none of the sentiment that you might expect among shipwrecked sailors on such an occasion.

"She was a hard-luck boat," he said. "The skipper was a good guy and he deserved better. It wasn't his fault we went aground. They decided that at the investigation, and he's got another command. I guess he'll get along all right now that the jinx is off.

"We did everything that could be done to get her off the reef. We flooded her to hold her down. Then we fired the fish and blew all ballast. But she was down for keeps. The tanks must have been punctured and she was sitting flat on the rocks. When a wave hit her the stern planes would jiggle back into the operating gear in the control room.

"So we busted her up. We did a pretty good job of it. The torpedo men rounded up the torpedoes we'd fired up onto the beach and took the works out of them. We soaked the clothes we weren't going to take with us in gasoline and oil and strung them through the ship. Then we broke what we could with hammers. A lot of the guys seemed real happy about it. G. I. Peterson, the chief electrician, wouldn't let anybody else bust the gyro compass. He said he was reserving that pleasure for himself, that he'd earned it. He'd been messing with that gyro for years and he figured it had finally done him dirt by piling us up where we were. When the hammermen got through, we set fire to our clothes and got away in the rubber boat. The Japs won't salvage that one.

"We left her there in the morning when the corvette's boat came back for us. She was red-hot in spots and sizzling, and odds and ends of things were blowing up inside her. It was a hell of an end for a submarine—high and dry on a coral rock. But we weren't very upset about it. After all we were alive and that was a better break than you'd expect to get in such a mess. You don't always get the breaks in the submarines. . . ."

PART THREE

THE MEN

27

THE BREAKING OF THE GREAT SILENCE

It wasn't until the surface fleet had come back from the raid on Marcus that a lot of war correspondents began to realize what the submarines were doing in the war that we had considered so exclusively our own. It came to us suddenly that the information about enemy ships and batteries furnished us before we set out to bombard the Gilberts and Marshalls had not been gathered from some admiral's ouija board. After we came away from Wake we decided it was no accident that the fleet had been able to slip in past the Japanese air patrols. But we were back in Pearl Harbor before the news began to trickle out about the activity of our underwater fleet around the Philippines, the Strait of Macassar and the Java Sea. Even then the communiqués were interesting but not startling. That the Japanese had begun to howl about "the Red Pirates of the China Coast" and "the ruthless barbarities of the so-called Western civilization" was a clue to the truth we failed to recognize.

About this time we were given our first chance to talk with a submarine commander who had taken his boat on a war patrol and had actually sunk an enemy ship. We journeyed out to the Royal Hawaiian Hotel—taken over by the Navy as a rest house for submarine men and aviators—less impressed by the prospects of a bit of news copy in a period when there was virtually no news at all than by our chance to get a close look at a man who had come from that incredible world under the sea.

While waiting we mumbled to one another that all this was a waste of time—that somebody in the submarine service was trying to cut in on the meager glory of the task forces. We asked one another what the submarines had done—and our questions fell into silence because nobody knew or much cared. But we were filled with an unexplainable curiosity none the less, and we were thrilled at the prospect of meeting this lieutenant commander not for anything he had done but for the life he lived and the manner of man he was likely to turn out to be.

Lieutenant Commander Edward Hutchinson, to whom we were presented by Admiral Thomas Withers, then commanding the submarines in the Pacific, turned out to be much like scores of other submarine skippers whom I have since come to count among my friends, a smart man with a pleasant face and a modesty approaching shyness. It was obvious that he looked on reporters much as we looked upon the submariners, as people outside the limits of understanding. He was polite and gracious to us and answered our foolish questions without indicating that he thought them foolish. But he volunteered little, and I couldn't but feel that he was never at ease with us. Manifestly he was one of the old school of submariners who had been taught early never to talk about their service, and old habits of reticence died hard even under the prompting of an admiral.

I think, in fact, that had it not been for Admiral Withers, we should have learned very little from Captain Hutchinson. We didn't know why we had been invited to the interview or what questions we ought to ask. But the admiral did. And he was an excellent master of ceremonies.

The significance of the incident, I suppose, was lost on all of us, but actually we were looking at the first effort of one in the high command to get the story of the submarines before the public. Admiral Withers, himself an old submariner, had to discard a lot of official ideas about such things before he could arrange this conference. Come to think about it the story that day was not so much in the accomplishments of Lieutenant Commander Hutchinson as in the admiral's upsetting of an old and exasperating precedent. When one looks back across the astounding chronicles that have since come from the submarines, what he had to say may not have been of any great dramatic importance, but it was of compelling interest, as he must have realized had he bothered to study his audience. We were hearing at last something of how these lone wolves operated. We were listening to the voice—incongruously human and well-modulated—of one who had known the life "down among the dead men" as a matter of routine. And we were beginning to realize, most of us, that we had been more intensely drawn by the mystery of the pig boats than by any other phase of the war. From then on nobody was going to tell us anything about a submarine that wouldn't be interesting.

"Captain Hutchinson has just returned from a patrol in Japanese waters and a successful attack on enemy shipping," Admiral Withers explained. And that in itself was startling enough to make the story worth the cable tolls. We had learned somehow that some of our submarines were in Japanese waters, but we had naturally supposed that they were just out there to see what they could see. It hadn't occurred to us that they'd be doing anything to betray their presence. Remembering the sanguine results of the last war, when it was held that the usual score was "one depth charge, one submarine," we had figured that for one of our subs to toss a tin fish at a Japanese ship in its home waters would be the equivalent of quick suicide.

"And you sank a ship out there—off the Japanese coast?" I asked him. I must have sounded surprised for he seemed puzzled when he turned to look at me.

"Oh, yes," he said. "I thought they'd told you that. We sank two . . . at least two. . . ." It seems odd to me now that at the moment I doubted my own ears. There was Waikiki Beach out beyond the terrace with its fringe of palms and exploding red flowers and purple-shadowed greenery. Over in the distance Diamond Head stood in the sun with mauve tints shimmering on its austere profile and the white boa of the surf breaking at its feet. And this was the Royal Hawaiian Hotel, and here was a man who had sunk a couple of Japanese ships in Japanese waters and not only had lived to tell about it but to tell about it with no more concern than he might have shown in a report on the condition of the ship's stores. I couldn't think up any more questions.

"Tell us about the first one," suggested Admiral Withers.

"Very well, sir," said Captain Hutchinson. "It happened a few weeks ago. I can't be definite about the time."

"They understand that they mustn't be definite about anything," said the admiral.

"Very well, sir," repeated the captain. "It happened one night about midnight when we were on the surface. I was down in my bunk when the general alarm sounded. That meant that a ship had been sighted. The men went at once to their battle stations."

"The men went at once to their battle stations!" I didn't know about any submarines except Jules Verne's *Nautilus* and the other similar contrivances with which Frank Reade and Jack Wright had filled the nickel fiction of my childhood, but somehow I could see a long distance beyond the skipper's unadorned report. "The men went to their battle stations." I could see a mélange of arms and legs as men in their bunks had leaped to the grating cough of the klaxons, the crowding of sleepy-eyed boys on the narrow iron ladders, the grim mobilization of the engine-room crew—the black gang—the quick end to disorder and the alert immobility of ranks of men at the wheels and levers and gauges and switches with which my imagination—or Jules Verne's—had filled these monstrosities. . . . Over the deck the gun crew would be spreading and in the torpedo rooms below gunners of another sort would be standing by. . . . Or at least I guessed that was the way it would be and the guess turned out to be reasonably accurate.

"When I got to the bridge the ship was ahead of us at about 8,000 or 9,000 yards," went on Captain Hutchinson. There was another picture but he gave us little chance to consider it. "We moved up on it," said the captain. "We had a little better speed. . . ." It was obvious by this time that we weren't going to get any scenery except what we provided for ourselves in the mind's eye. And probably that is just what we did do . . . otherwise I shall never explain why so bald a recital should have been so vivid and fascinating.

"At 7,500 yards the enemy ship showed a light," said the captain. "I said to the officer of the deck that the Jap was challenging me. He said he didn't think it was a challenge. He said he thought the s.o.b. was opening the charthouse door. . . . Anyway we kept boring in. It was a fine black night. You couldn't see a thing except the smudge of the ship up ahead toward the horizon.

"A little while later the light came on again. Nobody will tell me *that* wasn't a challenge, whether he meant it or not. So that time I went in as fast as I could go. The range when I started was about 7,000, so for the minute I was safe from any guns he'd be likely to have. I kept boring in and watching him, and nothing happened until at 5,500 yards he turned his stern to me. When he did that I got a good look and saw that he didn't have any stern gun. So I didn't stop. I came on in and fired two torpedoes right down his tail. They both hit. . . .

"That slowed him up but it didn't stop him. He swung around a little and illuminated me with a searchlight and I took a dive. . . ."

He took a dive! Well, there we had it. That was why submarines could do things that faster patrol boats couldn't do and go places where a destroyer wouldn't venture.

"As we went down, the moon came out of a cloud bank and spotted him for us," said the captain. "We trailed along watching him through the periscope in the moonlight. By this time I was sure he hadn't any stern gun. Otherwise he'd have been letting us know about it. I waited until he'd got a little farther away from me and then I surfaced to finish him off. I fired another torpedo.

"When I reached the bridge he was firing a pistol or a rifle at me. I still didn't believe he had a larger gun, so I started to attack. And then, just as I came up, he straddled me with a couple of shells from a four-inch or maybe a six-inch gun. It was firing from somewhere amidships. We went down and as we went I saw three or four other shots through the periscope.

"It was obvious that we had hit him. He was wallowing badly. After a while he disappeared from the periscope and I thought it was safe to come up. When we surfaced we looked for him but he was gone. It was certain that he'd gone under.

"We could see miles and miles of moonlit ocean but he wasn't anywhere in sight—not even any trace of him.

"These ships, this one and another that I met in a later encounter, were fast tankers. . . . And I guess that's about all."

We stood silent trying to picture some of this fantastic warfare and Admiral Withers resumed the prompting. "There was this second encounter . . . ," he said.

"Yes, sir," admitted the captain, "but I don't think it was very interesting."

"I think it was quite interesting," said the admiral. "I'm sure they'd like to hear about it." So Captain Hutchinson got on with his report:

"This other encounter was on the same trip," he said, "and with a ship of the same type though larger.

"Shortly after midnight we picked up this enemy ship in the moonlight. We approached on the surface until we got within close range. Then I fired some torpedoes. I heard the first one hit. His stern went up in smoke. His propellers stopped.

"Then the second torpedo hit. By that time I was doing things to get out of his way. I turned the periscope over to an officer, who saw him listing at a 60-degree angle and down by the stern. We followed him for twenty-eight minutes and heard numerous explosions as one after another his tanks went. While the ship was still afloat we kept hearing strange noises like iron smashing against iron. I figured that his gear was tearing away and rolling down the slanting deck. In about fifteen minutes more there was a big explosion and he was gone.

"Both these ships were heavily loaded and carried a lot of fuel." Thus starkly ended a tale which is worth repeating here only for its connotations and for the bench mark it provides in a study of what the submarines have done since.

Both the ships that Hutchinson sank were what the trade sometimes calls "sitting pigeons," merchantmen without escort. And Hutchinson got his bag in good season, for there have been few for the taking in that area since. The captain had one close escape —when the first tanker straddled him with a shell—but you marvel not at his luck in getting away but at his greater luck in failing to provoke a worse barrage earlier while the ship was still on even keel. He had no trouble with the second at all, and he reported further that he had been "picked up on several occasions by patrol boats," but that nothing had come of it. Nobody had ever hit him with artillery. Nobody had dropped any ash cans on top of him.

You come to the conclusion that submarine warfare was just about as new to the Japs at that time as it was to us. One must view Lieutenant Commander Hutchinson's experience as something in the shape of things to come, but not exactly. The pattern of war in the deep was changing out there. For against us was presently to be unleashed a relentless man hunt covering every channel, every port and cove and inlet. For the Japs was beginning the terror that the submarines have kept alive for them ever since.

There was one other little colloquy in the interview with Captain Hutchinson, merely to indicate how sometimes you fail to see the raw materials for prophecy when they lie close at hand. Somebody asked what could be done for sick people aboard. The captain answered that mostly they had to have luck. Keith Wheeler of the Chicago *Times* inquired what would happen to a victim of appendicitis . . . and maybe at that moment we should have heard the astral bells and looked into a future filled with pharmacist's mates performing appendectomies far below the surface with the aid of sharp knives and bent spoons. But we didn't, and the captain went on:

"I had a case of appendicitis on this trip," he said. "I read the book and prescribed a diet that amounted to no food at all. Then we packed the lad's stomach in ice and he recovered. It's not always that fine aboard a submarine which has to travel without a doctor. The ship goes out on her own. She does what job she has to do without hope for aid till she gets back and if a man gets sick he's in a bad spot. . . . There probably will be a lot of trouble with acute appendicitis cases in submarines before this war is over. . . ." And he didn't seem to be hearing any astral bells either.

28

"THEY FIGHT WITHOUT GLORY"

IT WAS sixteen degrees below zero, and the Thames River between Groton and New London, Connecticut, was frozen over for the first time since the big hurricane—or perhaps since the Revolutionary War which also seems bright in the memory of most of the folk in these parts. The admiral (Admiral Freeland Daubin, Comsublant, Commander of Submarines in the Atlantic), an old submariner and once the most famous of his kind, stood in motionless silence looking out across the snow-covered buildings and icy docks, past a long array of black iron whales at their moorings, to the solid white mass where an occasional red buoy under a frosty tam-o'-shanter still marked where the channel ought to be. Upriver, crashing through the ice with a racket that could be heard inside buildings ashore, came a submarine. She was enameled with ice until she looked like a floating Christmas-tree ornament, and ice encased the thick padded coveralls of the man who stood motionless in her bows. Crouched as low as possible against a forty-mile wind, the officers on the bridge could scarcely be seen. But she functioned somehow as if she were maneuvering in warm and placid waters under a summer sun. She made a neat, if abrupt, turn, piling quantities of slush ice on her deck, broke an opening for herself into a slip and came up gently against a pier. Reefered gobs appeared from nowhere to take her lines.

The admiral nodded with satisfaction. The other officers seemed pleased, and I shall confess to a sentimental sigh. For all of us knew that the spectacle we had just witnessed was something more than an experiment in ice breaking. The last time I had seen that boat was in Pearl Harbor in the days when the smashed battleships made a background for everything you looked at. And here she was tied up only a few miles from the ways down which she had slid in her launching. . . . A Pacific raider, and a highly successful one, had finally come home.

I remarked that for all I had seen of the work of these strange ships I would hardly have believed such a voyage possible. . . . The weather out there would be ghastly for the crew of a *Queen Mary*, the weight of ice across the Thames (Connecticut) had been enough to stop ferry traffic, and ships like submarines were never intended . . .

"You miss the main point," said the admiral. "It isn't the ships. It's the men. You remember the one about the submarine that surfaced in the Aleutians and kept going right on up through the fog? Well, to a submarine man that story would be only half silly. That crew down there, the one that just came through the ice, will never believe you if you say there's anything they can't do with a submarine. And many experienced Japanese navy men will now agree with them." He looked again at the river, where the churned wake of the incoming raider had frozen once more and was now a feathery ridge extending well down toward the red arch of the new bridge.

"No, sir," he said, "if you're going to set down the story of the submarines you must first set down the story of the man inside the submarine—the man who fights it and nurses it and whose life is bound up with it. Please God that somebody may find out about him someday. He is not yet the forgotten man of the U. S. military services because he has never yet been known. It's very doubtful—things being as they are—that he ever will be. . . ."

The submarine service—said the admiral—is necessarily a lonesome job. The boat leaves her dock and heads out over hundreds, sometimes thousands of miles of ocean—to her patrol area. And from the time she leaves until she gets back she is on her own and every man's hand is against her.

For weeks of such a patrol a submarine man may never see the sun. He may never come through a hatch into the upper air. He lives through days of excruciating monotony—a monotony in which he must be just as alert and just as precise in every movement as he was in the very beginning.

In time there is contact with the enemy and the submarine man helps to fight his ship. Nobody sees him do it. Nor does he himself see what he has done. There is nothing spectacular about what he does—nothing to distinguish it so far as he can see—from the routine of training. And this despite the fact that his work has become the most important feature of modern war.

Only the man at the periscope sees the target. Only that man—if anybody—knows the thrill of the chase. And quite often what little drama he finds in it breaks off in anticlimax. . . . Seldom is he able to stay long enough to see his torpedo hit.

There may be one brief moment of exaltation as the shot goes on its way. But even so, there is always the reckoning.

The torpedo is fired and inevitably—no question about it any more—inevitably the depth-bombing commences. Down below the man sits and takes it. There isn't a thing he can do to stave off this thing or to defend himself against it. He sits there and feels his nerves shrivel up inside him in the most harrowing experience in the world.

He hears the thud of the first blast—the ship trembles, things fall down. Sometimes the lights go out—frequently the lights go out. In darkness and dead silence he searches for leaks, both ears alert for the next burst. Maybe—please God!— there won't be another. Maybe the next one will be a hit!

("Oil patches on the water indicated to the captain of the subchaser that the target had been destroyed. . . .")

Anyway he watches and waits, sometimes for hours, as the dynamite rocks him and his chances under the law of averages run slimmer and slimmer.

The bombing stops. Drawn up within himself, he notices first that the interval after the last shot is increasing. . . . It's never the shot just past or the one that's bursting right now that concerns him . . . it's the next one. . . . He counts over the number of seconds that should mark the preparation for the next charge. There is no next charge. He knows he must have made a mistake. So he counts the seconds over again.

Naturally he doesn't dare to hope that the ordeal is finished for good. The slick Nip so-and-so up there is just playing tricks on him—waiting for him to move and tip off the sound detectors. In a minute there'll be another blast—a closer blast.

Sometimes the closer blast actually comes—infrequently, thank the Lord—and then there is truth in the communiqués about oil slicks on the water and floating debris. Sometimes, after enough hours of this torture to put an average man into an insane asylum, the periscope comes to the surface without provoking any new attack. The ride through hell in a glass-bottomed boat is almost completed. . . . Almost completed. . . . That is to say, the enemy ships are over the horizon and the TNT isn't churning the ocean hereabouts. But every ear in the boat is vibrating to the echoes of shots long dissipated—every diaphragm palpitating with the concussion of bursts that were never heard at all. The minds of the officers are too numb to work out problems in simple arithmetic—and for an appreciable time they will continue to be numb. . . .

Even the neurologists get tangled up when they try to explain what happens to these men. But they all know that it does happen. And, leaving out all medical terminology, they class it as a sort of delayed shock . . . the shock a man gets in an automobile accident when he walks away from the wreck and falls unconscious in the next street.

The odd part of it is that it's continuous. Men who have been depth-bombed a couple of times come out of it all right. That is to say they function all right until they get home. A couple of weeks of rest and sunshine rid them of all surface marks of their experience. But if, after that, they are subjected to another dynamiting, many of them get physically ill, nauseated. It doesn't seem to be fear, mind you, that upsets them. In actual fact they go about their work as usual. And, what is more to the point, their reflexes don't seem to be in any way impaired. Their conscious brain has pushed aside the unpleasantness of the last fight and is dealing entirely with the present. But something back in the subconscious remembers and rebels.

There is an obvious difference between this effect and that which men experience in land barrages or bombings. The latent claustrophobia that is in every man no doubt has something to do with it—the human dread of being buried alive or killed, helpless, in a box. Thousands of people have been bombed repeatedly in

London and Chungking Scores of Navy men and men of the Merchant Marine have been dive-bombed frequently at sea and seem to have suffered nothing from cumulative effect. It's being sealed in while death plays around that makes the difference.

The mental scars of the underwater-bombing experience may never heal. Men never really get used to the bombing. The fiftieth experience affects them just as the second one did. And yet they go out time after time until old age or the law of diminishing returns catches up with them. They are the hardest men in the world . . . the men who have subjugated their own weaknesses.

They fight without glory. It's the superstition, not to say the philosophy, of the service that there is safety in silence. It is also the policy of all navies to take advantage of the fear that comes of the submarine's ability to strike in the dark. Enemy shipping diminishes and the enemy wonders why. Enemy submarines fail to return and nobody knows what happened to them. Sub casualties in the last war, kept secret by the Allies, eventually caused Germany's homebound crews to rebel.

So there are few accounts of submarine exploits in the newspaper headlines, and this despite the fact that the submarine has turned out to be the most important single factor in determining the expense and strategy of this war.

The aviator goes into a battle for which he has been prepared. He is girded for the fight like a gladiator in the presence of his friends. If he dies in brief combat—as he is likely to die—some of his pals are around to mark his glorious end and he has a brief glimpse of immortality as he notices that they are watching him. Somebody will carry him along at least in wardroom conversation for some time after he is gone. As against that, your submariner travels alone in the shadows of his iron box. He is one of the most intelligent, one of the most highly trained artisans in any line of work, so he knows without anybody telling him the dangers that ride with him. He stands constant watch, a few hours on, a few hours off, and sleeps, when he does sleep, with all his clothes on. His vigilance relaxes only when exhaustion overtakes him; his nerves never relax at all until the boat ties up at her home base.

When he arrives at a fight he has been weeks getting there. He is physically and mentally as tired as you'd expect him to be. His moment of glory has arrived when he's wondering how much longer his legs are going to carry him. . . . "Take her down! Fire One! Fire Two! . . ." He lets go his shot in the dark, unknown, unhonored and certainly unsung. Then he stands at his battle station waiting for the depth bombs that won't be long in coming—ready to die like a trapped lion, alone.

29

SUB vs. SUB

THE more evidence you get about the lazy, dreamy days in Pearl Harbor while the peace workers were murmuring things about international amity in Washington, the more you become aware that one skeptic out there in the Pacific must have spent all his time getting ready for trouble. Others, repeating the maxims about our impregnable position and Hirohito's common sense, may have listened to the cuckoo songs that came out of the impromptu peace conferences. But all the while Admiral Thomas Withers, commandant of the submarine forces of the Pacific, was listening to "ancestral voices prophesying war." It was he who made a working base for his boats in Pearl Harbor, fought for supplies and parts from the mainland, installed an adequate torpedo plant and finally arranged for the physical refurbishment of crews who would one day come back blanched and racked by long and dangerous patrols. It was he who envisioned something of the sort of underwater war that was presently to be fought. And when the Japs came in on the morning of December 7, 1941, his forces had long been trained and assigned to fight it.

So most of the submarines were out of the harbor that morning of the attack . . . most of them in spots from which they could take on their new job with a minimum of effort. As a matter of fact they had been in such spots for months. It is significant that while Admiral Withers was running his expeditions out of Pearl Harbor—and he remained in command until well after the Battle of Midway—not one of his submarines was lost.

One of the few boats in the Honolulu area when the attack finally came—a bit late according to the admiral's calculation—was the one commanded by Commander J. H. ("Joe") Willingham, and Willingham was there only because he had just completed a patrol.

"We'd been expecting the war," Captain Willingham said afterward. "Admiral Withers had hammered that into us. We'd been on long patrols with everything set to fight and we'd been doing the hardest work of our lives getting the crews to realize that we were really going to have to fight a war."

The captain was in town that morning as were most of his battered crew. One of his men saw a lone plane flying overhead, noticed the red ball on it, and before the alarms had begun to sound had called him in Honolulu. The town was still peaceful. None of the terror had yet broken loose in Pearl Harbor. The telephone lines weren't congested nor were the roads that led out from town along the water front. In thirty minutes bedlam was to be loose in all that region, but Captain Willingham got out and past the gates into the naval base before the main wave of the attack had come over.

So he saw most of it. He was on deck when the low-flying V of torpedo planes came toward him over the oil dock, headed for battleship row. One plane stood out from the rest, and presently in the midst of the worst confusion he had ever seen he noticed that a couple of destroyers were firing at it. His own gun crews were in position and the 20-millimeter gun immediately below him began to bark along with the rest of them.

In a mess like that it is always difficult to determine who hits what or if anybody hits at all. But to Captain Willingham came an advantageous break such as comes to few men. At almost the same moment both destroyers ceased firing, and for a few short seconds the submarine had the target all to itself. The captain had a dozen other observers scattered about in the shambles between the sub-base and the battleships who saw his tracers running true toward the oncoming plane—a single arc of fire. And then they saw a hit squarely on the war head of one of the long glistening fish under the plane's belly. The torpedo blew up in a blast that sprayed the water with chunks beneath it and tossed up a mushroom of flame that broke into streaks across the smoke-fogged sky. One minute the plane was there and the next minute it wasn't. They never found any traces of it.

"That was a day," said the captain. "I hope I never see anything like it again. . . ."

All the time, the crew that had just come in from sea was back at work getting ready to go out again. All through the attack they worked, putting engines and gadgets back together again and filling up the boat with fuel and supplies. All through the afternoon they went on with it, sweating and weary as they waited for the next attack which fortunately never came.

The last wave of planes they shot at along about 11:15 A.M., this time in chorus with all the other antiaircraft in the harbor and without being able to tell much of what they had done. The planes spread their fish against the battleships and one after another the big flatirons went down. The *Oklahoma* shivered, careened and tipped over. The *Arizona* blew up and covered the harbor with oily smoke.

Along toward the last of it a big bomb hit the dry dock with a blast that threw a column of its own gas 200 feet in the air. The top of it exploded and put an umbrella of flame far across the harbor. Through this murk the Jap planes continued to dart—most of them unhampered. But not all of them came out of it. Willingham saw one take a hit as it was pulling out of its dive over one of the dim silhouettes in the smoke. It kept right on going and smashed into the side of the nurses' quarters by the hospital. After that there was no further shooting. Fire details got on with their work of saving what could be saved. Hospital crews and volunteer rescue parties did what could be done for the wounded and dying. The submarines got ready to go to sea.

One after another, the few boats at the docks slid out through the channel to join the rest of the underwater fleet already at stations. Captain Willingham was ready to go at 6:00 P.M. But by that time it was decided that it would be better for him to finish his repairs. So his boat lay there during the fortnight of the great jitters, while work crews swarmed over it as they would have back in almost unbelievable days of peace.

He went out from there eventually to look over some of the Japanese bases where the Navy was to begin its painful rehabilitation. And shortly thereafter Naval Intelligence began to realize the usefulness of submarines in scouting spots that no other ships—not even airplanes—could reach.

The submarine did little else on that patrol. But it was enough. Heat and sun produced a constant haze over the sea—a thin mist at times but always enough to make observation difficult and navigation precarious.

They got few star sights, traveled much of the time by dead reckoning and instinct. One morning they sighted their objective to the southward and lost it again in the rising mists. They closed in and found it in the night by the sound of the surf and the fishy smell of the reef. After that they stayed in close and studied its flora and fauna and particularly its shipping.

One day, offshore, they ran into a patrol boat, a wooden-hulled ship, and took a shot at it. They probably sank it, but nothing happened. Then a few days later as the captain was compiling his shipping lists he walked the periscope around. He discovered submarines moving along behind him on the surface. They were together, but in no particular formation, and they were just a little out of his reach. He swung about and went for them but they spotted him, dispersed and dived.

That, he thinks, was one of the worst days of his experience. Some of the crew suggested encouragingly that maybe they'd have a chance to get some more submarines and he said he'd certainly take care of them if the chance offered. But he didn't sound convincing even to himself.

He moved in then from where he had seen the submarines and got another disappointment. He sighted a fairly big ship as he approached the south shore and got all ready to make an approach on her when he saw breakers ahead of him. The ship was inside the reef.

However, the visibility was better from this new vantage point and he got a good look not only at the ship he had hoped to sink but at others in the harbor. He got their measurements and identified them all by name. That about finished the work he'd been sent to do in the sector, but he proceeded to the entrance of the lagoon and got there just ahead of a ship on her way in.

She was a setup, he reported later. He shot two torpedoes at her and one hit.

The story of what happened to him then is one with those of the other submarines that went into the war without ever having heard a depth charge, except that perhaps his spot was a little worse. There were plenty of planes protecting this base and several destroyers that had little to do but come out for ash-can practice. Captain Willingham didn't stay to see what he had done. The destroyers were after him almost immediately, and for hours afterward the planes came out to churn up the water around him with dynamite. The submarine was under for hours—so long that the air was blue and choking. It was the longest dive that any of the personnel had ever made or were to make in many months of war.

When, finally, the blasting stopped, they moved away and reconnoitered other islands in the vicinity. But after that they ran into no other ships. They went back to Pearl Harbor to complete the overhaul that had been started on December 5.

When they were able to put to sea again they were ordered into the Southwest Pacific. Things were quieter about the Hawaiian Islands by that time and they didn't expect to see any action for days. However, the Japanese submarines appear to have been more venturesome than they were to be later. Captain Willingham's boat was only a few days on its journey when the officer of the deck saw a flash on the water which he took to indicate a periscope. The captain looked and agreed. A Japanese sub was about one point on his bow, opening for a shot. He put the rudder over and sounded the call to make ready the stern tubes. When they were steady on his bearing the captain fired one fish.

He had already cleared the bridge and prepared to go under, but still he stood there watching the white streamer of the torpedo lengthening in the water behind him. It seemed a long time getting anywhere. He could no longer see the Jap periscope and there was always the chance that the target had gone a long way down. He was just about to give it up when he saw the water rise up and fall apart in a white froth as the smoke plume of a torpedo explosion came rolling out of it.

The captain had learned by this time that Japanese submarines were likely to be traveling in groups, so he kept his distance. He was approaching the scene of the explosion cautiously when a

U. S. plane came over. He signaled to it, explained what had happened and asked for verification.

He had a long wait. The plane came down low and circled endlessly. Captain Willingham was about ready to call off the search and get on his way again when he got another signal: "She's sunk all right. . . . Oil and debris all over water. She's unquestionably a submarine." So he sent a message to Admiral Withers, who checked with the pilot of the plane, and the submarine which had entered the war by blasting a torpedo plane out of the air got credit for the first verified sinking of a Japanese submarine by another submarine. The incident had wide repercussions because up to that time—despite the experiences of European fleets in two years of war—it was still believed that no submarine could ever do much against another ship of her kind. Captain Willingham went south with a lot of other ideas.

There were some boresome weeks after that—a little scouting here, a little there . . . an uneventful journey on the edge of the Battle of the Coral Sea. They heard nothing save reports of the war that other people were fighting—saw nothing for days on end save their own little ship and broad expanses of hot ocean.

They sailed on to an area off one of the westerly bases on the edge of the Japanese advance for some other quiet days. One night, an hour or so before dawn, the officer of the deck made out the shadow of a large passenger ship close in. They turned about and made an approach—and a very good approach—which got them into position shortly after the sun had risen. The captain was deliberate about it. The ship seemed to have no protection and there was no indication that his presence was suspected. But just after he had come to what seemed a proper range there was enough light on the towering hull ahead for him to see what it looked like . . . a fine ship and probably loaded, but filling the periscope scale was something else—a large red cross. So he lay back and watched her proceed over the horizon into the misty morning.

Later that day luck was kinder. They were loitering along off a coral island when they picked up a large freighter heading in. Captain Willingham got a torpedo hit on her, took a look around to make sure that she wasn't being followed by any destroyers or similar nuisances, and stayed where he could see the proceedings.

She didn't sink, although flame started to roll out of her and her bow came up out of the water. Instead, with a black plume from her funnel and white water spreading from her stern she drove on at full speed toward the island, where she ran halfway up onto the coral. The submarine moved away then and in a few hours was in the middle of a bad blow. She didn't get back for two days and when she did there was nothing to look at save some wrecked palm trees and a lot of debris on the beach.

Visibility was bad in this area. After the blow the water was fairly calm, with a hot sun and enough water evaporation south of the islands to keep the sea covered with a thin mist. When the breeze came from the north, as it generally did, the islands were shrouded. Yet occasionally they saw some signs of the Japanese shipping that infested the place. A few days after the storm they discovered a division of destroyers coming up from the south, and instead of running away they maneuvered for an attack. They put out a spread of torpedoes and missed.

The skipper has only one comment to make on that incident. "The attack was unsuccessful," he said. "We dived and they went over us." I gathered that the depth-charging was not worth mentioning or else that by this time the crew was getting used to such routine.

A few days afterward Captain Willingham was asleep in his bunk when a young ensign called down to him:

"Captain, there's a big liner in sight."

He got up to take a look for himself and discovered not a big liner but a Japanese submarine about the size of an S-boat. He fired one fish and missed by a close margin as the target went under. There was disappointment in that one. The captain was still nursing his theory that you could sink submarines if you shot fast enough, but the law of averages seemed to indicate that he'd be hardly likely to have any more chances for experiment. However, he was fully awake now and there didn't seem to be any sense in going back to bed, so he stayed at the periscope. Two hours later he picked up another submarine.

It took him about an hour to maneuver into position to do something about this one, but when he fired he hit. This time there was no doubt about it. The Jap came apart in small pieces.

Something like instinct kept him maneuvering in the same area. It might get hot there at any minute. On the other hand there was evidence that he was in a lane favored by Japanese submarines. . . . There might be some more of them coming that way, who could say? So he was in a fairly good position when the third one came along. He took after her unnoticed and unsuspected.

The mist came down again and part of his chase was by instinct but he never lost his target. His first torpedo was a hit and she stopped dead in the water. But as he cruised about, watching her, he noticed that she showed no signs of sinking. She'd taken enough of a blast to disable her but she apparently had plenty of buoyancy and was drifting right side up. As he came closer he could see the crew preparing to abandon ship. He fired another torpedo and that finished her. On a single patrol he had accounted for three enemy submarines, a record which is going to be difficult for any other submarine to better in this war.

There is something of a saga in the work of Captain Willingham's boat in its less spectacular but more dangerous phases patrolling the south side of the base. For two weeks the mists had clung close to the beach and he hadn't been able to see what was going on inside the lagoon. The main island was like others in the coral belt, fairly high inside and surrounded by low reefs—so low that the water doesn't break over them. It was easy to get into navigational difficulties in a spot like that. By night the treacherous rocks might be invisible. By day the spotters on the shore fortifications would be alert. So they had to feel their way in, a few feet at a venture, aware all the time that they might get within a few hundred yards of the beach and never know they were there. Every morning they had to dive, and not only that, they had to find water deep enough to dive in. It was a delicate problem to get close enough to make observations and still not spend all their daylight time running down their batteries.

Sampans rolling around outside the entrance were a constant bother.

"They might never have known we were there," said the captain. "But you couldn't be sure and in a place like that it didn't do to take any chances."

In spite of all that they did get close inshore, close enough to see things through the mist, and skirted the island till they came off the entrance to the lagoon. One evening they almost ran into a large ship—"a very large ship," the captain said—standing out to sea.

Before he could jockey around to make a run for it, however, some more surface ships started to come out and with them, presumably, an escort. The submarine withdrew and watched the convoy forming up outside the entrance.

They closed in again with the black of the island behind them and a black sea ahead. Captain Willingham had no trouble picking out the silhouette of the big freighter; it bulked high above the rest. And his weeks of caution paid dividends in that the escort ships apparently weren't worrying about submarines. He maneuvered till he found a good spot to shoot from, and fired his fish. He was aware in a few seconds that he had hit a loaded ammunition ship, probably one of those headed for the Coral Sea or the Solomons. She exploded in one of the most spectacular displays ever seen in the South Pacific.

There was some depth-bombing afterward but not much. The destroyers had all the work they could attend to sifting the debris that the blast probably had left in the middle of the convoy.

The submarine moved away from there that night and passed the next day in a lane approaching the island. At dusk the executive picked up smoke on the horizon. Captain Willingham ran ahead of it and spotted a small interisland freighter. He fired one and missed, closed in, fired two and hit. She was down in a matter of seconds.

The next two patrols were a little more disappointing. The skipper made a fine approach on one large ship in the China Sea and was ready to sink her when she turned on her lights and showed the red cross and white superstructure of a hospital ship. Not long afterward he saw a second large shadow approaching from the opposite direction and he got set for that. Her lights identified her as the exchange ship taking diplomats and refugees south from Tokyo.

It was all very discouraging, he thought. Two protected targets, a few miles from each other on the same day, and it was his luck to waste his time on both of them.

However, two days later in the same area he saw another ship without any badges or labels and apparently alone. He got in close to her without any trouble before moonrise, fired two fish at her and watched her upend. In his log he entered the notation that he had sunk what appeared to be a small freighter.

Later that night he surfaced under a bright moon and found a mystery. Ahead of him was an oil slick two miles long with a litter of debris in it. But nowhere was there a lifeboat nor a raft nor a life jacket nor any sign of a single survivor. The submarine officers studied that situation all the way back to their base and could make nothing out of it.

Back at their base for a brief leave Captain Willingham found the answer. Captain E. J. Hutchinson had been behind him on the way down and had passed through the same area, and the pair met in a local hotel.

"By the way," Hutchinson inquired, "did you sink a ship at such-and-such latitude and longitude?"

Willingham considered the matter.

"Yes," he said. "We got a ship there. It was a small freighter. . . ."

"Freighter, hell!" said Hutchinson. "When we were going through there the O.D. reported an awful stench. I went up to see what it was all about and by that time all around us we could make out hundreds and hundreds of legs—literally hundreds and hundreds —sticking up out of the water."

It was obvious then that Captain Willingham must have smashed up a large transport whose men had been promptly drowned by overweighted packs that upended them as they dived.

"But I didn't know," he said. "I saw his tail come up, and then his forecastle broke off and I went away. Generally I call some of the crew up to take a look at such things but this happened too fast. I just got the radioman to the periscope when most of her was awash. He said, 'She just turned over and sank, sir.' "

"Well," said Hutchinson, "she certainly did. . . ."

The next couple of weeks were uneventful, a fact which the captain remembers with some gratitude. Breaks like that, he says, help you to keep your skin on. Later on headed north they ran into a heavy rain squall and were plowing through it almost blind when they made out the contours of a ship. As she came in close they saw that she was a fast Diesel craft. Captain Willingham sent down the data for blasting her and was closing in when he heard a Filipino calling something. He was still cautious—fearful of aircraft with which the region was swarming—so he shot the boat's rudder off and she stopped dead. They came closer then, covering the decks with machine guns, and found only three men in sight— Filipino boys who dived overboard and swam to the submarine. They were thin and weak and covered with sores and said that they'd been having a hard time of it since the Japs took over the ship of which they'd been part of the original crew.

The captain told one of them to warn the Japs to get off, as he intended to sink the ship, and twelve of them came above decks, lowered a boat and got into it. He asked if everybody had got off and they told him yes. Then he gave them water and directions and opened up on the ship with the deck guns. The first salvo lifted her out of the water and then she suddenly began to erupt Japanese who had been hiding below decks. What they had intended to do even the Filipino boys didn't know, but they got no further chance to try it because the ship was even then falling apart.

She wasn't much of a ship, the captain recalls, but the attack was worth the effort because it provided the U. S. Navy with three new mess boys. The Filipinos were sworn in as recruits before the boat was under way again.

Up in the China Sea they ran into a typhoon, and after running north for four days they found themselves sixty miles south of the point from which they had started. Coming in their direction was an interisland steamship apparently trying to make the lee of a spit of land toward which the wind had been pushing them. They moved to attack in a gray and foaming sea but the ship zigzagged and they lost her in the rain. It was getting fairly late, and they figured she'd not be loitering long in the teeth of the wind. So Captain Willingham got behind the point of land and waited, and

THE CHRISTMAS TREE

A warrant officer at the controls which close main openings to
the sea. As the vents are shut the lights on the indicator board
above him (the Christmas tree) turn from red to green.

THE LONG VIEW

The deck and conning tower of one of the new U. S. submarines looking aft.

presently saw her rounding the point approaching him. He fired two torpedoes hoping to hit her with one. Both of them hit and she broke up in a few minutes.

It wasn't any free bag, however. They quickly discovered that all this region was swimming with patrol boats and airplanes, and in the shallow water behind the land spit the submarine had a harrowing few hours.

"It knocked a lot of things out of kilter," the captain said about the depth-charge barrage. "They ran us ragged. That was the first time I ever saw the crew really scared. . . ."

They got out of the danger but not entirely out of their run of trouble. Two or three days later they came up with a tender and an escort. The procession stopped. Captain Willingham fired a fish and missed and they took another working-over more vicious than the earlier one because there wasn't any doubt about their position.

When they were able to get up they saw a ship on the horizon and chased her until dusk. The captain fired one torpedo at her and missed. He knew where she was going, so he went after her again, closed and fired another one. That missed, too. Still all wasn't lost. The navigator calculated the ship's morning position and the submarine set out to intercept her. They caught up with her for a third time, fired a third torpedo and missed again. They gave it up after that and started for home.

In its patrols the submarine had been credited with sinking 50,000 tons of enemy shipping, three submarines and one torpedo plane, and the recruiting of three men for the Navy.

"We had only one really good patrol," says Captain Willingham looking back over the record. From which you may gather that he's something of a perfectionist.

30

SECOND BATTLE OF MANILA

LOOKING at the war from Battleship Row, Pearl Harbor, in December 1941, we couldn't see much defense against the indictment that as a nation we had very little business trying to get along in a world of realists. Observers in Manila Bay two days after the attack on Hawaii saw another disastrous raid and talked numbly about the end of our sea power and our prospects in the Pacific. To the Asiatic squadron had come the grim dispatch: "The Pacific fleet has been immobilized." One tough youngster who was presently to roll up an incredible record for destruction in the submarines went to his bunk and passed the most ghastly night he was ever to know . . . in tears.

Yet things weren't precisely the same out in the Philippines. For somebody—probably the same admiral who was about to go before the Roberts Commission and explain why our best strategists had been walking in their sleep on the morning of December 7—had mobilized a pretty good submarine fleet along the China coast. And the submarine men for months had been not only prepared for war but expecting it.

The fleet, considering that for months it was going to have to fight the Japs virtually unaided, was not too big. We had been just about as wrong in our estimates of the usefulness of these boats as in another generation we had been coy about the airplane.

The underwater fleet of December 7, 1941, consisted of 111 ships of all classes with another 73 building. Twenty-three additional were ordered almost immediately and Congress was asked to authorize 200,000 tons of construction, enough for 100 more, (which it did in April 1942). Obviously, with the Panama Canal and the coasts and Alaska and Hawaii to defend, the number of submarines that could be sent out to Asia was probably the absolute minimum that could be expected to do any good at all. But for all that the little detachment that moved out to the Philippines in the summer of 1941 was one of the best trained and equipped in the world and, as it was shortly to demonstrate, one of the most effective.

Among the skippers who were sitting about Manila awaiting the inevitable were eight or ten whose successes have placed them among the great ones of naval history—and this despite the official unwillingness of their service to look upon anyone as a hero. It's no secret any more that Lieutenant Commander Chester Smith was out there getting ready to pile up a record which submarine men say has not been surpassed, Lieutenant Commander Frederick Burdett ("Fearless Freddy") Warder with the *Seawolf*, Lieutenant Commander William Leslie ("Bull") Wright, Lieutenant Commander Eugene McKinney, Lieutenant Commander J. C. Dempsey, Lieutenant Commander R. G. Voge who survived the sinking of the *Sealion* and made an immediate scourge out of his next command, Lieutenant Commander Morton Mumma who drove the ghosts out of the old *Squalus*, Lieutenant Commander J. W. ("Red") Coe, Lieutenant Commander Wreford Goss ("Moon") Chapple who smashed up the Jap concentrations in Lingayen Harbor, Lieutenant Commander J. R. Wright, Jr., Lieutenant Commander Nicholas Lukey, Lieutenant Commander Frank W. ("Mike") Fenno who took the gold out of Manila, Lieutenant Commander C. P. Reynolds, Lieutenant Commander Michael Callaghan, Lieutenant Commander Theodore Alwin, Lieutenant Commander John Burnsides, Lieutenant Commander T. D. Jacobs, Lieutenant Commander Lamb, Lieutenant Commander Price, Lieutenant Commander Freeman, and others who have since won the Navy Cross and, what is more remarkable, lived to receive it.

Not all of these men were in Manila Bay when the Jap raiders came over on the morning of December 9 (E. Long.), 1941. But there was a pretty fair concentration of them at their bases—ships taking on supplies for the war that they knew was in their laps, ships in process of repair, a couple of ships awaiting complete overhaul in the harbor at Cavite.

The captains remember December 9 as a beautiful day, a day

filled with sunlight such as few of them were to see again for months. But it was a terrible day even before the Japs came over, because of the news that had begun to filter in from Pearl Harbor. Several of the boats lay alongside a tender where men were working at top speed to take on fuel and water. Most of them had boxes of food stacked high on their decks.

"It's hard to remember what that day was like," one of them said later as he waited for a new command in Mare Island Navy Yard. "I can remember the blazing sun and the streaks of purple and green across the bay and the palms on the shore and the piles of red and purple flowers along the Luneta. Manila Bay is one of the most beautiful ports in the world and you couldn't help noticing it on a morning like that when you figured that maybe you wouldn't be seeing it very long.

"Nobody had to send us any special orders to tell us what we were up against. The surface ships were out of business. We didn't know how long it would be before they could get going again. And in the meantime if anybody was going to fight the Jap navy and stave off the Jap convoys we were elected. Submarines haven't many friends at any time. Right then I don't think we had any.

"I suppose maybe we were taking a long chance to stick around Manila Bay, but there didn't seem to be any cure for it. We were right under the gun . . . more so by several thousand miles than Pearl Harbor had been, and we didn't know if we'd ever be able to come back once we got out.

"You must remember that at that time we didn't know how badly Pearl had been hit. We just figured that probably the worst possible had happened, that it had been so badly smashed that it couldn't be used as a base any longer. . . . And if that could happen to Pearl Harbor it certainly could happen to Manila. We weren't so far wrong about Manila at that.

"Well, in the circumstances we figured we'd better get all the supplies aboard that we'd need for months, and even at a risk we had to stay there and take them.

"We never completed the job. All of a sudden we heard an air-raid alarm. . . . It was so thin and distant that it hardly came out to us across the water. But we really didn't need it because in the next few minutes the Japs were on top of us. I don't know how many waves came because I didn't have any chance to count them, but the sky seemed filled with them.

"We were working like hell to get our fuel and water lines free. They kept yelling at us from the tender to dive, and I for one was certainly willing but we all knew it wasn't going to be any simple job. We were in thirty-seven feet of water and you haven't much room to dive a 1,500-ton submarine in thirty-seven feet.

"We were ready for it, though. We'd had all battle stations manned for some time. We had the engines going and the boat corked up, all except for engine exhaust and main induction and a couple of hatches. After what seemed like forty-seven years we began to get under way.

"The Jap attack, as I found out later, was just about like the one in Pearl. The fighter planes came low and strafed us with machine guns. I guess they got some men on the tender in the first few minutes. Those boys had guts. Instead of taking cover they stayed out where they could relay orders to us. They wanted us to get under before the bombs came, and they never seemed to think about themselves at all. A lot of them were still out on deck when we finally submerged.

"We didn't get down ahead of the bombs, though. The bombers were over right on the tail of the fighter waves, and all you could see were those golden sugar beets coming down through the sun and columns of water leaping all over the bay. If they brought any torpedo planes with them in that first attack I didn't see them. Anyway we didn't have that to contend with, which was at least a minor blessing.

"I suppose it was a matter of seconds between the time the first wave came over and the time we sounded the klaxon for the dive, but there didn't see to be any such thing as time any more. Hell was just loose all over the place and it didn't look like there was ever going to be any end to it.

"Antiaircraft batteries along the beach had begun to work. We didn't expect much from them because there weren't enough of them in the first place and the crews weren't any too experienced. It seemed to me we'd hear about ten bomb blasts before a shell would plop up above. But when the chunks started to come down you'd have thought there were a million of them. You could see the patterns of fragments like feathers on the water and every now and then you'd hear a clink when one of them hit the deck. I began to be afraid they'd put some serious holes in us before the Japs got a chance. We didn't try any of our own ack-ack. Our best defense was to get a few feet of water over us and when we'd got the lines cast off everybody scrambled off the deck.

"I knew of course that we weren't going to have any picnic below. Just as we pulled away from the tender I saw Lieutenant Commander McKinney's boat start down. Before we started to submerge he'd gone down as far as he could go, and believe me that wasn't encouraging. The top of his conning tower was still sticking up out of the water. By that time I was on my way off the bridge. We went down right after him.

"We felt a little safer when we straightened her out a few feet off the bottom, but not much. The bombs kept coming down for at least an hour, and if the Jap shooting had been as good as it got to be later I don't think any of us would have come out of it. The noise was just all over the place and there was no way you could tell direction or distance—not that it would have made any difference to us. We'd often wondered how depth charges were going to sound, and when we got out of there we knew. Dynamite is dynamite no matter how they deliver it to you.

"I don't know how the other skippers feel about it but I've never had a worse ride than that trip across the bottom. Fortunately we knew every foot of the bay, so we knew when we could get down another couple of feet. But all the way out to the breakwater and for a long time afterward we were practically doing a belly crawl along the bottom.

"We were making better speed than usual submerged because we weren't worrying about being picked up by sound apparatus. The Jap aviators already knew where we were. Most of the time I guess they could see us. And, boy, it was all six-two and even. We knew where they were, too.

"We got out of that with more luck than we deserved. Only one ship was sunk, the *Sealion*. She was lying next to a tender over in Cavite and they blew her apart with virtually all the crew. Only a few men who had been on the bridge when she was hit were saved.

"The ship lying next to her got away with part of her bridge shot off and half a dozen leaks that in peacetime would have looked like enough to put her out of action for good. But she was able to stay submerged the rest of that day without drowning anybody. Then she managed to sneak back to a tender where she found enough of a repair crew to close up some of the bigger holes. They patched her pressure hull enough so that she was able to get along for months, but she still had a lot of leaks. She was never really fixed up until she came back to the Pacific coast for an overhaul after more than a year of service down around the Solomons. Submarine men want to stuff her and put her in the Smithsonian Institution as an example of what one of these boats can take when she has to. She was the crate that plagued the Japs off Indo-China until they started to put out special communiqués about her. She was also the one that lay at sixty feet while all hands turned to to help the pharmacist's mate perform the first of those emergency appendectomies that you keep hearing about. . . .

"Well, we finally got into water deep enough to cover us, and we lay there until the row was over. When we surfaced at night we got orders to come back in, and we did and picked up what we could find in the way of supplies. We couldn't find much. All the stuff we'd had on our decks was on the bottom of the bay, and there wasn't much lying loose around the docks but rice and such stuff. We began to figure that we were going to be a lot thinner before we got another square meal and we were right about that, too.

"We hung around there for a couple of days and then they gave us our march orders and we started up north. It was a long time before we got back to a place where we could sit down again. . . ."

They got their orders and they started north . . . and it was a long time before they got back to a place where they could sit down again. It was a matter of routine as uneventful as all that. You pause to look over the meager but fascinating record of what happened down there during the next few months and you begin to wonder what it takes to arouse a submarine skipper's enthusiasm.

The submarines have had no press agents. What few stories have come to the surface concerning their work during those days, when the war was peculiarly their own, are as sketchy and devoid of wordy atmosphere as their skippers' official reports. But the world has heard enough to justify amazement that any of these ships ever came back from their first patrol and to make land-dwellers wonder what manner of men are the amphibians who from the very beginning set out to break the back of Japan in the South Pacific and have come very near to doing it.

They went out on that north patrol and they strewed the beach of Lingayen Harbor with wrecked transports. They ran arms and medical supplies into Corregidor in the days when MacArthur's battered army was beginning to die a slow death on its feet. They carried out intelligence surveys that took some of them well up into the waters held by Hirohito's home fleet. They took the gold reserve of the Philippines and generals and important officials and nurses and other refugees out from under the very noses of the Japanese. And eventually they became the greatest single menace that the Japanese navy was to encounter in this war.

And as they began to whittle down the tonnage of Japan's supply ships and transports and commercial carriers to a point where replacement began to look totally impossible, they developed a canny and murderous technique. When finally they had forced the Japanese to make up convoys with more escort ships than carriers, they proceeded to attack and sink the escorts with a boldness that would have seemed foolhardy if it hadn't been so uniformly successful. And with startling regularity they came back. Since that first week when they were still trying to prepare themselves to fight a war without bases, only five of them have been sunk, and of those five only three were sent down by enemy action. Of the original Manila patrol, virtually all the boats that slipped out from under the Japanese bombs on the morning of December 9, 1941, are still in service and maintaining an average of destruction that increasingly frenzied antisubmarine activity on the part of the Japanese has failed to affect. They still attack with the brassy boldness of the old privateers. They still furnish a startling proof of their own favorite theory that there is no death.

31

BATTLE ABOVE

WHEN the first clunk fell into Manila Bay on that morning of December 9, 1941, Lieutenant Commander Eugene B. McKinney, like the other skippers of the local submarine fleet, was on the bridge of his ship trying with some success to speed up loading operations. Like the others he heard the call from the tender to dive. Like the others he got out in a matter of endless minutes and "belly-crawled along the bottom" under the roaring bombs to deep water and safety. And like the others his only surprise at the attack was that he should have been able to come out of it with his ship intact and his crew alive.

McKinney, who has won the Navy Cross twice and a Silver Star and sundry other decorations, is no more introspective than others in his weird trade but something more of an analyst of human reactions. He is modest to an extent that would arouse the awe of men with better chances for remaining alive long enough to write their memoirs . . . which may explain why he rates so high in the esteem of his own kind. When he talks it is not about himself but about his ship and about his crew. Fights are won not by the commanding officer, he says, but by the men under him. And medals are awarded, he feels, not to skippers but to their ships. It's his theory that without personnel functioning like a high-class watch nobody would get any medals. His brother officers listen respectfully to this theory and then inform you privately that so far as his individual case is concerned they don't think much of it.

"That guy has done everything with a submarine except make it fly," one of them told me quietly. "He fights his ship as if he had a cruiser instead of a tin bottle, and he gets away with it."

And as I talked with him of the usual thousand things that a submarine officer can talk about I remembered that. I also remembered with some logic a brief remark of the late Cobber Cain (the first British ace in this war) and of its echo in the conversation of Lieutenant Edward ("Butch") O'Hare. Somebody had asked Cobber at a Christmas party in Paris in 1939 how it came about that he was getting a bigger bag of German planes than other men in his squadron and he said: "I can't explain it. All of them fly just as well as I do and they've all got guts. I haven't any special theory about fighting Messerschmitts except that I seem to do better when I can get close to them." Years later it was uncanny to hear Lieutenant O'Hare say much the same thing: "Well, there were a lot of those Japs and I was all alone, so I figured the only way I could knock 'em down was to get in so close that I couldn't miss. . . ." Lieutenant Commander McKinney didn't say just that, perhaps, but you got the idea. McKinney had been getting in close to them and he'd been sinking them. His pals couldn't say offhand what he had been credited with in the official score, but they were willing to concede that he'd put down about ten ships including a cruiser, and that he'd blasted another cruiser so that probably it hadn't gone anywhere except to the bottom.

"'Surface McKinney with the "Submersible PT-boat," ' they called him in them days," one of the officers quoted later. "He always made his own trouble and shot his way out of it."

Lieutenant Commander McKinney was one of the old-timers in the submarines—as old-timers go in the submarines—when his ship was ordered out of the Manila area to Lingayen. He accepted the job philosophically, just as he'd accepted the coming of the war.

"We were ordered up there," he said when asked about how he felt when he got the assignment. . . . It was an order and that's all there was to it. But not he nor any other man in the submarine fleet could have had any illusions about what they were being asked to do.

"I'll tell you," he said when this was pressed on him. "When we came out there in the summer of 1941 we were expecting the war to break out any minute . . . no use kidding ourselves about it, the situation was pretty rugged. We didn't want war. The last thing that a professional in the Navy or Army wants is war because he's been taught to know what war is. But it's his job, no matter how tough it is.

"We're not indulging in any heroics when we say that we didn't expect to come home again if there should be a war. Our lives were already dedicated to this business and already forfeit, if you know what I mean. I had a wife and a couple of children back here, but I couldn't allow them to enter into the calculations and I guess they knew that. Navy families are brought up on that proposition."

So he had come out to Manila and watched trouble building up on the horizon. Like the European sitzkrieg, that summer had probably been something of a nightmare. You sat there and waited.

One incoming submarine late in November had reported sighting a formidable array of supply ships headed apparently then for Truk, and putting two and two together some months later the submariners had decided that those ships had been taking out food and fuel and ammunition to the fleet that was even then massing for the raid on Pearl Harbor. But at the time there had seemed nothing overt in the maneuver. The Japs had obeyed all the rules and had gone their way, and that and other similar incidents had fostered a tenuous belief that maybe, after all, the old stories had been true and that Hirohito's admirals were not really so foolish as to risk certain destruction in provoking the mighty United States fleet. It is probable that nobody actually believed that. On the other hand it was comforting to hope that it might turn out to be true.

When the attack started, McKinney got his fuel and water lines off and his hatches closed and swung away from the tender full speed astern. His rudder fouled something and swung him stern foremost almost into the breakwater. But unaccountably it came right again and he eased around the corner of the breakwater and, as he expressed it, "pulled the plug."

"I didn't get down," he said dryly, "until a couple of bombs had lit right under my tail. That speeded things up a whole lot. It was a bad morning. I'll never know a worse one. . . ."

So eventually he was ordered to Lingayen and he went. His

order of going was left largely to his own discretion but the discretion doesn't seem to have involved a great deal of choice. Speed was an obvious essential and there was no chance that he could make any speed submerged. So, with the Japs swarming down on the Philippines with just about everything they had, he drove north on the surface as fast as the ship would go.

He arrived at his area on schedule and submerged for a while. Then he got orders to proceed into the bay.

Lingayen, any submariner of the Asiatic fleet will tell you, is a tough harbor. There is a lot of shallow water at the entrance barely covering a string of dangerous reefs. It seemed to him that the only way he could get in would be to surface and give her the gun. So he did. The ship came off the entrance about six o'clock. The tropical dusk was just beginning to come down thick.

Captain McKinney didn't waste much time reconnoitering and ordered a straight course for the slot. Then all at once he saw a ship over on the horizon. At first he couldn't make out what she was. By the time he was able to recognize her as a Jap destroyer she had gone up ahead and was turning around. Then he saw that another destroyer was with her.

What followed was one of the strangest episodes in a record that is full of strange episodes, and in many respects it lacks an adequate explanation. You get the idea that the Japanese destroyer commanders were just as afraid of submarines as they've had reason to be since. The pair of them came charging in the general direction of Captain McKinney's ship but a considerable distance off the port bow. They got way behind then, twisted about, came across the stern, and proceeded on a course parallel to the submarine, boxing her in. There wasn't any doubt by that time that they had seen her and knew what she was.

The captain, interested in this crazy performance, might have begun to take precautions. Instead he kept straight on his course because, as he said, "if we were to carry out our orders there was nothing else to do. I'll confess I felt a lot like diving but I was curious, too. I couldn't help wanting to see what the boys were trying to do. . . ."

The horseplay went on for perhaps half an hour during all of which time they withheld fire. The captain guessed that their skippers were just as inexperienced and puzzled as he was. The Japs just weren't expecting to see submarines maneuvering on the surface.

After a while he saw that they meant business, however long a time they might take to get on with it. Each time they criss-crossed his course they were getting a little nearer. Finally when one went past his stern at what looked to be a suitable range he fired two fish at her.

"I guess I had misjudged the speed of the things," he said. "It was easy to do when they were running rings around us as they seemed to have been doing all evening. I thought they were going about five knots faster than they really were. So the fish went a little ahead of the one in the lead. At that they probably would have hit him if he'd stayed on his course. But they were far enough ahead to give him a chance to turn out, and he did and they missed."

That ended the circus. The next thing the captain knew they were roaring in one behind the other, right down his track. Some-body on the bridge kept urging him to dive, which he admits was a good idea. But he was listening with detached attention. Over the stern he kept seeing them get bigger and bigger, and he makes the comment that until you are looking at it head on you'll never know how big a destroyer can get.

However, as you quickly learn in talking to these men, a sub-mariner's principal strategy is to attack. Captain McKinney knew that if he dived he wasn't going to be able to bother the pursuing cans any more, and he still had a couple of fish in his tubes. So, oblivious to all advice from others on the bridge, he stood there waiting.

Even with the destroyers charging in at full speed it seemed a long wait, and a landsman couldn't but wonder at the amazing emotional control that made it possible. When you consider that this skipper was in his first fight the miracle seems even more amazing. But he stood there looking at the widening silhouette of the destroyer with his hand on the button and his mind made up. He let the Japs get in close. Then he fired one fish, and after a decent interval the other one.

The leader saw the torpedo coming. You'd think that maybe he might have been waiting for it. But by the time he was conscious of what was going to happen to him it was too late for him to do anything about it. He started a swing to starboard and the first fish hit him right under the bridge.

"It blew him clean out of the water," the captain said reminiscently. "The second destroyer had swung to port, and the last I saw of him he was squarely in line to take the second fish. Then I pulled the plug. . . ."

In many details there have been few actions like this and it is unlikely that there are going to be many more. One destroyer had been totally demolished, and more than likely another one, by a floating sardine box on which they had been unable to get in a single shot. A submarine had fought a successful engagement on the surface not against a cargo carrier with slow speed and erratic artillery but against a type of ship specially constructed to destroy submarines. A captain totally inexperienced in warfare had calculated his margin of safety to the last split second and had finished the job with no trace of buck fever. Captain McKinney declined to discuss such matters as this but one must be permitted to draw his own conclusions.

The encounter was totally unusual in at least one other respect. Usually only the man at the periscope sees the action. All the men in the ship know about it is what he tells them:

"We fired two fish at a destroyer bearing so and so. . . . One hit . . . possibly two." That sort of thing. But in this case there were plenty of spectators on deck to look at a performance few of them would ever have a chance to see again. And there was no possibility of doubt about what had been done. Pieces of the first destroyer were still coming down as the order came to clear the bridge and the bow started under.

That wasn't the end of it—not entirely.

"We hadn't got far down when there was a second explosion," Captain McKinney said, "and it was a honey.

"I don't know what happened. It's possible of course that the second torpedo crashed into part of the first destroyer, but I give you my word that there wasn't much of it left to hit ten seconds after the first fish went off. I'm quite sure we got the second destroyer, too. But naturally we didn't get credit for it. What we did get was a fine boost in morale. You couldn't imagine any better boost for a lot of men just going into a war than to smash up a couple of cans that didn't have any other business in the world just at the moment except to finish them off. There was never any doubt in the mind of the crew about the second destroyer. They just knew we'd sunk her, and after that there was no holding them. You get to be a veteran in an awful hurry when you're on a hot corner. . . ."

Of course the submarine had no chance to get into the harbor after that. The men on her bridge weren't the only ones who had seen the blasting of the destroyer. The sound man began to pick up high-speed screws a few minutes after the second explosion, and the men stood by to take what is known in their own argot as "the working over." Even without immediate opposition they would have had to stay submerged, for surface fighting was going to be suicidal in that area for many a day to come. Submerged, with perhaps a dozen ships listening for them, they could have proceeded only at a speed of one or two knots, which would have brought them into the harbor and shallow water too late for them to operate. So they accepted the situation as they found it and prepared to make themselves as comfortable as possible in the hell that they knew was going to come roaring down on top of them at any minute.

"There was one thing about it," said Captain McKinney. "We didn't have long to wait. Patrol boats and corvettes and destroyers must have been on their way out before the first destroyer went down, and they plastered us for hours.

"We had a lot of disadvantages off Lingayen. Even as far out as we were the water was pretty shallow and the reefs were all over the place—not all of them on the charts. So we just had to take it. We've been in worse depth-charge attacks since, but there'll never be another like the first one. Even the bombs in Manila Bay hadn't prepared us for them.

"You had to admire the painstaking thoroughness of the boys up above. They'd just come walking down on top of us. You'd hear thumps, not so loud at first, and then some that would jar your teeth out. We were surprised when we discovered that the boat was holding together and that there were no leaks to amount to anything. . . ."

What was more to the point, the crew held together. There is probably no such thing as absolute fearlessness when you are cooped up in a pipe and a lot of skillful technicians up on the surface are setting out painstakingly to murder you. As Quentin Reynolds once said about air bombs and artillery shells, whatever else your reaction to depth charges, you can't be indifferent to them.

Another U. S. submarine in the neighborhood heard the racket, one of the most prodigious that the war had produced up to that time, and reported that Captain McKinney's boat had very likely been sunk. After two days the division commander was willing to take a realistic view of the matter and admit that no submarine could have survived such a savage hammering. When suddenly the lost ship came in on the radio and casually accepted orders to proceed to another area he admitted that he had been mistaken but continued to point out that he had had logic on his side.

32

NIGHT ATTACK

In MANY ways the most fascinating part of the story of our submarines was written in those hit-and-run exercises between December 9, 1941, and the middle of January 1942, in the neighborhood of Dewey's old stamping ground. Later, perhaps, these boats were to operate with greater technical skill and wreak greater havoc. But by that time the veterans who had slipped out of Manila Bay were no longer fledglings but experienced men who at the imminent threat of death had learned enough to upset the whole book of underwater tactics. Skippers who came out later in new boats may have been untried but they were under no necessity of learning their business empirically. By that time the routine of submarine warfare had been pretty well worked out and the skills of attack and evasion could be taught scientifically —and with considerably less danger—to men fresh from the service schools. Those first battles of the war were swashbuckling adventures, the like of which we may not see again.

When the first bombs dropped into the harbor at Cavite there wasn't a single man in the submarine service who had ever fired a torpedo in anger. Few of them had ever heard the burst of a bomb. None of them knew whether the book of rules so carefully learned in peacetime was going to be of any use against an enemy whose powers had been so badly underrated. Yet they rode into battle as they had gone to maneuvers off California, gloriously sure of themselves and gloriously willing to die proving themselves. They were going to have to find out about the truth or falsity of peacetime precept in a matter of seconds. They were going to be allowed just one false move apiece. They were going to have to succeed spectacularly and at once, whatever the means and however slim the opportunity. Thus must have reasoned McKinney in his unorthodox fight with the destroyers—thus Warder blasting a can out of his way to get at more valuable prey.

Captain McKinney, a few days after his spectacular performance with the destroyers, had to work out his own method for getting past the tightest destroyer screen he had ever seen and maneuvering to a position from which he could work on a big convoy with some hope for success. He surfaced at sunset and saw the ships streaming out of the harbor, darkly moving against the barely lighter silhouette of an island. There was a destroyer screen in front and other strings of destroyers along the sides.

"It was quite a problem," he said, "to figure how you were going to get in to attack a setup like that."

Quite a problem, and one for which none of the theoretical answers had been given a demonstration. In World War I the U-boats had quietly refrained from entangling themselves with any such concentration of hard luck. In maneuver, if such protective screens as this had ever been considered, they certainly had never been tried out.

"However," was McKinney's later comment on the situation, "I figured that if you get right in with them you can't go wrong."

(If you want a statement of principle from the U. S. submarine service you might stop at that.)

McKinney, it seems, got right in there with them.

The Jap lookouts are generally sharp-eyed and alert, as any U. S. submarine skipper including Captain McKinney will admit. But his very brashness seems to have given him greater advantages than he had any right to expect.

"The light was against me," he said. "I mean they were coming out from the land and I had the sky behind me which made it reasonably easy for them to pick me up. But still it was pretty dusky and I thought maybe I could make it."

So the captain maneuvered in his own peculiar way and presently was inside the screen undetected and well in front of the advancing convoy.

"There didn't seem to be any end to the ships," he said. "They stood out in front of me all over the place in wide black masses. There was nothing to it. You just couldn't miss."

"I picked out one principal target in the bunch—a big tanker—and when I fired a fish at that one it was aimed to hit. I spread out a couple of others. But I didn't have much time. The first one was still roaring when the cans swung around. They were right on my tail, of course—lots of them."

The tanker blew up and a fine spectacle it was. The submarine was on its way when the ship sank but the margin was slim. They'd hardly got the conning tower under when an ash can nearly blew them up. It put a big shove under the planes and they were in plenty of trouble.

The captain took a look at the depth gauges and saw he was about to surface and that was one time when he didn't want to. He ordered all-ahead emergency. The only way he could drive her down was under power and the noise at the time didn't seem to make any difference. For that matter, he began to think later that it wouldn't have been much worse if they'd come up. They gave him a working over that couldn't have been improved no matter where they were.

The destroyers never left him for anything. A lot of the screen went on, of course, and McKinney supposes he should have thanked God for that. But plenty were left. They cut out of the screen and went to work with the ash cans.

The submarine was in a tough spot because they knew right where it was. It wasn't as if they'd come in from a distance and had to guess where the boat had submerged. They were right on top of her when she got under and after that they knew she couldn't be far away.

"I thought most of the bombs were right in my pocket," said Captain McKinney. "Everything breakable inside the ship was broken up. The drawers came out of the cabinets and there was chinaware all over the deck. And stuff fell out of the lockers and things broke out of the wardroom cupboards. It seemed to me as though everything was loose and that everything loose was rolling everywhere over the deck at once. And the lights were out. They were out quite a lot of the time after the boys up on top really got going.

"We've taken it time and time again since then. But I've never had an experience like it. You see there was no guesswork about it—nothing haphazard—just them against us—a purely personal matter.

"You have to admire their thoroughness. When they finally did quit it must have been because they thought they'd sunk us. And you couldn't blame them for that. For a long time we weren't so certain about it ourselves."

33

MANEUVER ON THE BOTTOM

No MATTER who eventually writes a definitive history of the activities of the submarines in this war Lieutenant Commander Wreford Goss ("Moon") Chapple is certain to have an important place in it, for not only did he and his ship take part in the most harrowing adventure of the sea fighting for the Philippines but he was likewise the first captain to demonstrate what submarines can get into —and get out of. Furthermore the story of his exploit is the best documented bit of record that has come out of the Southwest Pacific. All in one dizzy day he slid over the reefs into a Jap port of disembarkation, sank a transport, rammed a lighter, went aground submerged on a mud flat that lifted his bow virtually out of the water where patrol boats were dragging the lagoon to find him, surfaced in broad daylight and survived. The most striking part of the record would appear to be that he survived.

From numerous sources people in the United States have been able to put together a fairly understandable picture of the unsinkable Mr. Chapple as a man of quick wit, keen judgment and great personal courage—a man who would take all of his crew on a picnic in Manila and a few days later be the first man aboard his ship to dive into a compartment filled with acid and gas after a battery explosion. He is shown as the man who could keep the respect of the personnel as he and they faced almost certain death . . . and above all as a good companion.

Much of this has come to us through the article which Cecil Brown wrote for *Collier's Weekly* a year ago, some from Captain Chapple's diary, some from his brother officers returning to the United States for new ships. But the most graphic description of the redoubtable captain was told to me by Miles Lasater, motor machinist second class, some time of Tucson, Arizona, at the New London submarine base. From a bit of biography accompanying Mr. Brown's article you learn that Wreford Goss Chapple was born in Billings, Montana, apparently the last place anybody would go looking for a submarine officer. He played football on the local high-school team, entered the U. S. Naval Academy in June 1926, and won letters in football and boxing. There also he received his nickname "Moon," based on a fancied resemblance to a comic-strip character. After duty on a cruiser he went into the submarine school in 1932. In February 1933 he was assigned to a ship and served in a succession of them, among them the *Perch* later lost in combat with the Japs. He received his first command in 1940 after a two years' post-graduate engineering course at the Naval Academy, and went out to the Asiatic fleet. He has been out there or in the immediate vicinity virtually ever since.

Young Mr. Lasater didn't know much about that.

"I don't know what he was but what he is," he said. "He was my captain and he had everything it takes.

"I hope I can tell the story of him straight but it ain't going to be as easy as it was because I lost my diary which was a very good diary. It told where every man jack of the crew was standing when every bomb dropped. I wish I still had it. . . ."

Even without his diary Motor Machinist Lasater was able to remember a lot of the detail of the trip north to the bay where the Japs were working.

"It wasn't a very gaudy trip," he said. "The old ship was no big bargain and we were crowded as the devil. We had air conditioning of a kind but, I'll be honest with you, it didn't air-condition very much. The air was just what you'd expect in a place like that, thick and hot. . . ."

Other commentators have mentioned Lieutenant (as he was then) Chapple's economy of words describing how he got into the bay. He just reported that he went over the reefs. It was obvious to anybody envisioning the chain of ledges protecting that bay in such spots as weren't being protected by destroyers that the lieutenant had left out something. It's a bit of a job to handle a submarine like a surfboat and finish the journey with the bottom intact. But what else was left out in this bleak statement you begin to realize only when you talk with disinterested witnesses like Lasater.

"When the war started we were in the harbor opposite Corregidor in the Philippines," he said. "We knew war was coming. Before December 7 somebody spotted a Jap carrier out there. The cans were sent to look at it and keep track of it. But they never found it. It was only spotted that one time. Admiral Hart gave us orders that showed he was expecting war too. All the submarines were moored in pairs instead of big bunches. All the surface ships were at sea. The Japs didn't catch anybody by surprise where I was. . . ."

He became lyrical about Lieutenant Chapple—although it must be said in justice to everybody that he was almost as enthusiastic about Lieutenant Commander H. G. Munson, who succeeded him. Captain Chapple was his first skipper in the roaring days of peace, and Lasater had more of a chance to study his attitude toward society.

"He was a swell guy," he said. "He gave us a good time on that old crate out in the Philippines. On all the parties the officers went along. There weren't any women or social-service workers— just ourselves. We'd get a lot of beer and a lot of things to eat that we couldn't get aboard ship and we'd have a high time. The captain was just like one of the crew.

"He had as much guts as anybody. That's one reason why we liked him so much. He was the first guy in there after the battery explosion. . . . I'll tell you about that later. The chief electrician was next, but the captain was first. Some of the crew thought maybe he didn't shoot torpedoes so good. I thought once or twice maybe his range was too long. On a submarine you get to talk things like that over. Every guy aboard thinks he can do anything better than anybody else that there is to be done. So he feels free to criticize. Nobody cares about it, including the captain—at least Captain Chapple never cared. And anyway, whether he could shoot torpedoes or not, he was as good a guy as I ever sailed with and we'd all be willing to sail with him again wherever he wanted to go.

"Chapple was always confident about everything and that helped the crew. The only thing really wrong with the service on those patrols was the boat herself. [She was old, small and uncomfortable as are all of her class.] She was such a miserable sewer pipe that it didn't take much to get a man down. I guess our nerves were always edgy—although we didn't take it out on each other. We left one guy on Corregidor whose nerves had cracked up. The Japs got him, I guess.

"The routine wasn't bad. In silencing ship you got some variety because everybody relieved everybody else on all sorts of jobs. That's why I liked small ships better than the big ones. . . .

"We were a pretty efficient crew, I guess. But sometimes things went wrong. One time the QM Second who was at the voice tube left it open on the dive. That really caused some trouble.

"At that part of the dive we were changing stations. I had the blower manifold and trim pump to take care of, and I wasn't paying any attention to anything else when a spurt of water hit my hand. The engineer officer came up and stopped it but we'd all got a swell shot anyway. The QM said that when he came down he knew he'd forgot something and he was just going to mention it to the chief electrician when the water began pouring in. The electrician certainly had an odd look on his face. You can guess how you'd feel if you were sitting at the controls and the Pacific Ocean began to land in your lap. . . ."

Well, there you have a little about Captain Chapple, his submersible sewer pipe and his swashbuckling crew. You begin to get some idea, perhaps, of what he had to contend with in the routine operation of his ship, why submarine crews must be always at peak efficiency and the skipper eternally alert. But there were other troubles that Lieutenant Commander Chapple didn't think worth mentioning in his diary. There was, for instance, this matter of wartime operation, much of it submerged, in heat that hadn't seemed so bad when you only got a couple of days of it at a time. Mr. Lasater recalled that phase of submarine life vividly.

"When we shifted out of Corregidor on December 9 we patrolled for a few weeks. The ship's spirit was pretty high when we heard we was really going to get some action. We were told to get up there to their landing port and head them off, and it was the hottest work we ever had to do.

"The heat all that month was terrific. The engines were too hot for you to go back of them and oil down. And there was lots of worry about that. It looked pretty sure we'd be burning out a couple of bearings. The engines just naturally never got a chance to quit. And the sea water you pumped to cool them was just about as hot when it came in as when it went out.

"I volunteered for one job of inspection because the engineer officer wanted to know how he stood. What he really wanted to know, I think, was when we were most likely to bust down or blow up.

"Well, the only way you could travel in that engine room was to get down as close to the deck as you could. And you couldn't lie flat on the deck because that was hot as a broiler, too. I tied wet rags on my face and got around there. I thought my eyeballs was going to bust out like popcorn. But I finally got back there and my eyes stayed in and I took a look at the cams and rocker arms, and then I came back in a hurry and reported that so far as I was concerned they was all burned out.

"They kept going, though. I'll never tell you why.

"You couldn't put a hand on the cans [batteries]. They were boiling and bubbling and gassing just on account of the heat. It was misery when we dove because then we'd have to shut up the ship without ventilation and live with all that hot metal of the engines shut up in there with us.

"We had a lot of diving. After we left Manila on our patrol we dove just as soon as we went over the reef. And it seemed to me that we was submerged most of the time after that.

"We didn't have much trouble while we were going to this bay the Japs had taken over. But after we got there we had enough to last us for the rest of our lives. Pretty soon it didn't look as though the rest of our lives was going to be very long. I'm telling you, boy, it was rugged . . . what I mean, *rugged*."

Thus Mr. Lasater brings the narrative to the point where Captain Chapple opens his . . . the time when he mentions unconcernedly that he went into the bay "over the end of the reef." It might be well to analyze this bit of news. In the first place the Japanese had taken over this bay for business reasons and into it they were bringing most of the weight of troops and equip-

ment with which they crushed MacArthur's little army and took
Manila and Bataan and Corregidor and the Philippines. Even then,
a few days after the beginning of the war, everybody in the U. S.
Asiatic service realized that Hirohito's high command was going
to have no truckle with shoestring strategy such as had been tried
out ineffectively in other parts of the world. Where Japan attacked, Japan was going to attack in force and crush the enemy by
weight of arms rather than military finesse. So she was operating
in the Philippines as she was later to operate in Malaya and Java
and at Midway and in the Solomons. Streams of ships were coming
down from Formosa and the occupied Chinese coast. Streams of
ships were flowing back for new loads of men and munitions. And
for the moment this captured harbor was one of the busiest in the
world. It stood to reason that the Japs wouldn't leave it unprotected.

To everybody who had ever looked at the navigational charts
of the district it was apparent that much of the required protection
was already there for them. The entrance to the bay is strewn
with reefs—dangerous shallows with jagged ranges whose peaks
are all near the surface although patches of them are awash and
some of them covered with a few feet of water at high tide. There
is some open water, and in there about a dozen Japanese destroyers and a fleet of smaller fast patrol boats kept up a constant
beat. There was apparently no net across the entrance but there
didn't seem to be any need for one—not to the U. S. submarine
skippers. Nowhere was the water very deep. And that's why,
when Captain Chapple was ordered to go into this place, he elected
to cross over the rocks.

He had a small boat which gave him some advantage over the
commanders of newer types of submarines. But to say that he had
an advantage is merely to say that his ship could clear some of the
knife-edged rocks by inches whereas a bigger one mightn't have
been able to clear at all. As it was he scraped the hull occasionally,
a performance that would have driven the commander of a surface
ship crazy in two or three minutes. Chapple also mentions casually
that he got over the rocks and into the bay in early morning, which
might mean nothing to a landsman but certainly means everything
to the men who have to maneuver the submarines in enemy waters.
He was sliding into a spot where discovery meant certain attack

and very probable destruction, and he was already under a rapidly lightening sky with the sun only slightly below the tropical greenery of the hills beyond the harbor. . . .

"Well, he got us in all right," Lasater reminisced. "But I don't know how he did it. I expected a spike of rock to be sticking me in the tail any minute. Once we got over the reef the water was pretty deep and he pulled the plug.

"It was all pretty quiet and we was glad to be where we was. I kept telling myself, 'This ain't going to be bad at all . . . not at all.' But after we'd been sitting there for an hour or an hour and a half and it was getting bright daylight up on the surface I heard Chapple say: 'God! There's a million of them!' I'd been on the stern planes when we dove. I went back to the motor room and I didn't get back to the control room until quite a bit later. By that time all hell had started to pop."

Chapple in his account of the proceedings says that he saw a whole mass of transports and supply ships spread out like cars in a parking lot, with some destroyers ringing them around in an endless beat. They were a temptation, he admitted, but somewhat north of the area to which he had been sent. So regretfully he left them and went about his business.

As it came out later, Fearless Freddy Warder was up somewhere in that vicinity preparing to strew the beach with pieces of transports and the unfortunate Japs who had been in them and it may have been his activity that made the going so tough for Captain Chapple a short time later. Maybe Chapple's own attack was responsible. At any rate the going got tough.

Before long the captain had maneuvered into his own area and had picked up a group of slowly moving ships within target range. Ten minutes later he fired his first torpedoes, one at the second ship in line, the others a little ahead of their targets, a spread from which he could easily hope for at least two hits, very likely more. All torpedoes missed. The skipper had no explanation for his bad luck except that the Jap vessels were all of an old type with shallow draft and that very likely his fish had gone under them.

He had no opportunity to mull over the problem because torpedo wakes in still water on a bright morning were something that the Japs couldn't very well have overlooked. He reloaded torpedo tubes as he dived and the express-train thunder of high-speed screws announced the arrival of trouble in the form of a couple of destroyers. Fortunately he was in water deep enough to conceal him, but even so the first depth charges rocked the ship and threw the torpedo men in the bow compartment off their feet.

From what his brother officers told me about his maneuvering during the next half-hour I got the impression that they respected his tactical ability as well as his unfailing brass. The water where he was may have been deep enough to hide in but it wasn't deep enough for him to carry out any elaborate program of evasion, and the Japs undoubtedly had a pretty fair idea of where he was. . . . The first blasts proved that. But in spite of everything the ship held together and slipped about like a silent if ungainly whale until presently the noise of the barrage was well astern. Then he stuck his periscope up once more and took another five-second look. A transport at anchor and getting ready to debark troops who were massed all over her decks was squarely in the middle of his scale.

He fired one torpedo as he gave the order to dive again. And that one hit thirty seconds after he let it go. The explosion was powerful enough to jar the submarine, and considering the type of troopship that was hit there has never been any doubt in anyone's mind that she fell apart.

The captain was in a worse spot then than he had been in before because there was considerably less water over his conning tower and presently virtually none under his keel. Once the ship hit a ledge and bounced so that he was afraid she was going to broach.

"I heard him call out, 'Flood the auxiliary tanks,'" was Lasater's comment on this. "I didn't need to hear the ash cans busting to know that we were in more trouble. Then I heard 'Stop motors! Listen all around!' I could hear Sound yelling something about 'High-speed screws off port bow.' But I kind of thought it wasn't going to make much difference where the high-speed screws were. I thought we'd gone aground. Then I knew we were moving. I could feel bumps along the bottom as we coasted."

After a while the ship ran into a mud bank and stayed there. All machinery was stopped except the motor generator on the lighting circuits. The boat was so silent that they could hear the movement of water above them and so it went for hours.

It became apparent pretty soon that the Japs' sound equipment was no longer picking them up, and they took what consolation they could out of that. The ash cans kept tumbling down on them, some near, some at a distance, but never very far apart in point of time. The men lay wakeful and tense in their bunks or stood in mute silence at the posts of their watches. In the control room some of them played cribbage with the captain— an endless, uninteresting game that occupied a little time but took nobody's mind off their unpleasant situation. Now and then slow boats rumbled overhead and at irregular intervals they could hear the roaring screws of the destroyers. It was like being under a viaduct, somebody said later, where you could hear the passing trains but not see them. But it was not exactly the same because trains wouldn't be likely to drop anything on you through a viaduct. Captain Chapple ordered the sound man to quit listening. When something's going to happen to you, he figured, there's no use knowing about it too far in advance. But that didn't keep the men from hearing the traffic overhead or from wincing as the bombs went off.

The air began to get thick and foul and the bulkheads began to drip with condensation. . . . Something else to worry about. Moisture, until the days of a perfected air-conditioning system, has been a bugbear to the submarines because it gets into electrical apparatus, rots insulation, corrodes points, causes short circuits. The engineer officer was less worried about the blasting outside than about what might happen when the motor switches were thrown again, and as it turned out he had reason.

During the long, terrible afternoon the men began to tire as the oxygen failed them and the carbon-dioxide content of the air rose. Soda lime was thrown about to absorb the carbon dioxide. But the atmosphere was still oppressive no matter what was done to liven it. The deck was slippery with sweat and condensation.

It would appear that nobody aboard the ship was cherishing any great hopes of getting out of this pocket alive although the thought became easier to bear as the air got thicker and brains and reflexes slowed down. Presently all movement of the crew was slow and automatic. The length of the vigil didn't seem to matter any more. There was no time. Then, after a while, somebody looked droopily at the clock in the control room and noticed the time. . . .

There was a moment's mumbling as the word was passed through the boat and then the crew began to fight against the lack of oxygen. It was evident that they might come through after all. It would be getting dark up there pretty soon. With the plaguing cans at the end of their beat they might be able to get away from the mud bank and head for deeper, safer water.

34

UNDERWATER NIGHTMARE

The feeling of a Doom searching them out and getting ready to strike did not leave the men in the boat until the captain thought it was dark enough on the surface to permit his moving out. After that the job of blowing ballast and backing and filling with the motors and still keeping the ship from popping out of the water did what cribbage and prayer had not done toward keeping the minds of the crew off the dangers that surrounded them.

They got out of the mud, surfaced cautiously, and headed for a safer anchorage.

Judging from Lasater's account of all this, I had come to the conclusion that whatever else might have happened to Captain Chapple's boat must be rated as anticlimax. When you come to the elastic limit of human endurance, I thought, you've had all the experience that will ever harrow you for all time. But I was wrong, as the sequel quickly showed. The troubles of this harassed submarine apparently had only begun. The weary crewmen were just getting on with their work again when the battery blew up.

"It was a pretty bad explosion," Lasater remembered. "Some of the men was hurt pretty bad. But looking back at it I guess it might have been a lot worse.

"We'd been up on the surface and I was sitting on the windward side of the conning tower. I couldn't hear anything account of the wind, and I was looking off into the air on the port side not thinking of nothing when I heard the quartermaster squawk. I looked around and I was the only one left up there. I didn't stay. There was a can coming at us off starboard. It wasn't hard to see and it wasn't wasting any time.

"I wasn't more than a couple of seconds getting off my tail and down the hatch but that was long enough for me to see three of those things coming just alongside. It looked like they was ready to come on board. They looked as big as houses—big houses—by the time I hit the ladder.

"Then we dived. There was one guy taking a bath and he never had a chance to get on his clothes. There was another one in the head and he was spilled a couple of times before he could pull his pants up from around his ankles. He was cursing plenty and it wasn't the depth charges that bothered him.

"Lots of fellas there had plenty of calm. I couldn't figure why they had it. I remember a torpedo man lying on the deck. All through the attack, and it was a long one, he lay there with his head bouncing up and down on the iron plates. I could hear the clink and it made my head ache just to listen. But he didn't seem to mind.

"Me, I just sweated it out. It was pretty tough business, though. I guess everybody knew what we were in for. There was a couple of gunner's mates near where I was after about an hour of it. One had a burning cigarette and the other was trying to get a light off it. And then the one who was trying to get the light said: 'Give me that cigarette. We're both shaking the wrong way.'

"Well, some way that had nothing to do with me we got out of it and surfaced. And then the trouble started.

"I was up in the forward torpedo room at the time and I couldn't see what happened aft. But I guess somebody started the blowers too quick. Generally you let the air circulate awhile before you turn on the blowers. It lets the gas in the battery room thin out. But this time the air didn't get going. When the blower switch was thrown there was a spark and the gas blew up.

"Not many batteries were damaged—two or three cracked. The gas had been in a layer above the cans, I guess. But it blew hell out of the deck. There was rice and potatoes everywhere because in submarines you haven't got much place for your stores except on deck and the rice and potatoes were in the way of the explosion.

"I told you the captain was the first man into the place. That didn't surprise us any but we was glad to see how good our judgment had been. There were some men lying around. Young

HOME FROM THE WARS

The gun crew of this boat, one of the largest of the U. S. submarines, comes in for overhaul with a crop of whiskers and a bag of eight enemy ships. (Rayed flags on conning tower indicate sunken warships, plain flags merchantmen.)

THE MARINES HAVE LANDED

And have returned from a Japanese base after a stiff fight
in which they wiped out most of the enemy personnel.
The man in the foreground is holding trophies including
a Japanese rifle.

Pasaretti got a fractured ankle. Another got two broken legs. One of the chiefs got a broken back, and two others were bruised and burned. The chief was pretty near death when we got to him.

"Later we got to transfer them to a hospital on Corregidor and the Japs captured them, I guess—all except Pasaretti. He got off in another submarine before the Japs came.

"The explosion happened in the wee hours of the morning and it looked like the beginning of a perfect day. We had to open up the engine-room hatch to get Hastings out. The gaskets had gone foul with the heat and we couldn't close the hatch. We worked and stewed around until just about daylight before we got enough of this mess cleared to work the ship. Just as we submerged we got a look at what was ahead of us . . . destroyers and plenty of them. And there we sat in shallow water with the damned gasket out and destroyers in front of us.

"We got our first break of luck soon after daybreak. The destroyers hadn't discovered us and they turned around and went back. We waited awhile and when nothing disturbed us we got the hatch fixed so's it didn't leak more than Niagara Falls. A few hours before that I wouldn't have believed that we was ever going anywhere again."

Lasater paused to turn the matter over in his memory. I mumbled something about it's being apparent that the law of averages didn't work in the submarines. Lasater nodded and recalled that the skipper had once told him there wasn't any such thing as the law of averages. The point seemed well taken as he went on, for it seemed that the battery explosion was not one single disaster but the beginning of a chain of them.

"We got the hatch fixed just in time," he said. "A patrol boat was coming at us. We finagled around and got out of his way but we didn't have much pick about where we were going. The Japs began to show that they were tired of having us around. . . .

"Like I told you I was on the stern planes when we dove. Then I went back to the motor room. We fired a lot of torpedoes that day but I don't know much about that because I never got out of the motor room until the real big trouble started. Fireman Ashcroft and I both passed out with the heat. When I come to we was laying on the bottom. I didn't know how we got there. I got up and started for some water. I didn't know why I had fainted and I didn't feel nervous at all until I got the water. Then I had to hold it in both hands to drink it. The cup was like to jump out of my hands or maybe my hand was trying to jump away from the cup, I don't know.

"Then I found out we'd run aground. . . .

"We was aground and at first we was all flat and everything shipshape. And then we come off a little and the bow was fifty feet higher than the stern. That was a hell of a predicament. The captain ordered me first to pump from main drain to the sea. But that was only at first. By the time we was at that angle on the stern I was pumping from main drain to the engine-room bilges. Nothing seemed as though it was going to do us any good.

"That was where I said the first prayer I ever said in my life and I said it right to a depth gauge. I looked at that thing and I prayed to it, 'Come up now, Baby! Come up! Please come up!'

"The electrician's mate at the same time was saying: 'Goddam you, come up!' So I don't know which one of us did it.

"While I was praying I could hear the captain saying over and over again: 'Blow 'em! Blow 'em!'

"We put forty pounds more pressure on the ballast tanks than they were built for."

An officer listening to this conversation seemed interested in what might have brought about so fantastic a train of circumstances and asked:

"Why were you so heavy?"

"Well," said Lasater, "we hadn't had any time to charge the can while we were fixing things up after the explosion. Another patrol boat had got after us after the last torpedo, and we had to go down with a weak can and we couldn't last. We tried setting on a ledge and flooded her so's we'd stay down. We'd just settled good when we slipped away. I thought we was never going to stop.

"The injured men in their bunks trembled. But they didn't let a peep out of them. You wouldn't have blamed them if they'd howled out loud because they were just about upended.

"All the time we lay there a lot of creepy things happened to us. We kept hearing a tapping just like it was against the hull. . . . And then there were creaking and breaking noises."

Somebody mentioned dryly that they were in a busy harbor. Lasater said he didn't think the amount of traffic had anything to do with it.

"It turned out that when we first found that ledge we was right on the beach. I've read reports that somebody tried to ram us while we were fiddling around in shallow water. But I don't think that's the way it happened. I guess it was us that tried to ram them. We run into a landing barge or something like that. We stove in a lot of superstructure. When we finally got up to look at it we found it was all busted up.

"After we crashed this thing, whatever it was, we laid low in water that barely covered us, and in the evening we tried to get away. By that time we'd settled pretty well into the mud and the port screw was out of commission.

"We tried to slip her off. The captain ordered to pump from the main drain when he gave the word and stop when he gave the word. It was a fancy job because he didn't want to broach.

"And how to ease her up without any fuss was a problem because we were stuck right there and I mean stuck. Well, we worked at it and the stern went down and the bow went up and as I said pretty soon I was pumping from the main drain to the engine-room bilge. And she wasn't going to take any soft treatment. When she did come off she shot up and she broached and the stern came up and the conning tower and the bows.

"Well, of course there was hell to pay right away. Everybody in the harbor had a chance to see us and they didn't pay any more attention to us than they'd have paid to a new geyser. The cans and patrol boats began to move and we dove again.

"But the captain outguessed 'em. He said the best place to be in a depth-charge racket is where they think you ain't. And wherever that was we went there. . . .

"We surfaced that night and charged the can. But we didn't stay there long. All at once the captain noticed a string of lights flickering between us and the beach. He looked at them for a long time. At first he thought they might be signal lights or marker lights. But pretty soon he saw that they were moving fast. They weren't no signal lights. So we went down.

"We waited a long time for the works. But they didn't bother us. I guess they was looking for somebody else. Some fast screws went right over us and didn't come back. There was some noise but the captain figured it didn't concern us any. We came back up and charged two more batteries. The lights were still flickering but farther away. They kept on flickering and they didn't come any nearer. Nobody ever did dope out what they were doing because they weren't putting over any ash cans out there.

"In the morning we submerged and tried to get in closer for an attack. On our course we ran into a bomb or light mine. It went off and set us on our tail. It was enough to bust your ears, too.

"Gunner Poole was on the bow planes. Chief Motor Machinist Ross was chief of Watch Two. When the smash came the outer glass of the gauges splintered. The inner glass stayed there. I was looking at the gauge when the bomb went off. And one second Poole was standing there and the next he had gone clear to the forward battery compartment and back. He wasn't running away from anything, I guess. It was just like something you do automatically. He still wasn't sure what was going on. The paint on the bulkheads had chipped and a chip hit him in the face. He thought it was glass. A lot of paint dust got him in the eye and then he thought he was blind. . . . Blind or not it was pretty the way he run up to the forward battery compartment and back.

"Mr. Melhopp—he was officer of the deck—he yelled 'Take her down!' But for a minute—it seemed longer—everybody was froze. Mr. Melhopp didn't get the order out any too quick himself. It was shock, I guess. I can remember how every face in the bunch around me looked but I can't remember what I was doing . . . not then or for some time afterward. We were all sort of numb. But pretty soon the gang began to move and the ship dived.

"We looked around for holes. It looked like it was going to be a miracle if the whole harbor wasn't in with us in the next couple of minutes. . . . Well, it wasn't as bad as that but we did take a pretty good beating.

"I've noticed that the black gang [the engine-room crew] is always more depressed than the other fellows on the ship. The shooting is always up forward and there's excitement and the captain and other fellows are always kidding each other and cracking jokes. But the black gang is back there in the heat all alone. And there isn't any excitement back there except when a depth charge smashes or something like that. The black gang is always more nervous than the fellows up forward and when trouble comes they've got a good start toward the jitters.

"My battle station was reloading torpedoes and I got forward once in a while. When I got up there this time Iron Mike Murdoch was lying on the deck with a pencil and notebook getting ready to mark off what might happen to us—a cross for each depth bomb and a letter to show whether it was far or close—a sort of box score on the bombing.

"Mike had been doing that since the war started and it wasn't such a bad idea. The captain used to call to him every now and then for a report on how the attack was going.

"It was only Jap shooting that Mike kept track of. When we were shooting he had other things to do. As a matter of fact we didn't expect to do much with our old crate. We figured if we did anything it would be a great surprise to everybody including us.

"Well, when we got conscious after we hit the mine we went on down and listened to depth charges. They weren't awful close but they were tough to listen to. They were long drawn out and we broke our ears trying to hear them go off before they had arrived. They'd crash out there and shake us, and when we'd start breathing again and move our hands and lift up our chins they'd fire another just to keep us reminded.

"Mack was listening on the sound apparatus and after a while he sang out 'All clear!' And just as he said it more came down.

"The captain said: 'Take those phones off, they're interfering with your ears. . . .'

" 'We're getting out of here,' he said. 'I think they know we're here.' So we turned around and started to move out.

"On boats of that class you have to vent the torpedo tubes once in a while because the pressure gets up. Well, as we're getting under way Pelley pushes the lever to vent things and it makes a hell of a *whish* and wakes up Big Mike who has got so tired waiting for the next bomb to come down that he's gone to sleep. He jumps up and smacks into a bulkhead and tears his pants just by momentum.

"All through the attack you could tell how tough things was

getting by Sound's voice. It started off soft and calm but it got higher and squeakier. And he was pretty tense by the time he gave the all-clear with bombs coming down. I've noticed that the way the sound man talks when he makes his reports has a lot to do with the way the crew feels about the whole business. On the whole Mack was pretty good and he got better. He was chief radioman then and he's up here in school now as an ensign. . . ."

Nobody had said a word through all this grim recital. Now, as Lasater paused, somebody said reminiscently that there's no sweeter sound in a submarine than the voice of the sound man reporting: "He's going. . . . He's gone. . . . He's over the hill."

"And the guys look after him, too," Lasater said. "Mack said that the cigarette smoke was bothering his voice. So all hands doused cigarettes to clear the air for him. . . .

"Well, when the fireworks were over we went on home. We laid in Manila a couple of days and went out again. We were all ready to go. The submarine service is always a funny thing to me. You wait and pray and swear until you get into it. Then when the bombs are falling you get conscious and say to yourself, 'What the hell am I doing here?' and you can't find any answers. I came to think that I'd like shore duty permanent. And now I'm tired of all this and want to get out.

"I didn't fear the depth bombs so much as other things. Planes made us a lot of trouble. And once a couple of tin fish missed us by a whisper. A destroyer fired them. We were diving at the time and I heard the sound man call: 'Why, they're firing fish at us!' He seemed like he couldn't believe himself. And I didn't blame him much. It seemed like shooting torpedoes was our business and not theirs. Nobody ever heard of a submarine throwing ash cans at a destroyer, did they?

"However, I wouldn't bet on it. Just about the time you think you've seen everything there is to be seen in the submarine service they spring a new one on you. . . . And I've heard guys around here kicking because they say it's monotonous."

One of those who say it's monotonous, it would be my guess, is not Captain "Moon" Chapple.

35

WAR IN THE JAVA SEA

EVEN before the Japs moved into Manila there were few in the submarine service optimistic enough to believe that the war in the Philippines could last a fortnight, let alone three months.

"The Japs had all the reserves and guns," said Lieutenant Commander Hiram Cassedy who at that time was conducting some practical tests on the old *Squalus*. "All our side had was endurance and guts, but plenty of those. I never thought they'd be able to last more than a couple of days, but they just went right on lasting. They were indestructible, those boys."

(I smiled to think of his failure to realize how indestructible he was himself.)

"They had dysentery and malaria and they were dying of starvation," said Lieutenant Commander McKinney. "I don't suppose any men ever did so well before under such odds. . . ."

And what odds did you work against, yourself, Captain McKinney?

Anyway the little army held out long after it had started to die on its feet and the last stand of the submarines stretched on indefinitely. When they weren't carrying supplies and ammunition they were out taking an occasional pot shot at the convoys, smashing the transports and filling the seas about the Philippines with flaming oil from sinking tankers. Quite out of proportion to the actual tonnage that they were able to take away from the invaders in those days was their effect on Hirohito's naval and plane concentrations. Hundreds of planes and scores of warships that might have found work in the overrunning of the Dutch East Indies were kept out of action by a little collection of boilers most of which were under orders to do no shooting at all.

If the record of the submarines had ended right there it would have been quite bright enough to justify whatever naval appropriation had been spent on them. But it wasn't the end, nor, as it turned out, a characteristic beginning. Long before the end of Corregidor, the submarine fleet which had been moved to bases farther south was forced to divide and lend a hand to the Allied Nations' fleet against a new peril that was sweeping southward over the impregnable fortress of Singapore. Somehow they accomplished this miracle as they had accomplished the more unexpected wonder of surviving the first onslaught of the war. Patrols began to range the China coast and the Java Sea and the straits through which Japanese ships must come in their descent upon New Guinea. Hirohito's tonnage losses in his new drive began to mount up. And all the while the ferry service kept working from the south to Corregidor and remnants of invasion ships continued to pile up among the rocks of the Philippine coast.

The Battle of the Java Sea, or rather the series of running engagements in the Java Sea, is still too much a matter of confused sidelights to permit any adequate analysis of it. One set of experts condemns the Dutch admiral for his refusal to withdraw his cruisers in the face of overwhelming superiority on the part of the Jap navy. Another praises him for making a courageous stand, that he knew from the first must be futile, in defense of the Netherlands Indies. And with sentiment and tactics, always irreconcilables, thus opposed, the right of the matter will probably be a long time establishing itself. From the deck of a cruiser some thousands of miles away it appeared to have been a battle of the tin cans—a battle which they would never win because there just weren't enough hours in the day for them to complete the job of sinking the endless array of Japanese escorts and troopships. Taking the long view of it, with returns far from complete, it would also seem to have been something of a success for the submarines, for it was there that they began to operate on a schedule of really scientific destruction that made their previous performances look like practice cruises. It was there that they broke at last through the silence of the communiqués and gave a promise of becoming what they actually did become—the barrier to Japanese expansion in the Pacific.

For a long time only the submarines themselves knew what they had done there. Only the grim-faced men who stuck pins in charts in the operations offices knew what anybody else had done there. Not that the little fleet of the Allied Nations was disorganized or that it failed to fight well. But there was a disastrous cruiser battle and a highly victorious assault on the invasion fleet by four destroyers. And there were sundry little encounters—little individualistic fights—on the surface and submerged at widely separated corners of the Java Sea. And there was a consequent incoherence about the ensemble that exists to this day.

From one of the submarine skippers comes a case in point. A U.S. cruiser which for some reason had been stationed in the Indian Ocean got orders to join the Allied fleet. She had barely started when the attack on the Dutch East Indies got under way. But she had no way of finding out, inasmuch as the radios on the Allied ships were suddenly silenced for business reasons.

So, all unaware of danger, she came charging into the Macassar Strait. How she got through and remained afloat is one of the mysteries of the war. Japanese submarines and patrol ships must have mistaken her for one of their own, basing their diagnosis on the fact that no Allied cruiser would have undertaken a dash through this narrow and dangerous slot unescorted.

She got to her rendezvous point and found nobody there and, still unaware that the battle had been joined ahead of schedule, opened up her radio to ask for instructions. Again nothing happened. The Jap radiomen may not have been listening that night. So she carried out her orders and proceeded westward preparing to take the USS cruiser *Houston* in tow. Even then the captain didn't know the magnitude of what he was getting into. His orders were specific only on one subject. And a lot of things might have happened to the *Houston*.

Some hours later he came to the new rendezvous and started a leisurely cruise up and down. His guns were manned as they had been since the beginning of the war. But that was purely a matter of routine. Officers not on watch lolled in the wardroom or on the decks and fanned themselves and complained of the heat and the luck that had assigned them to tugboat duty.

Along about midmorning a couple of cans went by, headed

south. The crew of the loitering warship watched them with interest. Then more ships began to slip past—all sorts of ships—and the captain began to be a bit disturbed. He was still disturbed when in the early afternoon a submarine with an identifiable number on her conning tower came along on the surface and fell in for a moment beside him. A blond youth with a puzzled face looked up from the bridge and asked an officer casually what the cruiser was doing there.

"Waiting to take the *Houston* in tow," said the officer.

"You'll never make it," said the lad on the submarine. "The *Houston* was sunk two days ago." The submarine turned back north and submerged. The cruiser took her place in the odd procession to the south.

In and out of this complicated action, in the crooked straits about Java and New Guinea and Borneo, wandered most of the medalmen of the Asiatic submarine fleet, among them Lieutenant Commander Frederick Burdett Warder, "Fearless Freddy," with the *Seawolf*. The fact that the Navy Department in conferring the Cross on him cited his ship by name gives sufficient indication of how exceptional that record was. Fred Warder was virtually the first of the submarine skippers to come out of anonymity.

Where his brother officers gather to spin yarns Warder is fast becoming the center of a complete cycle of folklore, most of which, I dare say, has basis in fact. They speak of him affectionately, amused at the intense seriousness he seems to have brought to his work, as if their grim business might be regarded more lightly. But when they call him "Fearless Freddy," they mean it. And when they tell you he probably would toss a torpedo at an airplane if he could get enough up-angle on the boat, they come close to meaning that, too. Generally you get the idea that he is a submarine man's submarine man. And after you've lived with them for a while you know that they could give him no higher rating.

Warder, who had been in the submarine service since 1928, a long time as they add up the hash-marks in that trade, was at the same starting line as the rest of the Asiatic submarine fleet when the war started—in Manila Bay—and his story for the next few days is the same as theirs. In and around Lingayen Harbor where the

Japs were landing he speedily took on identity as one of the whole-salers. He did a fine job on the inbound transports. To judge from such figures as have been made available, none of the leading aces did any better. And in a week everybody in the service was talking about his fine disregard for the people who were wasting their time shooting at him. Among the more apocryphal chronicles of those early days is the story of how he went into battle with a load of defective torpedoes. . . . Maybe the torpedoes were defective—complicated mechanisms have been known to develop "bugs" long before this. As against that he may have been unfamiliar with the shallow-draft hulls of Japanese ships. But the point of the yarn is that, whatever was wrong, his first spread missed and the raging destroyers began to close in on him. He didn't pay any attention to the destroyers. The problem in front of him was too engrossing. He just went right on firing torpedoes and he put out more than a dozen of them and covered the bay with a lacework of crisscrossing white wakes until finally two of them hit and blew a big transport literally to small pieces. Then, as the saying goes, he pulled the plug. Hugging the bottom, he paid less attention to the depth charges, the first that either he or his crew had ever heard, than to the study of what had been wrong, if anything, with his approach and firing technique.

You may take the ornamental detail of this story for what it's worth, although there is no doubt that he did fire several torpedoes and that he did blow up the transport as stated. What emerges from it all is a picture of two of the man's most important characteristics—his persistence and his complete lack of nerves. When he came back to Manila for another load of torpedoes he was shy about discussing what he had done—probably a little ashamed of it. But he couldn't escape the verdict of the rest of the fleet. He was "Fearless Freddy" from then on.

On his next patrol the torpedoes ran hotter and the Japs began to be unpleasantly aware of him. He quickly developed a knack for smelling out the enemy not only from things he saw but from things he heard—a gift which at times looked like second sight.

One evening Lieutenant Commander Eugene B. McKinney, diving to escape a ramming by what he took to be a lone destroyer, heard leisurely screws mumbling on and on over his head. He judged that he had got under a convoy he hadn't seen in the darkness and when there was silence again he surfaced to tell the world about it. A lot of ships, he said, were proceeding, as nearly as he could make out, somewhere toward the north of him. And he gave his position and the approximate bearing and speed of the convoy he had heard.

The incident is significant in that it appears to have been the first experiment in a technique of operation later adopted almost exclusively by the German wolf packs in the Atlantic. Having given his data, McKinney thought no more about it and got on with his immediate business, which was looking for a cruiser that he knew to be somewhere in his own area. He didn't know for months that anything had come of it. But in the meantime Warder had heard the news and had raised the glad cry of "View halloo!"

He charged at full speed to get into a position where he could intercept the convoy if it continued on its indicated course, and presently was technically out of his own sector. So he was lying in the jet murk when the destroyer screen went past and he had sunk three ships before the Japs had any suspicion of his presence.

He got down into the Java Sea and started a patrol about Bali. The Japs were still spreading themselves in their drive toward Australia, and inasmuch as about half the ships they were sending to that locality were transports no submariner had any fear about hitting an unimportant target. The Japs knew that, and no troopships sailed those waters without a terrifying array of destroyers and other antisubmarine vessels.

The captain of the *Seawolf* discovered this a few days after he had reached his area. He saw a familiar procession on the horizon and moved in on it. The destroyer screen was formidable but only one concerned him. That one, whether or not it had spotted the *Seawolf*, was streaking toward him, a threat which he couldn't very well ignore but an effective barrier between him and the line of transports. How another skipper might have met this situation is problematical. Warder solved it by blasting the destroyer out of the water, boring in before other ships of the escort could swing about, and sinking one transport and damaging an unidentified ship moving on the other side of her and slightly astern. They gave him a medal for that, as well they might.

Later the *Seawolf* was shifted to an island where the Japs had begun landing operations on a considerable scale and by this time Fearless Freddy appears to have grown tired of shooting sitting pigeons. Having discovered that torpedoes will crack up warships as well as barnacled merchantmen, he repeated his pleasing experiment with the destroyer almost ad lib. One morning he found himself mixed up with a sizable fleet, the most important feature of which was a light cruiser squarely in front of him and so close that she almost covered his periscope scale. It was a reasonably tight spot because one destroyer stood off on one side of him and another on the other side and a little off his bow. The opposition didn't bother his stance very much, as the sequel showed, but it did interfere somewhat with the deliberative quality of the attacks he had been able to make on transports. He hit with two torpedoes—which the Navy Department concedes was probably enough to take the cruiser completely apart—but he couldn't stay there to get any further data on the kill. He got down and plotted evasive tactics while the outraged Japs dropped depth charges close enough to rattle his teeth.

At that moment he was not at all pleased with his performance and cursed himself for his own precipitancy.

"We've got to get closer to them," he said with a sadness that members of his crew still remember. "The only way we can be sure they sink is to blow them into two large pieces."

So, having established a rule, he lived up to it. When he surfaced to charge his batteries, he saw another light cruiser girt about with four or five tireless cans. This time he got in so close that there was danger of the destroyers running him down in their patrol, and when he fired it was with leisurely precision. Three fish hit with a roar and a flash that must have been noticed by ships beyond the horizon. The cruiser was under before the destroyers could take up the chase.

He dodged ash cans all night to pay for that, and after daylight new relays of dynamite carriers came to do what might be done to the *Seawolf*. There was never a time that day when sizable opposition was far from him, but that did not prevent his sticking up his periscope every time the sound apparatus picked up propeller noises from ships larger than destroyers. So it happened that he wasn't forced to close in on the third cruiser mentioned in his log. It came to meet him and he hit it with two fish out of two. Regretfully he reported that one merely as damaged. There were immediate reasons why he couldn't give it further attention.

One of the remarkable things about these operations is that he was operating in seas as unfavorable to submarines as are to be found anywhere in the world. In most of this area the water is too shallow to permit much maneuvering up and down. Charts of the bottom are haphazard and inaccurate. Straits in which the invading Japs had to be attacked if they were to be attacked at all are narrow and twisting and beset by dangerous currents. With no targets to follow and no depth bombs to avoid, navigation of these traps would have been a harrowing adventure.

As for the actual opposition with which Captain Warder had to deal almost every day he was in the area, few submariners have had to meet anything approximating it. The ubiquity of the submarines off the island of Luzon had brought a swift revision of the Japs' invasion tactics. It was vital to them that they should be able to land their troops, and so they circled their transport convoys with steel rings that any tactician in the world might have considered impenetrable.

One of Warder's men months afterward put it succinctly:

"We didn't believe there were that many cruisers and destroyers in the world.

"But," he added, "we sank some of them."

Warder at that time was thirty-eight years old. The commander of the Japanese cruiser division probably felt older.

36

CATSEYE KELLY

It HAS been suggested to me by one who read the notes from which this book is being written that submarine warfare must be conducted by something like the sense of touch.

"You never see anything," he said. "You don't know where you are until somebody consults a gadget. You don't know how far off the bottom you are until you look at a fathometer. You can't even tell how deep you are without looking at a depth gauge. It's like trying to tell the time when you're on the inside of a clock."

It is surprising, all things considered, how much the men inside the submarines really know about what's going on in the hostile world outside the pressure hull. Shut up in their boiler they develop odd perceptions, not to say instincts, that substitute for the sight that wouldn't be of much use to them anyway on dark nights under black water. The Reverend John Wilkins of England, who advanced the idea that a special race of men might be bred to live in submersible boats, was not so foolish as he may have seemed to be when stuffy scientists were laughing at him. Bred for the job or taken from the ordinary run of men by skillful selection, the special race would seem to have arrived.

You might take as an example the case of "Catseye" Kelly Anastasia whose gifts were widely discussed by submariners until they discovered that while he was unusual in the service he was by no means unique.

Kelly, so go the stories that the sailors bring back from the South Pacific, was a member of the crew of one of the ships that carried on the first part of the war virtually alone. His greatest usefulness came from idiosyncrasies of his eyes rather than from any seventh sense. He served with a skipper who is said to have had an unusually keen sense of hearing, which would be a situation so logical that you are almost prepared to doubt it.

In the glare of the lights inside the boat, in the ordinary business of sailing or diving it, Kelly was so shortsighted that many of his mates figured he must have memorized the optical test charts.

"He couldn't find his own shoes when they were laced on him," one of them commented in puzzlement. "I used to wonder how he ever managed to get around the ship once he rolled out of his own bunk, and his hands were a lot of use to him. But he was a good guy to have around. On a submarine he was just as useful as another set of instruments."

Catseye Kelly's particular skill was that he was able to see in the dark. The man who might have had trouble finding his own shoes could look into darkness for miles after normal vision had stopped. So, with the simple logic of the submariner, his captain made him a lookout. He was generally rated the best lookout in the fleet.

Of course there were some skeptics who said that a long-distance observer can get along very well with no sight at all and a good imagination. It was easy enough, they said, to report "Floating seaweed, at 8,000 yards, five points off port bow," when nobody was likely to check up on it. And Kelly, like other lookouts, reported a lot of such things. But then one night he changed his routine. He turned about, looked up at the bridge and sang out:

"Something coming up over the horizon, sir. Dead ahead."

The captain studied the situation with his night glasses, and obviously found nothing out in the moonless dark to interest him. As a matter of fact he was having some trouble seeing a thousand yards ahead of the ship.

"Hell, I couldn't see the conning-tower hatch in this," he said and he called out to Kelly: "What's it look like?"

"A couple of black points," said Kelly. "They're coming up fast. Looks to me like the top rig of a destroyer."

The captain had too much respect for Kelly's weird talent to argue.

"Keep looking," he said. "And sing out if you see anything

else. But if there's a destroyer out there you're the only man who knows it except the people on it."

Then there was silence for a while as the submarine slid along on her course and Catseye leaned into the wind.

It was a bad night, threatening rain. The sky had been overcast when last the captain got a look at it through the periscope just before sunset. There were dense masses of cumulus clouds against the horizon and the moon wouldn't be up for quite a long time—not that anybody was likely to see it when it should come up. Somebody on the bridge grunted something about black mirages and floating seaweed. And then after a minute or two Catseye sang out again.

"It's a destroyer all right," he said. "New type. Slanting stack. Angle off bow zero-zero-ten."

"Why doesn't the Old Man ask him what the captain's name is?" mumbled a chief who had come up for some air. But he said it more in admiration than skepticism, for he had observed Catseye's work before.

"I still don't see anything," said the captain. "But we'll see about it." He ordered a slight alteration of course and there was more silence until Kelly reported:

"He's doing about twenty knots. Four thousand yards. Zero-zero-one-five." And then at interval with changes of bearing, "Three thousand yards, fifteen hundred yards, eight hundred yards . . ."

Kelly was calling out "Five hundred yards" before the captain saw anything much farther away than the top of Kelly's head. Then he wasn't sure what he saw or if he saw anything. There seemed to be a dark spot out there—unless it was one of those things that come of eyestrain. He got a bearing on the hole in the black, gave a few orders and watched the ship come about.

"Fire one," he said.

Then for a short distance into the night he had something to look at—the glittering phosphorescence of the torpedo wake lengthening from the bow, pretty and somehow thrilling but expensive if it should turn out that the torpedo wasn't going anywhere.

"It's on the target, sir," called Kelly. "Right down the alley.

It's . . ." But the captain never heard the rest of the report. There was a sudden orange flash dead ahead and for one instant the skipper saw what the lookout had seen—the black planes of a destroyer's turrets and bridge, the spike of a mast, lifting up and tilting forward in the weird light. Flame shot upward a hundred feet and the roar of blasting explosive caromed back.

"Right out of the water, sir!" Catseye screamed. "Right out of the water. . . . She's going down. . . . She's all under, sir." But by that time the captain didn't need to be told.

Several ships have had men who could locate and identify propeller noises almost as quickly as the operator of the sound gear. Whether they did this through exceptional hearing or an unusual sense of vibration neither they nor anyone else could explain. Some men, like "Big Mike" Murdoch, would lie with their ears to the deck to make out where the depth charges were bursting. Mike seems to have been the only one of them who gave a definite report on his estimates, but unfortunately nobody could testify to his accuracy save the Japs. Virtually all submariners back from patrols in which several ships have been sunk are acquainted with the characteristic sound effects that follow the bursting of a torpedo—explosions of fuel or magazines, the buckling of iron decks, the rumble of engines tearing loose from their beds, the crackle of bulkheads sinking into the relentless pressure of the sea.

From data thus mysteriously acquired these men are able to reconstruct the unseen spectacles of their war with remarkable accuracy. They are not prisoners listening to gunfire outside the walls but actual participants in battle. Which may account for the vividness and detail of the narratives they bring back with them. Even if you live inside the clock, it seems, there are ways of finding out what time it is.

Usually, of course, the captain's eyes at the periscope give vision by proxy to every man aboard the ship. But not always. Much of his approach in an attack may be done blindly with an occasional peep of five or ten seconds at his target. In evasion maneuvers to get away from depth charges he has to be as psychic as everybody else in the boat. Sometimes, perhaps, a skill at mind reading has been of more value to him than the fire-control apparatus or any of the intricate devices that clutter up his control room. And when you find a skipper with a talent for that sort of work you find the nucleus of a lot of interesting legend.

"The captain was a good chess player and he outplayed 'em."

"The Old Man was a good guesser and he outguessed 'em."

"The skipper always seemed to know what they was going to do next. . . ."

Machinist Lasater's captain, Henry G. Munson, seems to have qualified among the gifted. His ship had finished a patrol and was on its way to a base in the South Pacific when, in the cool of a starlit evening, a lookout whose eyes weren't so good as those of Catseye Kelly made out an odd-looking lump on the water a few hundred yards away.

He reported it to the captain, mentioning that it had a familiar look but he couldn't tell why. The captain through his night glasses furnished a dry answer.

"You naturally wouldn't know what it was," he said. "It's a submarine. And it's a Jap submarine. I can see the markings on the conning tower. . . . Stand by to fire Number One. . . ."

But right there was where logic and mathematics and the other skills of torpedo fire ended, and pure intuition began. The Jap lookout apparently had been faster than the American. While the captain was still speaking, the conning tower with the odd markings on it leaned forward and the end of the silhouette vanished under a white plume.

The American submarine had been tearing toward the Jap at full speed and, as it turned out, on just about the same course.

"Clear the bridge!" called the captain. "Take her down!"

There is a bit of legend that the diving officer asked what depth he was going to and that the captain said he'd decide on that later. But there, unfortunately, you have one of those apocryphal things that aren't readily verified.

It is certain, however, that the submarine dived at an angle which the skipper designated before he came down through the hatch. He'd calculated it, it seems, after a look at the slant on the black ship as the sparkling feather boa closed over her.

The crew didn't have to be told what was going on, or that

this trick was something that had never been tried since the days when Jules Verne was imagining things about submarines. By that instinct or telepathy or whatever it was that serves the submariner on such occasions, every man aboard the ship knew that they were diving right into the funnel the Jap had left, chasing her down and down into depths that might presently crush one of them.

They couldn't see the target. But this time it was all even. The captain couldn't see it either. The periscope was still sliding down into the well when they took a new angle. But they could sense what was going on out there in the inky water. They could see the stern of the submarine ahead of them, her propellers churning under the fat belly of her outer hull, the bubbles swirling behind the lump of her conning tower. For that matter they could see inside her. They could envision a lot of little yellow men, good sailors all of them, in a control room precisely like their own, watching the gauges and levels in their dive, sitting tensely before the levers in the motor room, and—although they shut their mental eyes to this—possibly manning the stern torpedo tubes.

As in most submarine actions it was only a few seconds from the time the American submarine started down until this, one of the weirdest battles ever fought, was finished. But it takes the better part of an hour for one of the spectators to describe it to you and, it is easy to understand, took a large part of a lifetime to experience. I recall a saying widely current in the surface fleet— "They get old fast in the submarines."

They had come down nobody is certain how many feet—no two agree at what angle—when the captain looked at his stop watch and peered out through steel bulkheads and lightless water toward his unseen target.

"Fire One!" he said.

The torpedo men fired Number One.

The men in the boat hardly heard the *whish* of the discharge. It was covered up almost instantaneously by a blast that almost threw them off their feet. They needed no Catseye Kelly now to tell what had happened to the submarine ahead of them.

"Stand by to surface," ordered the captain.

"Take her up!"

37

RESCUE AT SEA

THERE had been a storm, a tropical twister that for days had kept the USS *Toughfish* standing on her propellers or rolling, so that the men at the diving planes were piled up on their controls about half the time. Now the sea was covered with long glassy rollers in which at night the phosphorescence gleamed in patches like drowned constellations. It had been hot below decks in the submarine even when the gale was blowing. It was hotter now that the wind had died. The air conditioner didn't seem to be doing very well. Something had happened to it in the first attack of the patrol, and languid fans weren't cooling the ship any—just distributing the heat and the Diesel fumes and the other stinks from one compartment to the other and back again. You didn't notice the smells so much. In a month your nose quit paying attention to them. But the heat was something else again.

Even when she came topside, which was for a couple of hours every night, it didn't seem to make much difference. The outside air was just as hot and just as sticky as the worn-out atmosphere that the blowers took out. And it smelled worse . . . or at least it seemed to smell worse. The oxygen in it made you dizzy and the salt tang—if that's what it was—didn't smell like salt at all. It was sickly sweet with just a hint of fish in it. And it made you want to vomit.

Most of the time, though, you were submerged, because the wrangle for the Java Sea was still going on and no spot in these churning waters was ever safe from the Jap destroyers. Sometimes you made an approach to attack, but not often because shipping was scarce out here. That was one of the troubles with the place. You didn't get any run for your money and you had to take the plastering just as if you were actually doing something. So, mostly, you sat there and prayed that the patrols would find something to do somewhere else so you could go on with your business. You just stripped down to your skivvies and stewed in your own juice and watched the rivulets of condensed steam run down the bulkheads and spread out with the other puddles on the deck.

"My mother had an egg-cooking gadget once," the chief machinist's mate remembered out loud. "It was a sort of aluminum cup. You put the egg into it and submerged the whole business in a cup of water with an electric heater in it. And I know how that egg felt. It's just like being boiled in a submarine."

A torpedo man who had been wringing out the bottoms of his shorts joined languidly in the conversation.

"That thing must have been a great invention," he said. "I bet there ain't an egg in our locker that ain't cooked so hard it would bounce if you dropped it."

"I dunno," said the chief sadly. "I been cooked as long as the eggs and if you dropped me I wouldn't bounce. I wouldn't even move. I'd just lie there and drown in sweat."

Miles Lasater of the black gang looked into the far distance with eyes full of acid perspiration.

"I come from Tucson, Arizona," he said. "They say that's the hottest town in America. But, boy, I never knew what heat was before. I figure if I ever get back there I'll have to wear my overcoat all summer. That's what's worrying me. I can't think where I left my overcoat."

And then there was silence again, as there had been so continuously since the beginning of the storm.

Men drooped in every corner of the ship save the engine room, where the Diesels still held the heat of their last run on the surface. In a steamy murk like this they might be expected to hold it for hours, perhaps forever. Men, sprawled on the deck, envied those sprawled in the bunks next to the racks of fish in the forward torpedo room. It didn't do you much good to lie on a deck, even an iron deck, when it was just as hot as you were. The coppery fish might be greasy but they weren't so hot, and when you lay against them they seemed to take a lot of the fever out of you.

The ship looked hot. From the station in front of the air manifolds in the control room you could see almost to both ends of it. And even if the men hadn't been all over the place like wilting vegetables there would have been nothing in the sight to suggest green fields and cool waters. The lights blazed fiercely from the forward torpedo-room door back as far as you could see into the spaghetti of pipe in the engine room. You wondered if you'd have felt any cooler in a dimmer light. And under the blaze of the lamps everything looked mildewed and shopworn.

She'd been pretty clean-looking when she started out on this. Then the voice of Captain Munson:

"Stand by to surface!"

The drooping figures at the controls stiffened with a life nobody would have thought was in them. A rank of dripping, glistening bodies came up off the wet deck and out of sodden bunks into the blaze of the lights, and all up and down through the crowded corridor of the ship there was a scene like the yawning of graveyards in answer to the trump of Gabriel. . . . Men in rags and nothing at all . . . men with tired faces and tense muscles and wide eyes, weaving about in strange patterns through the chaos of machinery.

Nobody paid attention to this spectacle which had been endlessly repeated since the old *Toughfish* went down the ways at Groton, Connecticut, on a day that seemed a century ago. There was no novelty in the demonstration of how much you can torture a human frame without breaking it . . . nothing new in the continuing proof that a submariner is never really a corpse until he is dead.

However belatedly, however uselessly—considering the murk that would be waiting for them on the surface—the reprieve had come. The monotony was broken. They were coming up out of their eerie half-world to that stranger environment into which they had been born. The air up there would be dripping with warm water and in a moment they'd be complaining of its nasty sweetness and the nausea it brought them. But it would be something different from this . . . that was the main thing. It would be different.

"Pump from Number Two by the main drain," ordered the diving officer. This to lift the propellers clear of the mud bottom on which they had been resting. The pump rumbled. The stern came slowly up.

"Secure the pump," the diving officer ordered quietly in a tired voice. And a human echo answered him: "Pump secured, sir."

"All ahead normal," ordered the captain and the diving officer repeated the order. The ship began to throb a little.

The diving officer ordered an angle on the bow planes and stood with legs apart, his eyes fixed on the depth gauges. The men at the planes moved their little control levers back and forth ceaselessly, their heads bent over the bubbles in the spirit levels in front of them. And so to periscope depth.

"Stop all motors!" This from the captain. "Listen all around."

Another long moment of silence. Then the call of the sound man: "No propeller sounds, sir."

"All ahead normal. Blow One."

The boat shivered as compressed air forced the water out of the forward main ballast tank and she took an angle upward by the bow. In a matter of seconds there was another shiver as her bow came out of the water. The periscope meanwhile had been rumbling up out of the well. Slowly the captain walked it around, peering at 360 degrees of black horizon.

"Close all vents," ordered the diving officer and again the answer came from the man in front of the Christmas tree.

"All vents closed, sir." The diving officer half turned to the captain.

"Riding on the vents, sir."

"Open the hatch. Open inductions. Start the engines." The fresh dampness of the night swept down in a blast from the open hatch as the engines began to turn, and for a moment the boat seemed cool because it was moving. But only for a moment. The air was just the thick, sickening, barely breathable wetness the crew had been expecting, while hoping that somehow it might be different.

"Well, anyway," said a machinist's mate cheerily, "a match will light in it." And a dismal voice from the after battery room commented, "I wish I could teach my stomach to stay put in it."

"They say it does your lungs good," said somebody else.

"Not my lungs, it don't," said the chief of the boat. "It can't get through the enamel."

"Well, we'll just have to make the best of it till they take us down again and let us breathe the air we make ourselves with our own lungs," commented the cook. "It don't do no good to beef about God's blessings."

"And, boy! it's hot and it's going to be hotter," said the lad from Tucson, Arizona.

The patrol had been over for some days now and without looking at any charts the battered crew took some hope and stimulus from the sound of the Diesels. The Old Man wouldn't be wasting any time. He'd be making knots toward home—"home" being a base where they could go ashore and get a bottle of beer and show off a clean uniform to the girls across the street and see the sun again. . . . Not that anybody was too much interested in the sun. . . . You couldn't see so well in the sunlight and it was likely to be hot.

"It won't be long now," said the lad from Tucson as he overcame his squeamishness enough to light a cigarette. "Pretty soon we'll be ashore and I know a pub where they got an electric fan. And I'll ship in a honey boat before I'll come out in one of these sewer pipes again."

He was leaning over an engine and taking a scientific interest in the way the sweat sizzled and went up in steam when it hit.

"I'll be right alongside you, boy," said the pale fireman at the other end of the catwalk. "But if it's all the same to you I'd rather ship in a destroyer—that's the life . . . just hauling tail all over the Pacific dropping ash cans on submarines, with air to breathe and water to take a bath in and enough speed so's nobody can get at you. That's the life, boy, that's the life."

They'd been doing pretty well before they sighted the black patch on the water about 4:00 A.M. When chow came out of the galley at midnight they'd recovered enough to eat it. Good chow it was, too, some kind of pot roast with carrots and peas and things mixed in with the sauce—you'd almost have thought they were fresh vegetables if you hadn't known better. And the stuff was

well cooked—that went without saying. And there were fried potatoes and there was also some kind of fluff with peaches in it for
dessert. . . . Not bad at all. The boy from Arizona got up from
the table momentarily forgetful of the sweat that ran into his eyes
and the clammy discomfort of his wet skivvies.

"Well," he said, "I guess that does it. I'll live long enough now
to spit in somebody's eye and tell him I want a shore job. And if
I get another meal I may feel strong enough to take on some of this
high life on a tin can. . . . They say it's the life—nothing to do
but send down ash cans to the dizzy buzzards who work the submarines. . . ."

At four o'clock the ship was dropping the knots behind her at
top speed and there was a certain sense of well-being below. A
mumble of conversation was coming out of the messroom where
most of the men off watch had gathered—the homeward-bound
conversation that is always the most interesting if a guy has
strength enough left to talk at all. . . . That pub with the electric
fan in it . . . that swell house up on the hill where a guy was
always welcome to drop in for a home-cooked meal, that Dutchman who had a saddle horse and had said he'd let a guy borrow it
for a ride . . . that sort of stuff. Then the lookout sighted the
dark patch.

The first the crew knew about it was when the order came
down from the bridge to break out the small arms and man the
deck guns and stand by for attack. The lad from Arizona went
back to his engines inwardly cheered but outwardly discomfited.

"For the love of Mike, what now?" he inquired of the black
gang. "And just as we was getting along so well, too."

"There's just too damned many Japs," said his friend the fireman. "They're like the prickly heat on my back—all over the
place."

Up on the bridge the captain stood with his glasses fixed on the
unidentifiable shadow. It might be a cluster of sampans, he thought
—too low in the water to be destroyers—might be a clump of seaweed—you sometimes saw it like that in these waters—or it might
be wreckage. He looked again and decided it was wreckage. But

he didn't relax his precaution. Japanese sailors, he had found, weren't cheerful about being rescued. Sometimes the tougher ones had been known to take pot shots at you. With deck guns trained and no decrease in speed he swung to pass the floating mass on his starboard. But as he passed there were no shots, no sound save the rush of water from the engines and a low agonized cry: "My God! They're not finished with us yet." And he spun the ship about on her beam-ends. The voice had been English.

As he came about he noticed some details of what had looked like a solid patch of blackness. It was really several patches now, quite a lot darker than the surrounding water—a couple of rafts and some bits of plank and a wooden grating or two. And to this debris men were hanging, their oil-blackened heads only slightly discernible in the enveloping dark. He rang the engine-room telegraph for slow speed, leaned over the bridge rail and called out, "Who are you?"

There was a mumble of many voices, then one louder and steadier than the rest:

"Men of His Majesty's Ship *Electra*." After that there was silence again, a fact that the captain noticed with interest. They were disciplined, these men, and also men who could take the good with the bad as it happened to come.

So he hove to and got the ship's boat over and began a race against the dawn to get them aboard.

The incident barely figures in the official reports but it rates as another of those unbelievable things that submariners recount to one another. There were fifty-four of these men, most of them barely able to move. About half of them had to be lifted from the boat to the deck of the submarine and down the hatch. Seventeen of them were badly wounded.

The sun was well on its way up when the last of them had gone below and the boat was back under the superstructure. And on the horizon a destroyer was moving. For just a moment the captain wondered about how a hundred and four men were fitting into a space that fifty had crowded to stuffiness, how they were going to survive on half-rations of air, and with more immediate concern he wondered if the men on watch were going to be able to move about enough to handle the ship. He found the answer to the last question in a few seconds as the hull of the can followed her top rig up over the rim of the sea. He cleared the bridge and sounded the klaxon.

"We had to dive," the boy from Arizona explained later, as he sat in the shipyard that was to launch the new submarine to which he had been newly assigned. "We was still on the edge of our patrol area and the Japs was hot on our tail. But, boy, soon as we got down we was sure in a hell of a mess.

"There were fifty-four of these Limeys. And we'd thought we was hot and uncomfortable and crowded before. We put the wounded in our bunks and most of the rest of us just stood around on each other's feet. Most of the Limeys couldn't stand up at all. They just fell down wherever we put 'em. Men were piled up all over the place—even in the engine room.

"Then one of them died. He was just about dead when we took him aboard and he gave it up right away . . . just a few minutes after we'd bedded him down with the other wounded in the crew's quarters. The smell of death was in that ship for three weeks. We had him from four o'clock that morning until just about dawn the next day and you wouldn't think a dead man would get noticeable in that length of time. But he certainly did. The extra bodies in the boat heated it up a lot and it was already like a broiler.

"We began to notice pretty soon—in a couple of hours or so. But we were too polite to say anything about it. As a matter of fact we were just at the end of a tough patrol and we were so tired we thought we knew what it was like to be dead. I remember after we discovered that this guy was finished I was talking to a machinist's mate who owned the bunk he died in. This machinist's mate says, 'Hank, I'm so damned tired I think I'll just push him over and crawl in with him.' But he didn't. There wasn't room enough.

"I was at the foot of the ladder when this guy that died came down. He was so full of holes that I don't see how he lived to get aboard. He had one big rent in his chest right under the chin. I almost put my fist through him when I was handing him down. The others weren't much alive either—the wounded men, I mean.

But I heard afterwards just about all of them pulled through. Them Limey destroyer guys sure are hardy.

"The Limeys had just caught unshirted hell—worse than anything that had happened to us. I began to be ashamed about what I'd said about life on the cans being easy. They'd been hanging onto wreckage in that scummy water kicking away sharks for so long that their wounds weren't bleeding any more. They hadn't had anything to eat for days and no water. They were all gummy with oil and filth. What I mean is they'd been suffering out there. Hell wasn't going to be able to show them anything much they hadn't seen. But when we got the last one aboard and closed the hatches and started to take her down I don't think there was one of them wouldn't have been glad to be right back there floating in the drink. They was scared stiff—just simply stiff. It was dangerous down below the surface, they said.

"Well, whether they liked it or not, we just had to stay there. We kept picking up the sounds of propellers and we knew the cans weren't going to give us up—not that day. We figured we could expect the depth charges any minute. But we weren't worried about how they'd stand that. They had a lot of what it took, those guys.

"We couldn't communicate with the base while we were submerged. So we didn't know what we were going to do with the Limeys and naturally we couldn't tell 'em. That seemed to be the only part of the business that kept them nervous. They didn't like to think about being shut up in the box forever.

"We fed 'em all right. Those who were able to eat at all couldn't believe we could rig up that kind of a meal with conditions like they were. But we got everybody fed all right. We couldn't do much for the wounded. We didn't have any pharmacist's mate aboard, and all they had for medical care was a student who'd been on the destroyer with them. He was swell at first aid, though. He did a slick job trimming wounds and sewing them together with twine. There was nothing to ease the pain. But those fellows took it. You never heard a whimper out of them and seventeen of them was wounded bad—all ripped up with shell fragments.

"Some of us were detailed to take care of the wounded—that

is, to do things this medical student told us to do. We didn't mind handling the corpse, although we didn't have no experience at that sort of business. We could push him around and if we dropped him it didn't make any difference to him. But none of us wanted to handle the wounded men. Every time you lifted one or even leaned on his bunk you knew you were hurting him. Not that they said anything about it. They never complained about anything. But a guy doesn't have to tell you when you're half killing him.

"It was probably as hot that day as it will ever get inside a submarine. But I don't think we noticed it like we had the day before. Anyway we didn't dare to beef about it when we looked at all them guys we'd picked up. Hell, we didn't have anything to kick about. The fireman I'd been talking to about a shore job comes to me that evening and says he doesn't think he's going out of the submarines. He's going to stay where he knows what the pitch is. And I tell him I'm changing my mind, too. Life up on them surface ships is just liable to be too rugged.

"When we got up that night we got orders where to go, and a little before daylight a can come along and took off our passengers, including the dead man.

"Then we filled up the ship with what they call air out there and got going for home. It was funny how empty the old boiler looked when all them Limeys got off. And it seemed almost cool. And we didn't bleat about a thing till we got into port—not one damn thing."

38

THE PIONEER SKIPPERS

THE submariners who worked in the Philippines knew better than anybody else the size and equipment of the local establishment. Presently they knew also that there wasn't going to be any help. And they had little hope for miracles.

This, it seems to me, is one of the reasons why their own per-formance in that last battle has the look of an authentic miracle itself. They were busy piling Japanese wrecks on the coasts of Luzon and Mindanao when Corregidor fell. They continued to make the Philippine bays a nightmare for the invasion fleet long after their bases in the area had been closed to them. And at this writing, despite a full program elsewhere, they are still doing it.

It is difficult to say which action or which locale of the Pacific sea war gave the submarines opportunity for their most brilliant performance. You learn quickly among these men whose every work is incredible that you haven't any ordinary standards of com-parison. Is it more daring and spectacular, for instance, to bounce off the bottom of Tokyo Bay and sink a transport, or to fight a battleship at Midway, or to crack up a brace of destroyers in a sur-face action? Somebody else may have the answer, but until one is supplied it will appear to me that the submarines of the Asiatic fleet certainly set a pace. And it is a matter of record that at one time or another most of our best skippers were operating in that area.

For instance Lieutenant Commander Chester Smith showed up off Corregidor before the ghastly tragedy came to its climax. Where he had been before that it is difficult to find out even now. But he had already begun to roll up a record that led submarine men—Japanese as well as American—to judge him the best of their kind.

So far as newspapermen are concerned Chet Smith has been almost a mythical character and as illusive. In a business where ninety-nine percent of the men who do the work are nameless I kept hearing of him all the time and in places thousands of miles apart. Come to think about it, his was the first name I heard, and the record of his early patrols was the first to give us an inkling of what the submarines were going to do to the Japanese supply lines in the next few months.

There are two explanations for this. One is that his list of ships sunk was the largest in the service in a very short time. Another is that he was one of the few submarine skippers who started this war with a reputation. His ship, the building of which he had observed personally, had the top listing for gunnery and torpedo fire in the Pacific fleet. And in the submarines when you say the ship has an excellent record you are talking about the captain.

Civilians, naturally, did not hear much about Captain Smith or his accomplishments. But the fleet knew about him and talked about him much as they do now. What he had done was no particular secret. There was little nonprofessional discussion of it merely because such accomplishments in peacetimes are not rated as news. So it was not surprising to him or anybody else that the Japanese observers, attachés and peace emissaries knew all about it before he got his boat back to Pearl Harbor after the maneuvers. Commander Harley F. Cope in his highly informative book on the submarines, *Serpent of the Seas*, mentions that Smith's household for months thereafter was the scene of a parade of inquisitive Japanese maids, each of whom quit without notice after a week of service. It was said around Honolulu that he couldn't eat a meal in a restaurant without two Japanese waiters attending him, one to carry the food, another to stand at his elbow and listen openly to the table talk. The submarine officers thought maybe these people might be wanting to find out how an ace captain like Chester Smith was able to do his tricks. Smith himself was so impressed that in front of a Japanese he never talked about much except the weather.

If details are withheld concerning the location of his first patrol area, there was no such reticence about his initial performances. All that came out in the medal citations. It would appear that his

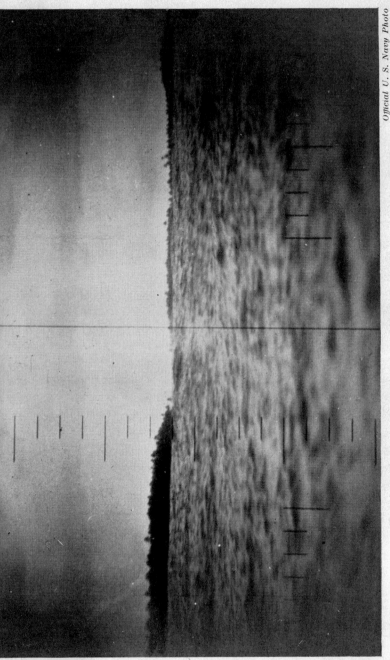

MAKIN ISLAND

As this strongly fortified Japanese base in the South Pacific looked through the periscope of a submarine which later rose to shell permanent installations and sink two ships with shell fire from deck guns.

A JAP TANKER BLOWS UP

first cruise took him to a spot where the invasion fleet moved in thick concentrations. If you can draw conclusions from one or two Japanese communiqués, it was probably somewhere north of Manila along the coast of Luzon. Wherever he was, he appears to have found no lack of targets.

He began his war work by boring into a big, well-protected convoy, and the first torpedo he ever fired in battle was a hit on a big supply ship. He lingered momentarily to estimate the damage, diving on a split-second safety margin as destroyers swung out of line to ram him. As he had calculated, he slid out of the way of the depth charges, and confessed to his executive that he considered the whole performance unsatisfactory.

"We blew a hole in him all right," he said. "But when I last looked he seemed to be holding together. It will take another fish to finish him off. . . . Take her up to periscope depth!"

So, with the clunks still blasting about him, he came up.

"Fire Two!" he said. "That does it! Take her down. . . ."

The blasting of the Japanese ship, which this time had broken in two, seemed squarely on top of them as they dived. The destroyers continued to look for him all day in the fashion of destroyers, and the crew got their first experience with the nervous torture of the depth charges.

"But it wasn't so bad as we'd expected," one of them said afterward. "Your state of mind has a lot to do with how you feel about depth charges and we were pretty cocky. We'd just picked a big one out of the pile and the skipper had come through just as we thought he would. We figured that no matter what the Japs did to us he'd get us out in one piece. . . ."

In the normal course of submarine tactics you might think Captain Smith would have avoided further action. That was probably what the Japanese thought, for while the destroyers were still looking for him the sound man reported the rumble of low-speed screws. The convoy, or another one like it, was moving up there—ten ships, perhaps, and all of them stomping over his head as if certain that he had been sunk or at least disposed of for the night.

So, at a moment when the order was least expected, he said:

"Take her up."

His first look through the periscope showed him a new and

heavier destroyer screen riding in formation. In the shadows behind them were great black masses of ships in parallel columns and moving slowly. He avoided the destroyers, a daring tactic but one calculated to give him only a few seconds for attack. Once in position, he fired three torpedoes—not fanwise but each toward its own target.

He got three hits. Not only that, but in the confusion that resulted when three ships simultaneously blew up he was able to stay up long enough to see them start for the bottom. The "workover" that followed has been reported as desultory. The amazed Japanese destroyer skippers apparently didn't know where to look for him.

When the time came for him to go back to his base he still had torpedoes in his tubes. So instead of heading directly for home he moved up into a strait heavily guarded but generally cluttered up with Japanese shipping. The report of that expedition is just as laconic as his other narratives of battle. He didn't delay long. He hadn't enough fish to fight a lone-handed war in this spot, whatever the Japanese might offer—and besides, officially, he wasn't there at all. So, in the cool of the evening, he spotted a long tanker, closed in on her under the noses of the destroyers and patrol boats and fired two torpedoes. Both hit and the ship took fire and went under by the stern.

The Navy Cross was waiting for him when he returned to his base, and the admiral suggested that he and his men might be in need of a rest. He accepted the Cross with pleased dignity but he asked to be excused from the vacation.

"We don't need any rest, sir," he said. "Not yet awhile. The ship is in good condition and the crew are on their toes. So if you'll just give us some more torpedoes we'll be getting back."

He went out on another trip. "In Japanese waters," one gathers from his second citation. He sank another list of ships. Someday the Navy may get around to telling where and how and how many.

Largely through Mrs. Francis B. Sayre, wife of the former High Commissioner of the Philippines, one learns of his definite connection with the fighting about Luzon. For she identifies him as the captain who evacuated President Quezon and returned to

Corregidor to pick up the commissioner's party. She quotes Admiral Rockwell as having said to her: "You are going out with our ace submarine skipper. He'll get you through." And Commander Cope, commenting on it, says, "I could have told her the same thing."

Every now and then you continue to hear of Lieutenant Commander Chester Smith, a ship here, a ship there. And it becomes apparent that whatever he had in the beginning is still with him. I asked a lot of his associates about him, and from Lieutenant Commander Hiram Cassedy, himself an ace, I got a fairly comprehensible answer.

"It's just that he's good," he said. "He's the best of them all. He has a knack of judging speed and distance such as I've never seen in anybody else. In addition to that he has guts and calm judgment and he can outthink any Jap who ever sailed a ship. When he goes out after them they might just as well turn in their suits."

A number of the submarines were in cargo and taxi service during those first weeks of the battle for the Philippines. Toward the end, when the malaria-ridden defenders of Corregidor were looking at the Japs across the sights of empty guns, ammunition hauling had become one of the most important jobs that the subs were likely to have. It was likewise one of the most dangerous and seemingly most unheroic jobs.

Back and forth between Corregidor and the new supply depots in the south the submarines shuttled, as vulnerable as they had always been, as much alone and unprotected in everything they did. And, hunted continuously by everything that the Japs could send into the South Pacific to intercept them, they were forbidden to fight. Hirohito's high command apparently knew all about this traffic and realized its importance, until every sea lane and strait among the islands were covered with destroyers. Against this disheartening array the submarines could make little progress by day and could move only with daring abandon by night. Yet the ammunition continued to roll out onto the dock at Corregidor and not one of the boats was lost in transit.

Once, before the "no fighting" order went into effect, Lieutenant Commander Frank W. ("Mike") Fenno came up to the Rock. His ship had been lightened of everything movable, including a large part of his provisions, to make more room for his shell cargo, with the result that when the ammunition was delivered he found himself riding high in the water and in immediate need of ballast.

A lot has been written about Mike Fenno's removal of the gold reserve from Manila, and there was something in the idea of saving so much tangible wealth in an undersized boiler that took hold on the public imagination. But nobody apparently bothered to record the incident from his point of view.

As nearly as one can reconstruct the affair from the accounts of men who were in Philippine waters at the time, his attitude toward great wealth was that of the typical Navy man. Treasure, however large, was something far from the perilous realities of running a submarine. Gold, considered merely as metal, however, has a specific gravity close to that of lead. A million dollars' worth of gold would weigh somewhere around a ton, and he could use a few million dollars' worth to steady his hull.

So, when somebody mentioned that all these riches were piled up waiting transportation, he volunteered for the job. The gold was taken aboard and stowed where it would do the most good. After which Fenno started the long trek to Pearl Harbor.

The Japs may not have known anything about the gold transfer until long afterward, but whatever Fenno's ship was carrying, it was still a submarine, and with planes ranging over him and destroyers working their sound gear on him he wasn't out of trouble for more than a week, if you can say that a submarine is ever out of trouble.

Not all of his danger, however, can be charged to Japanese initiative, for there were still plenty of ships about, and along with the gold in his hold he had a load of torpedoes. So, knowing the nature of the submariner, one is not surprised to learn that one evening when he ran into a convoy with a destroyer escort he paid no attention to evasion tactics but bored in. He sank three ships, then took his gold below, where, it is said, he listened to the snarling depth charges with pleased complacency.

Some publicity has been given to the odd hegira of Lieutenant Commander James Charles Dempsey who took thirteen nurses off Corregidor. Submarine men are generally chivalrous, but never since the days of Bushnell's *Turtle* had one of them been that chivalrous. Submarines are built without accommodations of any sort for women. And the costume of the crew in tropical waters was never invented for a mixed society.

"But the girls were all right," the captain reported. "They kept to their own part of the boat and didn't get into anybody's hair. We gave them the chiefs' cabin, which had four bunks in it, and somebody found a piece of mirror to put over the washstand. With four bunks a dozen of them had to sleep in three eight-hour shifts. The other one just shifted for herself, I guess. A couple of them blew themselves up by turning the wrong valves in the head, but we could be tolerant of that. You can't expect nurses to have an engineering education.

"They didn't kick about anything. They didn't do any back-seat driving. All things considered they weren't bad passengers at all. I was greatly surprised." And the submarine warfare is unlikely to produce another commentary so startling to the submariners themselves.

Lieutenant Commander Frederick Burdett ("Fearless Freddy") Warder was in these waters for a long time and his ship the *Seawolf*, about which more has been told elsewhere, took much of her toll along the coast north of Manila. "The Red Pirates of the China Coast," the only submarine fraternity on record, plied a similar beat, as did Lieutenant Commander McKinney, Lieutenant Commander Cassedy, Lieutenant Commander Morton Mumma and sundry other aces. And while some of the boys were fetching and carrying for Corregidor, others went on with the program of destruction.

How well they did is something for which one must take the astounding unofficial score although much may be deduced from reports of minor incident. . . .

One day after the fall of Manila a U. S. submarine so far unnamed was on patrol outside the harbor when destroyers stood in, escorting a lone cargo ship.

"Obviously that's the last of the convoy," said the skipper. And he called out his course. "It would be a shame to have them bother any more with this. . . . Fire One!"

The ship blew up and sank and the submarine went down toward the bottom to take the hammering that one might have expected from destroyers with nothing left to do but drop ash cans.

A tired crew listened to the bursts in unsmiling silence. They had been taking a lot of this up and down the coast and they didn't seem to be getting any more used to it.

Under the circumstances they winced when the captain burst into a loud guffaw that echoed interminably among the bursting clunks.

"And what's so damned funny?" the executive wanted to know.

For a moment the captain controlled himself.

"I was just wondering," he said, "what the commander of that destroyer division is going to say when they ask him to explain what happened to his convoy."

39

ENSIGN COOK GOES ASHORE

WHEN they gave the Navy Cross to Ensign George Cook they cited him for meritorious conduct above and beyond the call of duty aboard a submarine in the South Pacific. . . . But this, if one puts a strict interpretation on it, is not entirely correct. What Ensign George Cook might well have been cited for was a well-done job as a one-man landing party from a submarine, and a single-handed raid on a Japanese camp.

Lieutenant Commander Hiram Cassedy is proud of the fact that he first introduced young Mr. Cook to the service and prevailed upon him to stay.

"He's got the right stuff," said Captain Cassedy. "And I'll tell you about it from the beginning. . . ."

Captain Cassedy, after sundry patrols about the Philippines and the usual amount of fetching and carrying, was given a new ship and sent somewhere in the Java Sea. Cook, fresh from the merchant service, came along on invitation just for the ride.

"I didn't have any doubt he was going to get one," the captain reminisced, "because things were pretty hot up in that corner all the time. Well, anyway, he got it. And so did the rest of us.

"Nothing much happened during the first few days of the patrol. Then one evening we picked up a merchant ship traveling alone. . . . Or at least it looked to be alone.

"It was a squally night—patches of rain all around and you couldn't see much. The ship was making knots off our starboard bow. So I got up on the surface and took out after her. It was a funny experience because we kept losing her and finding her in the rain.

"I didn't think she had seen us because after all we didn't have much silhouette and the weather was all in our favor. She was going pretty fast but we were faster, and I thought it wouldn't take long to intercept her. Then Sound reported that he was hearing depth charges off to port.

"I couldn't figure that one out because I knew we were the only submarine in the area. I looked out there and couldn't see a thing but clouds and waves. And while I was looking the ship went into a heavy patch of rain and we lost her.

"Sound called out that he was still hearing things. And then I did something nobody ever ought to do. I stopped dead to listen. Sound reported that the blasting off to port had stopped but that he was hearing something over on the starboard side and forward.

"All of this was very mysterious and we hadn't learned much, but I got a hunch that I'd better get out of there. Whatever it was, I didn't have any business sitting down there like a dead duck. So we started up. The screws were just turning over and we were just beginning to get a little white water under the stern when I saw what the trouble was all right. Two Japanese antisubmarine ships came charging down on us. Maybe there was a third one. I didn't stop to see. The two that I was looking at had us pretty well boxed in, but by that time we'd got moving and we dived.

"I knew we were going to take a shellacking. Which we did. But all of this is just incidental to what I started to tell you about George Cook. He looked more or less interested when the blasting began. But he didn't seem to be any more upset than anybody else in the boat. When it was all over he took a deep breath and said to me:

"'You know I used to hear fellows talking about things like this on the sub tender in port. . . . But they really do happen, don't they?'"

So it looked to the captain as if young Mr. Cook would be a good addition to the submarine service. And thus he happened to be on the next patrol, which had nothing about it that resembled the normal activities of the submarines at all.

Captain Cassedy had orders to proceed to an island and take off thirty-five marooned men, the remnants of an Australian force. He had been told what the recognition signals would be and warned of a trap. The Japs had been active in that part of the ocean for some time—almost without opposition. And nobody knew exactly how far they might have got.

The submarine came off the island in good time and pulled up in a cove at the entrance to the lagoon. Cassedy had to feel his way in at dusk, and even then had trouble with reefs and shallow water. He decided that the only way he could carry out the rest of the plan would be with the ship's boat. No submarine could have gone anywhere in the lagoon.

The submarine had been at sea for a long time and had taken the customary beating from the depth charges, and nothing about her superstructure was quite right including, as it turned out, the ship's boat. Nobody had used it for months. Nobody had had a chance to look at it. And when they got it out onto the deck they discovered that what they had been afraid of was true: they couldn't get the little Diesel engine started.

That meant that there could be no immediate expedition ashore. So Cook walked to the end of the ship and signaled with a flashlight to the beach. There was an immediate response. Cook signaled that the boat would be in presently, and there was no answer to that.

The repairs were difficult. Eventually they took the engine out entirely. They tore some two-by-fours out of a rack in the falsework and attached flattened tin cans to the end of them for oars. They made rowlocks out of scrap iron in the engine room, and along about midnight got the boat over the side and manned, with Cook as chief of the landing party.

While this work was going on, the captain saw the glow of a fire in the jungle beyond the beach. Now and then through the glasses he could see men on horseback crossing the light.

His instructions had not made it entirely clear just who the men were that he was supposed to rescue, so he came to the logical conclusion that somebody had sent him after a troop of cavalry. He mentioned it to Cook, who was apparently willing by that time to believe that Captain Cassedy could do anything with a submarine but haul horses in it.

The captain said that a horse was about the only thing that remained to be hauled in submarines, but assured the ensign that he wasn't thinking of that. He said that if the stranded men turned out to be cavalry there was nothing to prevent their swimming their horses out to the ship and taking the strain off the boat. Eventually Cook set off with his oarsmen and got into the lagoon to a spot where surf was breaking over a reef. He stood there and signaled the shore again.

He got no answer, although he repeated the signal every few minutes for an hour. The glow of the fire died down and the jungle was jet black behind the white ruff of the surf. Captain Cassedy, who had seen what was going on, signaled him to come back. The submarine submerged, and that was the end of the rescue for that day.

The next morning the captain looked out through the periscope and got something of a shock. A Jap destroyer was off the outer reef and apparently heading in. The submarine moved slowly out to fight in deeper water for, what with all the crazy signaling and the deserted campfire and the romping horsemen, he was prepared to believe that the Jap strategists had lured him in here for slaughter. No matter where he elected to fight the destroyer—or dodge it—he could see he was going to be in a bad spot. And while he was considering these matters the destroyer suddenly swung about and headed for the horizon.

Thinking it over, Cassedy decided that she had been merely sticking her nose into coves and inlets in the neighborhood without definite advance information of what she might find. So he was encouraged to resume his vigil on the bottom until night and try again to make contact with the Australians.

The second night, except that the boat needed no tinkering, was about the same as the first. The signal from the ship was answered promptly. The signal from the boat after it had gone as far as seemed safe in the lagoon was ignored. Ensign Cook stayed at his work that night for several hours and then came back to the ship. As he returned, the campfire started up again in the bush and the horsemen passed back and forth. But when the captain worked a blinker in the direction of the light nobody paid any attention to it. Eventually, toward morning, after repeated attempts to get some further recognition from the Australians, the boat was secured and the submarine dived for another day of waiting.

"It was beginning to get on my nerves," Captain Cassedy said in discussing it afterward. "There was something screwy some- where and I couldn't figure out where. . . . However, we had our orders and we tried it a third night."

This night, when the boat had come to the breakers, Ensign Cook went over the side and swam ashore. It wasn't easy because there were currents about the reef and he finally reached the beach in the middle of a thicket about a quarter of a mile from the glow of the fire. By walking out onto a spit of land he could see the fire among the trees and dim figures moving about it.

He flashed the recognition signal, then turned the light onto his face so that the Australians could see he was white. When that brought no results he shouted out who he was and why he was there, and put the light back on his face again. When nothing came of this, Ensign Cook shoved his flashlight into his belt and started to make his way through the swampy fringe of the jungle in the general direction of the fire. There was no secrecy about his progress. He crashed through the brush and splashed through water, and startled macaws woke up and flew overhead shrieking.

In spite of that there were still several men sitting about the campfire when he broke through enough of the screen to see it again. As he called out to them they scattered into the woods. He went up to the fire and examined it without learning anything. Then for half an hour he floundered about in the underbrush try- ing to catch one of the men to find out what he looked like.

He didn't find one, which was probably fortunate. Apparently they knew more about the jungle than he did.

He made his way back through the swamp without adventure, save that at one point he fell flat over a pig. That puzzled him, he told the captain when he got back to the submarine, because he couldn't figure out what they were doing with pigs in swamps. The captain looked at him quietly and pulled out for open water.

They made contact by wireless with their base that night, and received the disquieting news that this was no hoax, that com- munication had been established with the men on the island—who were in desperate straits—and that Captain Cassedy could pick them up the next night if he went to a designated cove on the other side of the entrace to the lagoon.

So they went there. Cook made another journey in with his boat and brought off seventeen men, all of them malarial, several badly shot up. Eighteen were left ashore—the ones least able to make the trip. A young lieutenant reported that Jap patrols had finally cornered them and had sent them an ultimatum—expiring the next morning—to the effect that if they did not surrender in a group they would be attacked and killed individually.

So Cook went back and brought out the other eighteen in two trips. Two men were so badly wounded that they could not swim out to the boat, a matter of only a few yards. Cook swam out with one strapped to his back. The other was brought out strapped to the back of another man whose name also turned out to be Cook. The captain thought maybe a numerologist or somebody could make something out of this, as a coincidence.

From what the Australians were able to tell of the matter it became apparent that Ensign Cook, after identifying himself, had actually raided the camp of the Japanese patrol, but in struggling through the jungle he had come into the back of it and so had encountered only the camp followers and bottlewashers, who were not armed. They hadn't allowed him to overtake them in the jungle because they didn't know whether he was armed or not.

Cook sat down on the deck in his wet skivvies as the ship began to get under way, and he gave this considerable thought.

"You were right about the submarine service, Captain," he said. "You said it had a lot of variety and it certainly has. . . . Japs in forests . . . pigs in swamps."

"I'll tell you about that pig," said the captain. "I asked the Aussies, and they confirmed my suspicions. The pig was a crocodile."

40

IDYL OFF JAPAN

CREED Burlingame has won the Navy Cross with a couple of buttons and is rated by his fellow officers and friends as one of the great individualists of the service. What with the secrecy that has covered submarine operations in the Pacific, I heard considerably less about his activities with his medal-winning ship than of his interesting ventures in ports—and quite a folklore has grown up about them. His days ashore seem to have been filled largely with carefree argument with brass hats, including numerous officers'-club managers and one or two generals of whose policies he did not approve. He keeps on going, with the accolade and prayers of the Navy Department, not because he adheres much to tradition and protocol but because he's good. As his executive officer observed, "A guy with his ideas has to be good."

He was in Honolulu when the war started and went out on one of the first patrols to the coast of Japan. In the patrol area he ran into the usual ring of trawlers, and so was one of the first of the submariners to learn about surface fighting. He learned with considerable blood, sweat and tears but he did learn, and his report of what he found out is still studied by the tacticians despite its discouraging detail.

Lieutenant Commander Frank Selby, who served with him on repeated patrols and is still his most enthusiastic biographer, is of two minds about what you can do with wooden-hulled spitkits, but he echoes his old captain in the certainty that one of the things you shouldn't do is fight them with 3-inch high-explosive shells in a rolling sea. Burlingame's submarine learned these things the same way the destroyer skippers learned at Wotje and Wake—the same way the gunnery officer of one rapid-fire cruiser discovered for himself at Shangri-La.

Captain Burlingame spotted the sampan. The sampan spotted the submarine. The skipper closed in for what he hoped would be a bit of morning machine-gun practice.

But it was rolling weather up there off the Japanese coast at that time of the year, and a submarine is no more steady than a destroyer under similar conditions. The gunnery officer posted his crews, figured his data and started to shoot. But, of course, neither the submarine nor the target would stand still. Fire control on a submarine at best can never be what you'd expect to find on, say, a battleship, so every roll meant new difficulties of calculation. The gunnery officer had with him the human element —the normal error that a man may be expected to make if he is required to pull a lever at the precise moment when the bubble on the quadrant centers. In addition to that there was a movement straight up and down in the long swell that automatically changed the angle of site, and there was little anybody could do about that except guess. At the same time, the target was rolling and changing its silhouette, and also rising up and down, so that a shell on perfect range when the sampan was low in the trough would be short when it rose to a crest.

"Well, anyway," said Lieutenant Commander Selby, "we closed on this thing and went to work. After the first couple of shots it didn't look as if he had any guns. Anyway he wasn't answering us. We could see men jumping around. I remember one guy came up out of what was probably an engine-room hatch forward. He took one look at the splashes around him and went down again and closed the hatch. There was no sign of a gun crew on the deck.

"The first couple of shots came fairly close and encouraged us. I believe we really got a couple of hits. But there is one great trouble when you start to use that kind of shell on a wooden ship. The slugs go right through her without causing too serious damage. Those crates will take an awful lot of holing above the water line before they get to the point where they won't function.

"After the first salvo we didn't do so well. The Jap skipper had all the advantage of maneuver. He kept swinging his stern to us to narrow the target, and he was bobbing up and down like something in a shooting gallery. So were we. He had pretty good speed, although that wasn't so much of a factor. We didn't want to get too close to him because we still weren't sure what he had.

"Well, we plastered that spitkit for a long time—it seemed to most of us like hours—and we certainly tossed a lot of shell at him. We knocked some of his superstructure off and he was still going.

"The gun crew was taking a hell of a beating. It's bad enough pasting shell when you're not being knocked all over the place. Two or three of the men went into the sea and had to be fished out again. It was almost impossible for anybody to stand up to his job. The waves were breaking over the deck most of the time and the water was cold.

"After a while we started to move in closer. There didn't seem to be any other way out of it. Somebody asked Captain Burlingame what he intended to do and he said maybe he ought to ram the thing. He didn't intend to, of course, but it began to look like a healthy idea.

"Getting closer didn't improve the artillery situation very much. When we'd about halved the distance a good roller would hide the target completely and we'd have to wait till it bobbed out again before taking another crack at it.

"Well, we got within a couple of hundred yards of it before we found out what we were in for. The Japs had a quick-firing gun and they suddenly turned loose a blast of it that threatened to take us apart.

"The first blast hit around the gun crew. The Number One loader got a smashed right arm in some fashion. The Number Two loader was dead before anybody could pick him up.

"It was bad medicine because they were so close in. The executive, who'd been out on deck, dodged behind the fairwater of the conning tower just as a slug hit the outside. It knocked a lot of paint chips into his face, went through the steel about half-way and left a dent sticking out right at the level of his eyes.

"All this happened in seconds. Even before the Japs turned loose their gun, our small guns were firing, and we cleaned off their deck at the second or third blast. And just about that time we began to get results with our big gun.

"There was one fantastic thing about it. We socked a shell

amidships and we knew that was the end of everything. Her bow began to come up out of the water and she was stopped cold. But before she had settled, the forward hatch opened again and a Jap —I supposed it was the same guy we'd seen before—shoved his head out. He took a look at the water breaking over the deck, and instead of making a dive for it he just went down the ladder again and closed the hatch behind him.

"The gun crew came staggering off the deck and they were as far gone as I ever hope to see human beings get. For that matter the tension had gone all through the boat. Nobody aboard was feeling very bright. The Number One loader got to the hatch, holding his arm, and then he fell through it. With his right hand smashed he'd been loading the gun with his left hand most of the time.

"We submerged, presumably to find out if we had any leaks but mostly to check up on the human damage. There was nothing we could do for the Number Two loader but the pharmacist's mate had plenty of work with the rest. Not that we had any list of wounded. But there were plenty of cuts and bruises and everybody was on the verge of collapse. I've never seen a ship in a worse state.

"I've seldom known it to fail that hard luck stacks up on you once it starts. If we could have put back into port somewhere for two weeks' rest it wouldn't have been any more than we needed to get back to battery again. But, so help me, we'd hardly begun to feel conscious again when we got a report of a mast over the horizon.

"It's situations like that, of course, that make you realize why submarine crews have to be trained the way they are. The word was passed, and the corpses got up off the deck and manned their battle stations and we went in. We didn't get that ship. She was a fast tanker, and what with the sea and our distance to begin with we couldn't hope to get in and out. We suspected that she probably had some friends with her but we never got a chance to find out. We were pretty low-spirited that day. It looked as if submarine war was going to mean work to the limit of human endurance with nothing much to show for it. . . ."

That night, as soon as the men had got somewhat settled and

were able to walk around again without stumbling, Captain Burlingame arranged for a burial at sea. . . . "They buried him darkly in dead of night. . . ." It was new work for a crew that had that day heard a hostile gun go off for the first time, and a dismal ending to a dismal battle. But there have probably been few more impressive funerals in the service. They sewed the dead gunner up in a canvas sack, took him up to the rolling deck and laid a flag over him. All of the crew who could be spared from their stations mustered before the conning tower, and the captain, a bit nervous, conducted the burial service.

"He made a brief talk," Lieutenant Commander Selby recalls. "Considering the circumstances nobody will ever make a better one. This was our first casualty and it couldn't help but have its effect on the personnel. I could see the executive looking now and then at the dent in the conning tower and I knew he was thinking how close we had come to having a double funeral.

"The night was overcast and the sea still rolling. But we were a little glad of that. I don't think we could have stood the sight of another mast on the horizon right then. There's something depressing about leaving a man out there in an empty sea with the whitecaps breaking over him and the wind howling. It gives you an idea of the permanence and loneliness of death as you'll get it nowhere else except maybe in a prairie cemetery in a blizzard. And every man in the ship's company was just about at the end of his tether anyway."

Captain Burlingame finished quickly with what he had to say about what it means to give up one's life in line of duty and then he recited the Lord's Prayer. The body slid over the side and everybody went down to take up his business again.

When they got down to the wardroom they could see that the captain was still upset.

"It was a tough job," he said. "I was halfway through the prayer before I could be sure that I was saying the Lord's Prayer and not 'Now I lay me down to sleep.' I haven't a very good repertoire of prayers."

The other officers told him that he had done well and he seemed cheered up a little.

"I wouldn't want that lad, wherever he is, to think that I'd let him down at a time like this," he said.

So they went on to the coast of Japan without incident and, one judges, without much revival of spirit. Technically they were a crack crew, one of the best organizations of their kind in the world. In practice of actual war they were tyros. Save for the fight with the sampan in which they did not feel that they had conducted themselves with much distinction, they had had no experience in battle. They had met the enemy and they had lost a man, and they had taken a severe blow to their pride. It was only normal that many of them should have been wondering, during the long perilous miles between the outer patrol zone and the end of the island, whether they were going to turn out to be any good or not.

A week later they were in their area off the coast of Japan and they began to hope again. They didn't do anything immediately. Coastal shipping in and out of the port they had been assigned to watch was well protected and took a lot of study. They were in a difficult zone with a narrow strait between them and the port and shallow water on all sides of them. To the south of them, however, there was opportunity in plenty. The deep water runs close to the shore and all the Japanese ships had to follow this route. This meant that submarines operating in the area also had to get close to the shore—so close that it's not remarkable some of them saw horse races and roller coasters and railroad trains and airfields. There is something weird to think about in their unending vigil— the eyes from another world ceaselessly watching an unsuspecting enemy and occasionally checking up on his finish.

They watched the toil in the rice fields and along the loading platforms and docks at the seaside. They studied with interest the scenery of tidy landscapes rising in steps to the blue hills. And they reported appreciatively on such things, for they were paying a longer visit than most tourists to one of the most interesting spots in all Japan.

They marked the traffic that ran like something in an old-fashioned magic-lantern slide down the thin little band of road beyond the sands, trucks and army cars mostly, the only proof from where they could look at it that this toy kingdom was actually at war—actually the conscienceless menace that had wrecked a fleet in Pearl Harbor and was strong enough to send hordes of vicious little soldiers armed with vicious little machine guns and deadly little shoofly-kite airplanes to threaten the continent of Australia.

On days of religious significance they could see crowds of old women in gray kimonos and streams of little children in flowery wrappings pass through the red torii to shrines back in the greenery. There was a solemnity about these processions that they could discern even though they were unable to see the votaries save as masses of shadow and color, for the movement was slow and rhythmic with none of the lively disorder that travelers' tales have always associated with Japanese holidays.

It was a strange world—a world filled with unexpected flower gardens and gracefully curving roofs of yellow tile—and an unreal world, like that of the old colored travelogue movies, with no dull commentator's voice to interpret it to the men from the deep who lay unseen and unsuspected a few hundred yards offshore.

At night when the engines were quiet they could sometimes hear temple bells thin and tinkly in the distance behind the more familiar sounds of rattling trains and locomotive whistles. But that was not often. Generally the pictures that they built up for themselves from the odd fragments that crossed the periscope scale were silent.

There was a house on a point of land where Captain Burlingame's submarine did most of its patient cruising . . . rather a good house as such things go in Japan. And in time the crew got up an imaginative interest in its occupants. The beach was blacked out at night—much more efficiently than some of the rest of the world is blacked out. But even so there were nights of brilliant moonlight and there were moments when the life of this region had few secrets. Captain Burlingame declared that he had learned all about the intimate routine of the folks in the house on the point and he enlivened otherwise dull hours of the patrol with a sort of impromptu society column, recounting his discoveries.

He issued sundry bulletins about the daily doings of Papa San and Mama San and Baby San and the lesser people in the house—

where they went by day . . . what they had to eat in the evening . . . how they amused themselves. Nobody aboard the boat could find any fault with his accuracy since he was in sole charge of the periscope most of the time. And as for his sources of information, aside from the ghostly visions in the lenses, the men all knew that time after time the submarine had gone in almost to the beach, chasing the shadowy tankers and cargo carriers that were almost continually passing. . . . And while targets take up a lot of one's attention there seemed no reason why the trained eye of a submarine skipper could not have taken in a lot of interesting detail about less important things.

This region, naturally, was not the most populous part of the coast—otherwise it probably would not have been selected as a good spot for submarine operation. But it was populous enough. And what was more important, the people minded their own business. Even after the wreckage of ships that Burlingame had sunk began to clutter the beach, and the deep blue water was black with oil, the activity ashore went on unchanged. There was something idyllic about it all.

Each night the radio was tuned in to the English broadcast of Radio Tokyo, and Tokyo Rose became a favorite with the crew as she had already become with the bored men of the surface ships. They liked particularly her stories of the efficient iron ring that protected Japan against marauding submarines. They applauded her announcements of new arrangements to protect Japan's shipping against this puny and ineffectual menace. They felt, almost, that they were a part of the celebration which greeted the returning submarine skipper who had shelled the Pacific coast. But it puzzled them a little to hear her indignation against American submarines lying off Japan while she recited the brave deeds of Japanese submariners who, full of righteous zeal and *Bushido*, were trying less efficiently to do a similar job off the coast of the United States. It seemed to some of them that from Rose's point of view submarine warfare could be justified only to the extent that it didn't do much damage.

In one way they had a nice spot for their work—good scenery, avoidable competition, a constant supply of targets. But there were drawbacks. Ships following the deep water close to the land were hard to see at night, particularly when there was no moon. Some of them, with the rising greenery behind them and a light haze on the shimmering sea through which they rode, were hard to follow in daylight. In the matter of lighting, a submarine was necessarily at a disadvantage because it must always lie with the sea and sky behind it. Maneuver out from the beach was restricted by shallow waters which sometimes were as clear as a mountain lake. Maneuver in toward the beach brought complications from airplanes, patrol boats and similar nuisances.

"One got away from us that I shall always remember," said Lieutenant Commander Selby. "We were only vaguely aware of her. Not until she was almost on top of us could the captain be sure that he was looking at a ship at all and not some play of the wind in the foliage ashore. We had made an approach, but since it had been impossible to make out what we were approaching, we couldn't judge her speed. And when finally we saw her, bulking up like a block of houses in the gloom, we were in a position from which we couldn't fire. She went by us, towering over us, one of the biggest ships I ever saw—loaded, I suppose, with troops and supplies for the Southwest Pacific. She was over us and then she was gone. We felt pretty low about it for a long time. A little more light, a little more luck and we'd have piled her right up on somebody's front lawn. But the luck wasn't there. . . . Not that night."

The submariners noticed that one patrol boat had a permanent beat along their area—much as they had themselves. But in time they came to resent it. They had been there first.

There were other patrol boats—a string of destroyers taking turns at making life unbearable for underwater visitors. But no matter how many or how few of them joined the parade back and forth from the port to the north, *Old Nuisance*, as she was affectionately called, was always there. The boys came to plot her harm with considerable more energy and intent than they might have wasted on a larger ship. They felt that as a matter of pride they ought to eliminate this pest before all others.

So they made a couple of other unfortunate approaches. *Old Nuisance* was coy. *Old Nuisance* was wary. *Old Nuisance* had good sound apparatus. She dodged them as they came in. She lambasted them plentifully as they went out.

Once they almost got her and missed. She swung about with considerable courage, as the torpedo cleared her, and began to spread out her ash cans. But by that time Burlingame had figured out just what she was likely to do and he was behind her and coming up when she was outward bound. He might have eliminated her then but there was a distraction. Ahead of him was a tanker proceeding like a duck down toward the corner where Papa San lived. So he made a half-turn and blasted the tanker.

It was light on the beach that night for the first time since the coming of war and the blackout—a gala night for everybody except the Japanese. . . . Burning oil spread out into the water so far that *Old Nuisance* was in trouble of her own. And though the depth charges came down with regularity the direction was nothing to brag about. The U. S. submarine came up that night as usual to charge batteries, and in the smoky light of the fire got a good view of what was going on ashore after dark. After that night Captain Burlingame had no need to guess the activities of the family of Papa San and Mama San and their friends. He knew.

The destroyers prowled the area all the next day and spread their bombs recklessly. But the crew of the submarine took it in their stride and somewhat contemptuously. They were pretty sure of themselves now—confident that they could get on pretty well with their jobs.

A few hours later they crossed in toward the beach again. A convoy was coming down with a sizable escort. They joined up with this procession in the darkness, turned with perfect timing and put two fish into a ship which may have been a cargo carrier or a liner converted to transport duty. Pieces of the ship were on the beach when they went away.

They got their comeuppance for that—or they nearly did. The frantic destroyers zoned every part of the ocean with depth charges. And the submarine learned a lot about the difficulty of evasive tactics in water at times hardly deep enough to cover the conning tower. By daylight they had come back to deep water and drifted south. The bombs were no fewer but the maneuverability was better and they got out of trouble eventually with the luck that Burlingame had contrived out of his own skill.

They surfaced and charged back to their old parade ground. Then they resumed their pleasant inventory of the doings of Papa San and Mama San and the lovely Japanese scenery.

A few days later they blew a ship apart and blasted another ineffectual fish at *Old Nuisance*. Then, reasonably well pleased with themselves, they turned around to go home.

They were south of Japan one day when they discovered another submarine lazing along on the surface, presumably headed for Tokyo Bay. Captain Burlingame studied the Japanese characters on her conning tower and readied a torpedo.

"It's a shame to do this," he observed. "Strictly unprofessional. If submarines take to shooting at submarines there'll be no living in them. Fire One! Fire Two!"

The Japanese submarine disintegrated before his eyes as he resumed his course to Honolulu. No destroyers chased him. No patrol boats came out to drop their ash cans. Submarines have only themselves to protect them from other submarines. And nobody's submarine can be expected to have any friends.

On the way around the end of the island Captain Burlingame sighted another trawler or patrol boat and, briefly, he closed in to do battle. But there are difficulties about battle at night. You can't tell how big your enemy is—nor exactly where he is. Maybe it's a small boat close at hand. Maybe it's a big boat far away. And what armament it carries is something you don't discover until you're committed to battle. The submarine maneuvered about for a while trying to get an advantageous position from which to fire deck guns and then discovered that the target was trying the same tactics.

"We'll wait for daylight before monkeying with that one," the captain decided. And in the morning it was gone.

On another patrol Captain Burlingame was assigned to his old corner. It had been the intent of Comsubpac to send him somewhere else but at the last minute he was headed west out of Pearl Harbor to resume his studies of Papa San and Mama San. They probably never knew he was there—the pity of it!

Nothing much had changed in the old neighborhood. The debris of sunken ships had been swept up off the beach. People still wandered the roads or worked the fields or passed to the hidden shrines under the red torii that stood out like Chinese hieroglyphics against the hills. *Old Nuisance* was still running up and down the deep-water channel near the shore, and Burlingame fired a few fish at her just as a matter of routine. He missed, what with the dark masses of the land confusing his sight and the sound apparatus of the patrol boat announcing his advent. He took up his old stand and skated about much as he had done before. And when time and light permitted, he drove in once more toward the beach. . . .

He sank several thousand tons of shipping that time and got another star for his Navy Cross. It may not have been a spectacular accomplishment but it was skillful work and the score was good. Papa San and Mama San and Baby San didn't have far to look to see most of the blasting. Tokyo Rose, speaking no doubt in their behalf, said that it was a very great outrage.

PORTRAIT OF A LETTER WRITER

To MUCH of the Navy—surface and submarine—Lieutenant Commander J. W. ("Red") Coe is known as a handy letter writer with a gift for upsetting the well-figured routine of distant supply officers. In a way that is as it should be, for no better communication on its subject is to be found in the English language than the masterly composition reproduced in the Appendix of this book. A couple of fleets laughed at it at a time when laughs were few. An admiral gave it his personal attention. A lot of lesser figures will be haunted by it for the rest of this war if not for the rest of their lives. But it occurs to one who has talked with the men who served with "Red" Coe in the Southwest Pacific that some of his other skills may have been overlooked by the friends of literature who mimeographed his work and spread it broadcast. It doesn't seem likely that they hung the Navy Cross on him for writing letters.

Coe, whom I met in Portsmouth and in subsequent scientific research in New York, is a quiet, companionable young man whose ways are marked by modesty and gentleness. Like the other submarine skippers, he has a ready sense of humor and a bright acquisitive mind, which attributes, coupled with a wit sharper than most and a gift for facile expression, might deceive one unacquainted with his branch of the service. That a world so ruled by people with long faces and undertakers' voices should appreciate him is remarkable. But he retained the respect of the people he had set to laughing. Alongside that, the fact that he is rated as one of the best commanders in the underwater fleet seems an accomplishment hardly worth mentioning.

Back in port in the early days of the war he wrote his famous requisition for paper. Nothing came of it—not until long months afterward when somebody in the Navy supply office at Mare Island sheepishly made it public. In the meantime Coe, who through force of necessity had forgotten all about it, had other things to occupy his time.

He was stationed in Manila before the beginning of the war, and like many another of the Asiatic fleet started for battle in one of the antiquated S-boats. He was ready for it, although as he says himself he didn't have much idea what it was going to be like.

All during the fall he had been running pseudo-war patrols from Manila along the obvious invasion route from the China coast, and he was out on his station one fine December morning when he learned that the Japanese had blasted Pearl Harbor. He sat down at his desk in the crowded pipe that was his home-from-home and tried to realize what it all meant.

From where he could see, across the still waters to the palm-fringed shore and on into the mountains beyond, nothing had changed from the time he had first looked at it. There were the contours of the land just as they had always been on the charts. Up over the horizon was a sleepy port in and out of which a lot of third-rate shipping occasionally crawled. The sea was just the same as it had been during his years of service. And yet, of course, nothing was the same. . . . The sea was a wide highway over which the enemy must presently come charging. The land over on his quarter was land occupied by the same unscrupulous horde that had descended upon Hawaii. The port up ahead was an enemy port. And when next he looked at a ship flying the white flag with the red ball in it, she would be an enemy ship. This transition from peace to war was something that it was going to take the crew some time to understand. For that matter, as it turned out, it was going to take some time for him to understand it himself. He got under way and approached the north edge of his patrol.

It would have been simpler at the moment if trouble had developed immediately. There would have been less time to look out at a peaceful, familiar scene and try to imagine it as something else. But the war did not come to him immediately. The Japanese, even then gathering for their attack on the Philippines, were deliberate about it. Life in the port seemed unperturbed. What ships were inside on December 8, 1941 (East Longitude), stayed where they were and no newcomers came over the horizon.

Then one morning there were signs of activity in the bay—smoke in the sky and the hazy silhouettes of vessels moving about in the mist. While he was studying these signs and portents he caught sight of masts on the horizon and then a funnel. A merchantman came over the rim of the sea standing in. He made out briefly a feathery streak off his port bow that he thought might be a submarine—a Japanese submarine, he knew, because no other boat of ours was in the vicinity. The boat had submerged, and he could see no luck in looking for it, but even so he knew that he wouldn't have to wait long, now, for the war to begin.

He was fairly close to shore when the merchantman came into view steaming squarely for the port, and for a long time he studied the lines of a ship whose type had only recently been a common sight in all the ports of the world. He noted the white flag with the red ball and reminded himself that this was the enemy. It still seemed difficult to believe.

He has said since that nobody in those days knew much about submarine warfare . . . a lot of things were to be done wrong before a great proportion of them were ever going to be done right. But he knew his boat. He knew the technique of maneuver as taught in the target practices. He took his sights and moved in for his approach.

He was between the ship and the land when he fired his first torpedo—a good position in some respects but lacking in others if you consider that a well-established enemy base was behind him. The fish hit squarely and the Jap merchantman lifted up out of the water.

It was a tremendous spectacle and for a moment it hypnotized him. The red ball seemed to fill the periscope and under it a ship was trembling and putting out great doughnuts of smoke and starting to sink. He stood there so fascinated that he never noticed the destroyers coming out after him until they were well on their way.

He recovered in time to swing the periscope and take a short look at them. He dived then—in time—but not before he had seen the awesome picture of the ship's stern coming up out of the water, her nose going under in an ocean that no longer looked familiar.

Things went smoothly and with peacetime precision after that. The boat was rigged for depth charges as she went down. A calmly expectant crew stood at battle stations awaiting the blasts with which they were acquainted so far only through hearsay. "Red" Coe in a few seconds was aware that he had a good crew— a crew that would stand up to it no matter what happened. He waited a few tense seconds while the screws of the destroyers went growling by overhead and then realized that nothing was happening. The bombs weren't falling—neither then nor later. Then presently Sound reported that the cans had circled about and were on their way back to port.

During the next few hours, submerged, he tried to figure out what had happened. The cans had been on top of him and the ship taking her final shiver out there beyond him had been proof enough of his presence. It still seemed impossible that he should have escaped a blasting from everything that they could bring to dump on him. And then he remembered the glimpse he had had of the periscope feather off his bow. That, and bull luck, and the fact that a lot of the Japanese were sharing his own trouble in remembering that a war had begun, had saved him from a raking. The Japs undoubtedly knew that one of their own submarines was in the area, and with their sound apparatus picking up a pair of them they couldn't be sure which was which.

"I was thankful," he said. "I didn't quarrel with my luck. But it taught me one thing: It's bad policy to stay up admiring your own handiwork when destroyers are coming after you. . . ."

On his next patrol Captain Coe was sent out on a rescue mission. Some fifty Australian aviators who had been moving a base had grounded on a little island in the Java Sea, and the Japs who knew they were somewhere in the vicinity had been looking for them. After some delay the Aussies had got a transmitter working and sent out an S.O.S. Captain Coe's boat was ordered to locate them on their island and take them off.

With time an essential factor it was discouraging work. The little submarine had a long haul to get to the spot, and, once arrived, found itself in a zone that promised plenty of trouble.

Japanese destroyers and patrol boats were ranging the area. Japanese bombers were overhead. To approach the island at all was a ticklish job.

Despite all that, the submarine got to the rendezvous point in good order and in good time. There were no indications that the Japanese had occupied the place. It seemed that all that remained to be done was to signal the aviators and take them off.

But it turned out to be not so simple as that. Captain Coe moved as close inshore as he dared and began to flash cautious signals into the bush. He got no answer and at daylight had to withdraw and submerge.

The next night he tried it again, hoping that no loitering cans were any place near enough to see him. But the mat of palms and scrub stayed black while the flasher worked, and a tentative radio call brought no response. So went another night.

On the third night Captain Coe and a few of his crew went ashore. They started at one end of the island and worked their way through it to the other but for a long time they found so signs of life. The aviators were gone undoubtedly. Where they had gone he could guess when one of the men picked out the outlines of many footprints on the beach. Significantly all of them were leading down through the sand to the water's edge. . . . The captain for a moment felt something as Robinson Crusoe must have felt . . . and then he was suddenly sorry for these aviators he had never seen and never would see. The Japs had just been there.

He got back to his boat before dawn and was on his way just as a pair of Japanese destroyers came nosing along the coast looking for him. They probably had been around the island most of the night.

He was ordered back into the war after that and started to earn the title that his crew was to give him throughout the service: "Oil Tanker Coe." One morning among the Javanese islands he came upon an oil ship of the new naval type, well down in the water. She was traveling with an escort of destroyers.

Because of her position off land and in shallow water she was difficult to approach, but Captain Coe, who had learned a lot since his encounter with the merchantmen off the China coast, evaded the destroyers without being seen, jockeyed himself into a position forward of the tanker's beam, and put two fish into her. She blew up while he looked at her although this time he didn't waste many seconds on inventory. Fire burst from her all along her length and her bows were under when he dived and heard the cans come streaking after him.

The spot where Captain Coe went down wasn't very deep nor well charted. He was in an awkward position for the usual evasive tactics, but even so he was surprised at the persistence of the bombing. The ship stood up to it well—as was the fashion of those old boats—but she took some jarring that smashed part of her electrical apparatus and chipped off her ancient accumulations of paint. Captain Coe was not disturbed so much about that as by the fact that the blasting seemed likely never to stop. No matter where he went or at what speed, the cans followed, and the clunks came down with the same accuracy he had noticed in the string that followed his dive.

He cut down his speed to virtually nothing save what was needed to keep the boat down—a speed at which he would have been certain no sound apparatus could have picked up his motor noises. And still the attack went on.

At that point the diving officer reported that they seemed to be slithering along in mud, and he got a flash of second sight. He took the boat up to twenty feet less depth and began to move again. The crashes diminished in intensity and then in number. And after a while Sound called that the destroyer screws seemed to be "going over the hill." He had figured it out all right, as he was able to see as soon as he could stick up the periscope. The submarine had been scraping her keel through liquid mud and, turning her propellers over slowly, had put up dense yellow-gray clouds of this muck to guide the huntsmen on their way. . . .

"The chart showed plenty of depth," he said. "But it just wasn't there."

Up off China again they blew up another ship, a freighter. They made good diving time on that one because somebody threw a slug under their tail and helped them. But they had no unusually harrowing experience. A few ash cans came from somewhere but presently there was silence in the sound apparatus and they went up to look around. The ocean was littered with floating stuff. Apparently the ship had been carrying something in bales and most of the bales had come loose when she broke up. It looked as if there might be several acres of this stuff and to Captain Coe it seemed that there were at least fifty Japs hanging onto every bale. The skipper and his crew began to realize how many people any Japanese ship was likely to be carrying.

A few days later he came onto a convoy of ships and an escorting destroyer. The captain, reversing his usual tactics, went in and picked off the last ship.

"I let them go in a spread," he said, describing it. "One of them hit the ship right in the duff and he just folded up in the middle. He was sinking, tail down, in a couple of seconds. Whether any of the other fish hit anything else or not I don't know. It seems very likely that they did."

He dived at once and the destroyer came over and dropped depth charges—a vicious and well-calculated bombardment. The boat was in dead silence for some time after the last blast had gone . . . something of an ominous sign. And then, suddenly, one of the black gang piped up cheerily:

"Say, Captain, this is payday, ain't it?"

"It certainly is," said the captain. "And believe me, boy, you just about got paid off."

They checked for leaks and the usual damage, and found nothing much to worry them.

"But I learned another lesson," the captain said. "When there's a destroyer around, go for that first. If you get him, he'll not get you."

On the way back from that patrol they ran into two transports escorting themselves. The submarine was on the surface charging batteries when these big blots came up over the horizon. Captain Coe put on speed and ran around them. He fired at the first and missed. He fired at the second and blew it to bits. The first one came back to pick up survivors and at that point, the captain says, he got buck fever or something. He fired another and missed. The ship turned tail and went over the horizon.

The one he had sunk didn't seem so large or so important as the one that got away, and he was much concerned about it until he came into port. Then he learned that this ship had been bringing troops and technicians to work the oil fields and rubber factories and other industries that the Japs had taken over in occupied territory. Their loss was undoubtedly one of the worst blows Hirohito had so far received.

Captain Coe left his S-boat after that and went aboard a more modern command. He went up onto the edge of the spreading invasion, and just outside a flourishing base found a target that came close to finishing him. He closed on some sort of Q-ship that looked bigger than she was and had virtually no draft at all. The fish he fired at her was straight in line but went under.

"After that," he said, "she let us have it, and she was certainly loaded for us. She must have hit everything in our neighborhood except us."

The men were somewhat shaken after that experience. Luck didn't seem to be riding any too close to them. And then of a sudden they saw a tanker coming out of a hazy evening to stand almost alongside them. Captain Coe sized up the situation in a quick glance around. A couple of destroyers were coming out from port to escort her, and it occurred to him as he pressed the button that she had certainly chosen the wrong spot for a rendezvous. He blasted her with two fish and had time to see the usual Vesuvius of flame from her middle as she started under.

There was no doubt in anybody's mind that she was finished. Even over the bedlam of the depth charges the crew could hear the characteristic noises of her breakup. But nobody saw her finish this time save the Japs. She was another naval tanker such as the one Captain Coe had sunk on an earlier patrol.

Some weeks later he was north of the Solomons cruising about, and one night met two ships apparently heading for Rabaul. He shot a spread of torpedoes and sank one. The other, instead of running away, came about and began to throw depth charges. The captain felt exasperated at this foolishness and chased her.

Most of this maneuver was guesswork because he was able to see her only once or twice under an overcast sky. In the morning, however, he found that the navigator had figured her course accurately. He caught up with her unseen, fired another torpedo and missed again.

END OF A SURFACE FIGHT

Japanese supply ship set afire by gunfire from deck of U. S. submarine is listing to starboard and about to sink.

BATTLE STATIONS

"I can't explain stuff like that," he said. "It just happens. They were certainly expecting us on that second attack. Everybody on the ship was above decks along the rails and in the rigging watching for us. In spite of all that, we got in for a shot and it didn't do us any good."

They blew up a freighter on that patrol. It was carrying a load of bombers on deck.

"I should think," Captain Coe said, "that a ship carrying a deckload of bombers would be likely to run into pretty heavy tonnage. But of course our estimates have to be based on the silhouettes and other information available to us."

He returned to the Solomons later and ran into a lot of well-protected shipping. At that time the Japs were relying on the ability of fast merchant ships to get away from submarines and to protect one another. All had depth charges and deck guns fore and aft. Whenever he attacked one, the other was certain to close in and drop a load of bombs. Also they had developed a new technique of counterattack which wasn't so bad except that it seldom worked.

After a couple of months in that area he was called into Pearl Harbor for overhaul. On the way north he came onto a tanker all by herself and he made an approach. He was just getting into position to shoot when a patrol boat came out from the blind spot behind her and charged at him. He fired his fish and thinks he may have hit but he had no way of finding out.

"The going-over we got," he says, "was something unforgettable. It was pretty apparent then that the Japanese sound men were getting better. Another patrol boat came out from somewhere and we thought for a time we were going to stay right there. . . . When we got up finally and found we had no bones broken we decided maybe we'd better get on about our business, and we headed for Pearl."

The captain came into Pearl Harbor unsuspecting that his fame had preceded him. He got up to the dock and threw over his lines and then became aware of a brass band and a large reception committee. He noticed vaguely that the trees and lampposts along the shore had been hung with streamers of white tissue paper. Some sort of gala was in progress, he felt, but he couldn't see that it had anything to do with him.

He went ashore and met the admiral who was standing with a large retinue behind him. Prominent in the assemblage were two large men carrying on their shoulders a long rod like the support of the chairs in which Hong Kong coolies once used to bear lazy riders up the hill. But on the rod was no chair—only about fifty rolls of paper, labeled and easily identifiable even by a Mare Island supply officer.

"Welcome home and congratulations," greeted the admiral. "And here's the stuff you requisitioned a couple of years ago."

42

A FISH-EYE VIEW OF THE BATTLE
OF MIDWAY

I FIRST met Commander William H. Brockman one midnight in San Francisco when I came aboard a naval supply ship, the first vessel to venture westward after the Japanese visitation on Pearl Harbor. And from him, also, I first learned a few things about U. S. submarines, for he was not only the first but the only one of our underwater skippers I had ever seen. I recall that as he came into the little wardroom and genially poured a cup of coffee for me I was definitely puzzled. He wore the dolphins and he talked easily of his service but he certainly shocked my preconceived notions of what a professional submariner would be like. In the first place he was a big, well-muscled man who looked as if he might have been a pretty good fullback somewhere. And I had imagined that only the thin sailors and the short ever could bear the life in what we used to call pig boats. In the second place he was pleasant, humorous and thoughtful of other people, and I had believed that all submarine officers must live in eternal consciousness of the perils of their trade and meet the world with grim faces and harsh manners. It was a little disconcerting.

His good cheer was the more remarkable in that he had no illusions about where he was going or the job he was likely to get.

"At the moment I'm a relief skipper," he said. "But they'll probably give me a boat. The submarines are going to have to fight this war just about by themselves for the next few months and there'll be plenty of work."

He laughed at my suggestion that life in the submarines might be tough going even without any war. (I recall mentioning that I considered them all potential *Squaluses*.)

"A lot of people think that," he said. "But it's not true. You can live a long time in the submarines, and you can live fairly well and comfortably. It's really the safest service in the world. But you mustn't make any mistakes in it."

So I was surprised to see him come in from a watch at midnight a few nights later genuinely disturbed.

"We're taking our lives in our hands on this ship," he said. "The funnel out there is sending up flame and sparks until we look like a floating volcano. We're a setup for any Jap submarine that happens to be in the vicinity. And just to make it easier for an attack we've been putting out clouds of smoke all day." He wasn't smiling as he sat down and stirred his coffee. "Honestly," he said, "I've never felt more uncomfortable in my life."

And I thought of that many times later. The idea of a submarine skipper worrying because he might be killed before he could get his duffel stowed in some submersible deathtrap in Pearl Harbor seemed incomprehensible. I was only just beginning to understand last summer when they pinned the Navy Cross on him and dispatches from the Pacific began to refer to his utterly fantastic accomplishments.

I said good-by to him when the surface fleet started for the Marshalls. He was still on the beach but still hopeful of getting a command soon. When we came back to Pearl Harbor he was somewhere on his way and I did not see him again. It was from Lieutenant Commander Thomas Hogan, his former executive waiting for a boat of his own in New London, that I heard his story. I am putting it down here as told to me, briefly and somewhat baldly. It needs no embellishment.

Lieutenant Commander Hogan was already second in command of the boat when Commander Brockman arrived as a relief captain. Where the new skipper had been in the months before that I haven't heard, but nowhere could he have been any closer to potential trouble.

"We had been expecting orders to make a patrol off Japan," said Hogan, "but instead we got orders to an area not far from Midway Island. We left Honolulu without much enthusiasm. . . ."

Honolulu was jittery at that time with tales of strange wars being fought in the neighborhood of Wake Island, and the alert had been on continuously for a couple of days. But the submariners, who knew that the gossip had no foundation, were unable to figure what good they were going to do up there with the gooney birds for their sole companions in a watery wilderness. And, wondering, they set out for their post.

They got to their area without incident or enlightenment, and then began to cruise about.

Then, on the morning of the fourth of June, they intercepted a report from one of the Catalinas that a big flight of Japanese planes had been sighted heading toward Midway. The bearings were given to Captain Brockman who traced them on the chart with his finger.

"My God!" he said. "They're almost on top of us."

Brockman moved over as fast as he could and got there just about the time the planes did.

"They spotted us right away," said Lieutenant Commander Hogan. "They took a little time to drop bombs on us but we dived and got out of it. We came back up in a different spot and kept sticking up the periscope every few minutes and then all of a sudden the captain began to mumble something. We were right in the middle of the whole Jap fleet.

"It was something to raise your hair when the captain began to inventory what he saw. He was calm about it but I don't know why.

" 'On the port bow, a battleship and some cruisers. Ahead, more cruisers and destroyers. To starboard, cruisers, cruisers, cruisers! Behind them, four carriers. . . . Cruisers and destroyers alongside the carriers.'

"The captain made up his plans in a hurry.

" 'Ready all tubes!' he said. 'The battleship is one of the *Isei* class. Our target is one of the carriers. But we'll take a shot at the battleship as we go by.' "

(I have since thought that one should take a high place among the great phrases of the war.)

"He gave us our bearings and we started for the attack," said Lieutenant Commander Hogan. "A couple of cruisers over to the starboard looked as if they might be taken although they were too far away for a good shot. But we didn't have to worry about them very long because we heard a roar astern and a couple of blasts and a destroyer came right over us. Before we could haul in the periscope a cruiser came bearing down on us from the opposite side doing about thirty knots. We heard that one go over, too.

"We didn't have to make any run for our target because it was still coming straight at us. When we came up again we were really in the middle of the fleet. The sea fore and aft of us and on all sides was literally covered with ships. The battleship was only a few hundred yards off our port and she opened up on our periscope with her main battery. A couple of fourteen-inch shells were almost on top of us but we dived before they could close the straddle. We got down and meditated and heard the battleship rumbling out of the formation. . . . We'd done that much anyway.

"While we were down there we first learned that a battle was going on. Before that we had figured everything was one-sided. We began to hear a lot of shooting and any number of surface explosions. That was the time Squadron Eight came in with the torpedoes.

"Of course by this time we knew what the setup was. That is, we knew what the Japs had and something of what we had. And in the circumstances it wasn't very heartening to listen to a battle that we couldn't see.

"While the rumble was going on we did all that we could do. We kept shoving around toward where we thought the carriers were going to be. The Japs in the meantime apparently had forgotten about us. They had quite a lot of other things to think about although at the time we didn't realize that. The sound man kept reporting heavy screws over us and every once in a while we could hear the rumble of a fast destroyer. But there weren't any depth charges.

"When the noise had quieted a little we came up again. The fleet had scattered. We didn't know then how much of it was on the bottom. Three or four piles of black smoke were billowing over toward the horizon. Three of the carriers had disappeared but one was still with us. She was moving about six knots and she was burning like a haystack.

"We moved on over there and then a cruiser came around the corner. We hadn't seen it in the smoke. We fired a couple of fish at it and dived. We heard a crash and thought we had hit it but we couldn't be sure because just about that time the depth charges began to come down. The sound man reported that he hadn't been able to hear the cruiser's screws after the first explosion, which is a pretty good sign. But we had no way of looking out through the hull to see whether or not she was coming down alongside us. I'm quite sure that at any rate we did her some damage. When we came up again about half an hour later there was no sign of her.

"We'd been taking a pretty bad beating through all this and the men weren't used to it. Somebody suggested to Captain Brockman that maybe we'd better stay submerged until things sounded a little better up topside.

" 'Hell, no!' he said. 'We're going to get a couple of these things.'

"So we came up again and this time we were only six or eight hundred yards from the carrier. She had a couple of cruisers with her. They'd got the fire out and she was picking up speed.

"We maneuvered a little to try to get into a better firing position. We hung onto the parade for a couple of hours because the escort kept getting in our way. But pretty soon she'd got a couple more boilers going and we figured that in another few minutes we'd lose her entirely. So Captain Brockman swung into the best angle he could get and fired four torpedoes. Three of them hit.

"We took her down and listened to the depth charges. After about an hour we came up for another look and she was really afire this time, and down by the stern. We thought maybe we could stay there and see her cook. But a destroyer was on our tail almost immediately and we had to dive again. I don't know how many depth charges we got. It seemed to me that there was never a minute when we weren't hearing them. But everybody was so keyed up by that time that they didn't seem to count.

"About 6:00 P.M. things quieted down again and the captain and I went into the wardroom for a bite to eat. We were just sitting down when there was a terrific blast.

" 'Who's depth-charging us now and how did he get there?' the captain wanted to know. We got up and ran into the control room. The sound man was standing there looking sheepish, and the officer of the deck was white as a sheet.

"The O.D. was at the periscope. He'd been shoving it up and down every five minutes.

" 'But there's nothing up there,' he yelled before the captain could say anything. 'Honest to God, there isn't a thing. And there wasn't any sound of anything either.'

"Just then there was another explosion that set us rolling. The captain took a look through the periscope for himself and mumbled something. The horizon was empty all around and there was nothing on the sea except a lot of oil and scraps of wreckage.

"Then we began to hear other sounds—smashing, crackling sounds. The boat was full of them. . . .

"Once you've had a chance to hear a ship sinking and have identified the sound for what it is, you'll never mistake it for anything else—the breaking up of the underwater compartments and the grinding of steel bulkheads under pressure. We just stood around and listened to the *Soryu* tearing herself to pieces on the way to the bottom.

"We came on up and all was serene. There wasn't a sign of a ship anywhere or any sign of a battle except for the stuff floating around in the water. The *Soryu* was certainly gone. But we hadn't seen her sink. So we turned in a report that we had hit her and damaged her. We still had no way of telling how the battle had gone.

"We surfaced and charged batteries, and we were pretty glad when we got the job done without any interruption. We knew that all sorts of Jap ships were in the vicinity and figured it was quite likely that some of them might be on the prowl looking for us.

"In the morning, just as we were ready to dive, we got orders to close in on Midway. We couldn't tell what that meant, either. It looked, of course, as if the Japs had not yet finished their attack.

"It took us all day of the fifth to get down to our new area. We were traveling on the surface with everything we had and we naturally expected trouble. But nothing happened to us. We didn't see a thing or hear a shot all day.

"We got into position and sat down. We didn't know but

what the Japs had taken Midway. Our orders didn't explain anything. We didn't get any real proof that we were even holding our own until the next day—the morning of the sixth, when the Fortresses began to come over. We couldn't know, of course, that they were trying to find the remnants of the Jap fleet, but we did know that they were coming from Midway—which meant that we were still on top.

"Nothing happened that day, either. We sat there putting radio messages together and decoding everything we could hear until we began to get some picture of what had happened. It was the sort of good news we could hardly believe in spite of what we'd seen. The next day we were ordered to Midway to refuel.

"An oil tank was burning and one of the hangars was still smoldering but the place wasn't damaged much. We went ashore to talk over matters with the Marines and so it happened that we met Ensign Gay.

"You remember Ensign Gay. He was the flier who was shot down and watched the whole battle from a rubber boat. Well, it seems that his rubber boat was almost alongside the *Soryu* when our three torpedoes hit. He heard them hit and identified the bursts as torpedo explosions.

"Soon after that, he said, the ship burst into flames from one end to the other and began to sink by the stern. As he watched, her magazines blew up and she went to pieces and sank. A second explosion threw up pieces of her as she went under. And that story, of course, verified our report. From that time on the *Soryu* was officially in our bag . . . and a very good haul it was. . . ."

43

THE ROAD TO TOKYO

AFTER such beginnings it seemed natural enough for Lieutenant Commander Hogan to minimize some of the subsequent performances of Captain Brockman's boat. But his summary of a voyage that took them almost to the door of Tokyo seemed a little bald even for a submariner.

"We hung around off Japan for a couple of weeks and sank several ships," he said casually. I pressed him for a little enlargement on this matter but there were other things that interested him more.

"We went out there on the surface most of the way," he said. "There wasn't any incident to the trip until we were almost there. We figured that we'd have to begin regular daytime diving pretty soon, but we hadn't run into any signs of trouble at all. Everything was peaceful up beyond Midway. There were still oil slicks on the water and the contented sharks were rolling around like porpoises.

"One morning when we were getting pretty close to our area I woke up the captain about 2:30 to get a bit of air. He came up to the bridge in his pajamas. He'd just about got there when the sound man reported to me as officer of the deck that he had heard the sound of heavy screws.

"Well, I had the periscope up as far as it would go to give me a glimpse of what might be over our horizon. But there wasn't anything in sight and we could see about ten miles. The screws kept pounding—getting louder all the time and coming straight toward us. There was only one thing to do. I called to clear the bridge and dropped down to the control room. The captain came tumbling in after me and wanted to know what it was all about. I told him I was taking her down.

330

" 'It may be a submarine,' I said. 'The sound man reports heavy screws, and a torpedo wouldn't sound like that. There certainly isn't anything on the surface in ten miles.'

"The captain said he doubted it—that a submarine wouldn't make heavy screw noises either. But I said the sound man had made his report and that if he wanted to he could listen to the noises himself.

"By this time there was no doubting that heavy screws were making the racket. They came closer and closer until they were almost on top of us and we knew then that we must be running into another submarine submerged at just about our depth. We swung to port and just then the other boat swung too. We ran parallel for a minute or two and then we swung another ninety degrees, putting us on a course opposite to the one we'd been on when we dived. Almost at the same time the other ship turned around and the propeller noise got dimmer and dimmer. After a while it stopped. We surfaced and got back onto our course.

"We didn't see any signs of the other ship and we couldn't figure what it had been trying to do, or whether or not it had been stalking us, until nearly daylight. Then, with the periscope lifted, we saw a couple of patrol boats coming up to our horizon. We got ready to dive, but before the order could be given, both boats turned around and started back. Apparently they were walking a beat. They had come to the end of their run and were heading for home. And that gave us a partial explanation of the spooky doings of the last couple of hours. Something of the structure of the ocean floor in that region or the density of the sea water had done freakish tricks with sounds. We had heard those boats as clearly as if they'd been on top of us and they must have been miles away.

"Off Japan I spotted a large blot in the darkness—so big that it looked like an island. The chart showed some islands in that direction but they were about fifty miles away and I was puzzled. I called the captain's attention to the blot and he looked at it awhile. Then he said:

" 'If that's an island, it's moving. Clear the bridge!'

"We moved over and pretty soon the detail began to come out

of the darkness. The island was a big tanker. She was loaded and low in the water, and she seemed to be all by herself.

"We fired a torpedo, but whether it was a defective torpedo or we'd miscalculated, it went past the bow. We were getting all set for another when we discovered that we'd made one principal error. She'd been masking an escort destroyer, and the destroyer was coming across her bows toward us at better than thirty knots.

"We dived in a hurry and the clunks began to come down. We sat there expecting the worst for a while and then we noticed the bombs weren't getting any closer. We'd made considerable progress underwater during the dive and apparently we'd stepped out of the ash-can barrage.

" 'Take her up!' ordered the captain. And I began to blow tanks.

"One officer who was pretty disturbed wanted to know if the captain hadn't heard the depth charges.

" 'Certainly,' Brockman said. 'Of course I heard them. But they're all back there and while the can is dropping them he'll be doing us no harm.'

"So we came up and had another look around and Captain Brockman's judgment turned out to be perfect. The destroyer was still over there dropping charges into the hole where we'd gone down.

" 'Pay no attention to him,' said the captain. 'Stand by to fire torpedoes. . . . Fire Two! Fire Three!'

"Both torpedoes hit. The tanker buckled up and there was fire all over the Pacific. We dived again and the can came over to work on us some more.

"We stayed down that time counting the bombs until no more came down. Then we figured that the destroyer had just about run out of material . . . or rather Brockman did. And he came up again.

"By the time we got the periscope up the destroyer was moving around the edge of the fire, probably picking up survivors if there were any. We moved into range and fired a fish at him. He saw it coming and dodged. But apparently it was enough for him. Instead of rushing at us he swung about and headed for home. We watched the rest of the tanker burn up.

"The next morning we came in a little closer. The day was clear and the water calm as it sometimes gets in that region. We were hardly moving in the water when we saw a destroyer coming out. A spit of land or something had screened him and he was almost on top of us before we knew about it. But it was obvious that he hadn't sighted us. He was moving in a straight course at an angle. We turned about a little, and when he crossed our bows we let him have it. We blew him in two.

"I suppose he'd been sent out to look for us but he never got any chance to make a report. So we kept on moving toward the harbor. We got in and sat down.

"When we got a look at what was going on, we saw plenty of activity. A couple of transports and a tanker were on their way out with a cruiser escort. One of the transports we recognized right away. She was a liner which used to run between Yokohama and the Pacific ports.

"We didn't waste any time about it. We let a cruiser go by and put a couple of fish into the liner. She went down almost as fast as we did.

"There was unshirted hell in the bay for the next few minutes. The place was cluttered up with destroyers and patrol boats and they were all dropping depth charges. The first one almost got us. It rolled us over sidewise and knocked men clear across the boat. I sat there in front of the diving wheels expecting the depth gauges and all the diving controls to come right into my lap. But the next ones weren't so close. We'd done our job and we moved away fast —once we found out that the boat was going to hold together. We got into the channel and the current was with us. We were doing about seven knots all the way out.

"We went out to sea and tried to patch up the damage the bombs had done to us. Nothing very important had happened.

"However, we did the best we could and went back toward the bay still wondering what course we ought to take. While Captain Brockman was mulling over this problem a freighter came sailing by, all alone.

"We moved in and knocked her off. It was the easiest target we'd had since we'd gone into business. Captain Brockman waited until it was all under and then he waved his hand over his head.

" 'And that will be about enough,' he said. 'Let's go back to Honolulu.' "

Comsubpac was surprised when the boat opened up her transmitter and announced that she was coming home. The Japs had reported her sunk, and with some logic.

44

GREEK FIRE

THAT wasn't the end of the Brockman blitz on Japan. He went back there again shortly afterward although not to precisely the same spot. His new area was in a strait and, as Lieutenant Commander Hogan remembers, it was a weird experience.

"The first night we were in there we had an adventure with a blind patrol boat," Hogan said. "Maybe her skipper mistook us for a Jap submarine—they have a model about the same size. Maybe we were masked by something. He wasn't so easy to see, either. He was coming in fast when we picked him up—cutting right across our stern and only a couple of hundred yards away. As he went by we put two fish into him and he dissolved.

"A couple of days later we did a battle surface to blow up a sampan. Japanese sampans, we had learned, may be just sampans and they may be something else. We don't know what this one was except that it was masking a destroyer. We had put one shell into her and another in the gun when the destroyer arrived and we went down in a hurry. We left one slug in the gun as we went.

"When we were on our way again a couple of hours later we almost ran into a big trawler, undoubtedly a patrol boat, which we could see wasn't carrying guns equal to ours. The ship was a setup but small, so we came to the surface again and fired our leftover shell.

"The trawler was maneuverable, even if she was slower than we were, and she managed to keep her stern toward us through most of the maneuvering. She yawed as we fired and the shell went straight through her without exploding. Then we closed in and fired with the machine guns. We raked her fore and aft with solid shot and incendiary bullets but nothing happened. She was about the most durable tub I ever saw. When we stopped to look she was still maneuvering without the sign of a leak or a spot of fire on her. And while we were marveling at that we ran out of incendiary bullets.

"We loaded up another shell and I told the gunners to put it closer to the water line. They did. It was a perfect shot but it got turned upward somehow and came up through the deck and blew away the pilothouse. The ship was still moving. There were a lot of dead men on the deck forward.

" 'Well,' the captain said, 'what are you going to do now? I don't want to waste a torpedo on a thing like that.'

"So I called down to the engine room. I told them to make a dozen balls of waste with a bolt or nut or something in them to make them heavy enough to throw, and to soak them in oil and to send them up in a bucket.

"They did. Then we came alongside, lighted the balls and tossed them onto her deck. She burned up quickly after that. I guess that was the first time the Greek-fire idea was tried out by a submarine in this war.

"A few nights later we ran smack into a convoy. We didn't see at first that it was a convoy. All we saw was one ship that seemed to be about half concealed by a point of land. She was a small freighter and didn't look to be making very good time. It was 11:30 P.M. and we'd been on the surface for a couple of hours.

"We had no trouble catching up with her and the guns were ready when we arrived. We fired twenty shots at her and got eighteen hits. We know we did because we could see the flash of the burst and the long gleam on the oil slick in the water around her. But she didn't go down immediately. We were still shooting when we saw the rest of the convoy with a couple of escorting destroyers between them and us. The destroyers started to herd the other ships to the south and for a time left us with the freighter. The captain looked over the situation.

" 'Okay,' he said. 'You fire the guns and I'll fire the torpedoes!' And he fired one into our target. She went down about fifteen feet by the stern and a couple of lifeboats came away from her and men began to spill over the side into the water.

"The next few minutes were a little confused. We were proceeding parallel to the beach and about a mile and a half out. One lifeboat had drifted between us and the beach. Another was on the other side of us. The torpedoed freighter was still ahead of us.

"Two men were swimming about in the water near us and Captain Brockman ordered them taken aboard. When they got his idea they swam back to their ship. What happened to them I don't know because everything exploded at once.

"I heard a crash and saw a slick of water on the port bow. Then there was another blast and water splashed over the deck from the starboard. There were flashes from the shore and we didn't need anything to tell us that we'd been straddled by a land battery. At the same moment a destroyer and a PT-boat came charging from starboard.

"I got down to my diving station. The captain had an agreement that when he wanted to go under in a pinch he wouldn't give any depth orders but just say 'Dive emergency!' and I waited for the order. Nothing came. There was another crash outside and then the word came: 'Take me down! Take me down!' He'd forgotten the talismanic word.

"Searchlights were working on us before we got under water—a couple from the beach and one from the destroyer. And we were in a pocket. The charts showed hardly any water under our keel . . . not enough anyway to do us any good.

"Well, we got down in what there was and there we stayed while they dropped twenty slugs. We heard the destroyer and the PT-boat go away and we risked coming up again. We couldn't very well sit permanently in water no deeper than an umbrella trickle, and there's always the business of charging the can. But they were only fooling. We hadn't been up five minutes when I heard three bursts ahead and saw a shadow streaking across the rising moon. The airplanes had taken over.

"We went down again and we stayed there. They kept plastering us all night—although the attack got less murderous toward morning. By that time they were putting down nuisance bombs at the rate of about one every half-hour. The last one went off at 11:00 A.M.

"By that time, however, there wasn't any doubt that we'd sunk our ship. She turned out to be the *Shoei Maru*—9,246 tons.

"We sank another freighter in the same locality a short time later. She was 5,000 tons. And that was the last one for ten days. A typhoon hit us and most of the time we had to lie submerged.

"Submarines are equipped to get out of storms, but this one was a honey. We had a roll of ten degrees at a depth where usually there was no motion at all, and when we went higher we were on our beam-ends half the time.

"When the storm started the rain was coming in horizontally. When it hit you in the face it would spatter. After the worst of it was over we could hardly stand the cold topside. We had arctic-issue clothes but they weren't good enough. The only consolation was that it was as bad for the Japs as it was for us. We couldn't work at all while the worst of the blow was on. You can't shoot a torpedo in a sea like that. They'll prime and explode as soon as they leave the tube and maybe blow you sky-high with them.

"Coming out of the storm one day I saw a ship just on the horizon . . . a fairly large ship with two masts and a stack. We headed over and caught up with her. She was a patrol ship but a handsome one—shiny-new and beautiful. We stayed off a bit, figuring that our guns would outrange hers. We began to fire a matter of seconds after we surfaced, but even so we expected to see some sign of life on her. There was none. Our first shot took away her radio antenna and after that we whittled her down. I didn't see a single man aboard her during all the shooting. She didn't zigzag. She made no effort to get away. Nobody fired a gun. After a while we put a slug in her engine room and she blew up and sank. She put out no lifeboats. Nobody came off her. I kept feeling that she was something like the *Flying Dutchman*. . . . But anyway she was down.

"It was funny that while we were on that beat we didn't see a single ship coming up from the south. Lieutenant Commander George Porter was down there and he took care of all of them that were headed our way. We reciprocated by cleaning up just about everything that was going in his direction. All in all I guess you'd call it a profitable patrol."

45

COMMANDO RAID

LIEUTENANT COMMANDER HOGAN looked out across a terrace of the officers' club where tables were set with delicate glassware and smooth white napery and women in spring finery circulated about, preparing for some sort of party. Outside, the lawn just turning green sloped down to the river, and in the thin haze beyond glistened the white spires of a New England village.

"We were in a commando raid once," he said as if all this civilization and peacefulness reminded him of it. "We went with the Marines to a Japanese island base in the South Pacific and helped them take it apart. . . ." They did take it apart, too, if he was talking about the same raid we've been hearing about. But he didn't go into much detail concerning the action. It wasn't a submarine expedition at all, he felt. The Marines had put on the show and the Marines were entitled to tell about it. However, there were one or two incidents. . . .

"We sank a couple of ships there," he said. "We smashed them up with gunfire, which shows you something of what kind of a job it was. . . . But it was really pretty good shooting.

"Our area for the purposes of the raid was outside the lagoon. The ships were inside behind a wooded island in a harbor that we couldn't even see. We knew they were in there. We had advance information about that which was verified by some of the raiders.

"We sent a couple of men ashore to spot bursts for us, but there was plenty of hell going on and they got out of communication. It's pretty hard to shoot blind when you can't be sure of your adjustment, but eventually we worked it out with a sort of zone fire. We picked out a tree in the distance first as a registration point and then as an aiming point. After we'd got the range on it we came up a little and traversed right and left from it.

"Once we hit we didn't need anybody to tell us about it. The ships were both pretty fair-sized freighters and apparently both were carrying munitions. When they blew up we could see the smoke and flame shooting up over the trees."

The excitement continued right up to the end of the raid. After the first bombardment the sub headed into the lagoon to pick up the Marines who were coming out in rubber boats. One boat-load was aboard when bomber planes came over from another island and started to work on them. They had to dive. A second boat was between them and the beach when they went under and the planes strafed it. All the men in that boat were killed.

"We took most of the raiders back to their base," said Hogan. "They brought nine wounded men aboard . . . some of them in pretty bad shape. One was a kid sentry who had been jumped during the night by eight Japs. He had only a Garand rifle to defend himself with but he got three of them before they shot him down. He had eight or ten wounds across his chest.

"They rolled him into one of the officers' bunks and gave him some morphine, and when we started away he was more dead than alive. About eight o'clock that night I was off watch for the first time in seventy-eight hours and I went into the wardroom for a drink of water. I heard somebody in the passageway outside and looked out. This kid was walking toward the control room, his chest crisscrossed with bandages like a mummy. The morphine had worn off and he was wide awake. I asked him what he was doing.

" 'Well,' he said, 'I heard them say I was going to die. And I figured that if I got up and walked around a little maybe I wouldn't.' He didn't either. I knew he wasn't going to die when I took him back to his bunk.

"There was one sergeant who got a CPO's bunk. He didn't seem to be wounded. He just got the bunk because nobody was using it at the time. He walked aboard without help and wasn't complaining to anybody.

"The Marine Corps doctor didn't do any operating that night. He said he was so tired he was afraid he might kill somebody so he put it off till morning. The next day we fixed up an operating table for him in the wardroom and he began to put the boys back together again. He worked steadily for two days. Then, finally, he got around to this sergeant. The man just walked into the wardroom and said he thought something was the matter with him.

" 'And what would that be?' the doctor asked him. 'Did you stub your toe or something?'

"And the sergeant said, 'No, that ain't it. I got a scratch somewhere and I can't sit down and I can't bend forward.' The doctor put him onto the table and dug a soft-nosed bullet out of his back. . . .

"There was an interesting guy with the Marines that I particularly remember—a second lieutenant. He was born in Japan, the son of missionaries. He'd lived in Japan until he was sixteen years old and then had come to the University of Oregon for his education. After he was graduated he stayed on at the school as an instructor in the Japanese language. He'd got a commission early in the war as an interpreter but he wasn't much interested in interpreting. When the raid got to the island he could have stayed with us but instead he went with the troops. He said, 'I got into this thing as a fighting man and I'm going to fight.' They had him firing a 60-millimeter gun which in their business they call the 'elephant rifle.' It was a frightful weapon and manned by an odd crew. Aside from the Japanese linguist the most interesting member of the outfit was the man who carried the gun. He weighed 200 pounds and walked around with this gun on his shoulder and 1,200 rounds of ammunition slung around his neck. They called him 'Tiny,' of course.

"They got hell right away. The planes picked them out and ganged on them. And they fought back. It was all one-sided. The language professor knocked down a couple of planes and did a lot of other havoc with the elephant gun, but eventually they got him. A slug took the top of his head clean off. We were all damned sorry about it."

The oddest story of the raid, as the captain recalled it, was that of Oscar Peatross of Charlotte, North Carolina. The original landing place had been changed and he never got the order. When he landed he was behind the Jap lines. From there on what had started out as a commando raid became a pitched battle with his outfit raising hell in back of it.

"His pals were taking cover in a ditch alongside a road when a Jap came by on a bicycle. They all shot at him at once and blew most of his face off," Hogan reminisced. "He must have died instantly but that didn't stop him. The bicycle continued along down the road, his legs going up and down automatically as the pedals moved them. The bike went about 150 feet before it collapsed.

"Just about that time a motorcycle messenger came along from the opposite direction. He saw a dead man with no face riding toward him on a bicycle and he stopped to investigate the miracle. So they shot him, too. . . .

"I left the ship after that patrol and came home. I was touched by the farewell a couple of the crew gave me.

"To understand it you have to go back a little. When we first began to do a lot of diving, we got a couple of tin cans to make seats for the men who operate the bow and stern planes. We upholstered the tops but they were still tin cans.

"In depth-bombing the men of a trained crew don't get jittery, but you can't say they're not tense. There's nothing in the situation you can ignore. I've had a lot of them dropped on me and it's not the kind of experience that seems old to me even yet.

"To provide against carelessness that might possibly come of shock or fatigue, we had painted orange all the controls that had to do with closing outlets to the sea. That made them stand out from the mess of gadgets and easy to find. And that's the background of the story.

"When the lads at the diving planes had been on duty for a long time, they got the habit of kicking to take the cramp out of their legs and in kicking they'd bump the tin cans. You might not think that such a bang would bother men in a depth-charge attack but it did. There was a lot of protest and finally I told the boys about it. I said in conclusion that if they persisted in their error I'd have to treat their shoes the same way as we had treated everything else connected with promoting care in emergencies and paint them orange.

"They laughed at it and I forgot the incident until I came up before the muster to say good-by. The two lads from the diving planes were out in the front rank with their shoes painted orange."

46

THE GANOMIE FACTOR

LIEUTENANT COMMANDER L. S. ("TEX") MEWHINNEY came out of the underwater riot in the Southwest Pacific with sundry decorations and a fair bag of Japanese ships. It's worth mentioning merely because you'd never get much of it out of Captain Mewhinney. He spent most of his time at Mare Island, while waiting for his boat to be refitted, complaining about a general suspension of the law of averages and trying to nominate himself for place as the worst of the submarine skippers, and to one not in his own line of business he might have sounded convincing.

Not that his self-castigation ever seemed to bother him much. He is one of the most pleasant young men in the service, with a gift for humorous expression, and he can contrive to make a chronicle of peril, disappointment and exasperating hard luck sound almost hilarious. Which he did repeatedly as his brother officers smiled at him and murmured the sea-going equivalent of "Horse-feathers!"

The other skippers will tell you privately that he is a "Human Is-Was," a natural calculating machine with a fine fire-control apparatus in his blond head. They mention casually that he took over a jinx ship and made it fight, and they agree that nobody in submarines is more willing to get into tight places or more able to get out of them. They are willing to concede that he is one of the smartest mathematicians in the Navy. If they were to vote for the most popular man among their number, Tex would very likely be their choice. But they admit that with all his accomplishment he logged a most phenomenal run of bad luck. It's the "Ganomie factor" or something, they say. You can't hit 'em if you can't get at 'em and sometimes you don't hit 'em if you do get at 'em. . . .

"But don't make any mistake about it, he's a good submarine captain," Captain Hiram Cassedy told me. "He came out all right."

So I sat beaming like the rest as Tex recited his comical history of trouble.

"Most of these stories about submarine skippers give me an uneasy sensation," he said, conveying the impression that he never had really had an uneasy sensation about anything. "All of these heroes are described as men of magnificent and abiding calm—fearless gents with no nerves, and all that. Well, I never met any of those people. Everybody I ever knew in command of submarines had shaky legs and I certainly had a shaky pair myself. I remember one fight we were in when my knees were beating out such a tattoo that I almost had to sit down on the deck.

"I don't say, of course, that anybody else had the jitters as bad as I had them. I'm the most scared guy in the Navy all the time. That's partly on account of the ship and the men I have to look out for. . . . Partly because I'm the only guy responsible. But mostly, I guess, it's because I'm just plain scared."

His brother officers laughed heartily at that and he protested.

"I mean it," he said. "And you fellows aren't going to get anywhere trying to be polite.

"They used to call my boat 'the zero fighter' because that's the kind of score it had. We used to go out on long boat rides. Most of the time we never saw anything. When we did see anything I couldn't hit it. And I'll confess I worried a little about that. No matter how rotten I was I thought I ought to get a salesman's percentage. I used to blame the torpedoes. But that didn't make me feel any better and it didn't sink any more ships.

"Once I thought I had a fine break. I was cruising around on the surface one dark night and a big ship with an escort came up on me from behind. Well, I fired the classic system, zero angle from stern. They'll tell you shots like that are sure to hit. Anybody else in the submarines would have blown up the transport or whatever it was and a couple of cans besides. But I had to be the guy to make a clean miss. The ship turned out or the torpedoes went under her or something."

The officers, remembering his record of authenticated sinkings and likely hits, murmured their condolences with a mixture of Bronx cheers.

"You're breaking my heart," said Captain Cassedy. "You make me think this business will never amount to anything."

"Maybe not," conceded Tex cheerfully. "But you'd better ask somebody who knows more about it. Twice on that patrol I made approaches on big ships that had cans hiding in their shadows. The cans came after me and I had to make long-range shots as I dived. And it didn't worry me much when I missed because I knew I could miss 'em at short range in broad daylight without any cans to bother with."

His audience, for a wonder, took up this matter of long shots seriously.

"Sometimes they work," one officer said. He mentioned the case of one skipper who had been in the Southwest Pacific from the beginning. "He was always a nervous operator. But he fired at least three impossible ones at ships a couple of miles away and he never missed. It's all a matter of luck."

"I don't know anything about luck," said Tex. "I never had any. About the time I missed the third one I got the idea that the crew were looking at me queerly. Maybe I was wrong about that. Maybe I just thought I saw them reflecting the things I was beginning to see in myself.

"One night a little later I was wandering around on the surface with a flat can, and I spotted a cruiser. I started to move in on her but I knew that the minute I fired a fish at her I was going to have lots of trouble. So I wanted to know whether or not the battery would last us long submerged. The electricians broke out their slide rules and did a lot of figuring and then I got the kind of answer that does you a lot of good when you're trying to break up a cruiser. They said maybe it would and maybe it wouldn't.

"I kept on moving in but I told them that wasn't what I wanted to know. I didn't want to hear anything about maybe. I wanted to be sure one way or the other, yes or no. Still I didn't get any sense out of them. The next time I got a report that perhaps it would last another day, but as against that there was the possibility that it might not.

"By the time they got around to telling me the glad news I

was in a good firing position. So I let go my fish, and missed and dived. We got a good working-over that it seemed to me we didn't deserve—after all we weren't doing any harm to anybody. I figured the Japs ought to be sending us medals instead of wasting ash cans on us. Anyway the battery held out. That was a break I didn't expect to get.

"I hardly thought I'd be with the boat for another patrol but it turned out I was. After the first week out I didn't expect much. We had a leaky exhaust valve that flooded the engine. We got into a nest of surface patrols and they kept after us all the time. There was no reason why they shouldn't have. Our pumps were going all the time and they kept looking for us. We were making more noise than a school of whales. It was almost continuous hell but the men didn't seem to mind that much. They were all going around with heads hanging. I guess they figured it would be nicer to get knocked off right there than to have to go back to port again and start fighting people who wanted to talk about 'the zero fighter.'

"We got away from the patrols after a while. I think we just wore them out. We surfaced one night and did what we could to get our damage fixed up, and we'd made quite a lot of progress when I saw a ship ahead. She was a big one. . . . All the ships I missed were big ones. I never wasted torpedoes missing little ones.

"I closed in on this black lump just out of force of habit and figured I'd have to go a long way. I couldn't make out exactly what she was except that she was big. My night vision isn't very good anyway.

"But I didn't get a chance to come into close range. I saw that a couple of cans were moving around on the edges of the shadow. So I said to myself, 'Well, here goes another one.' And I fired a long shot in the dark and pulled the plug.

"The wake of the torpedo churned up a lot of phosphorescence. A blind man could have seen the streak. So the two cans came after us and with them a lot of other cans I hadn't seen. There seemed to be a dozen of them. We could hear their propellers coming right down the track and we pulled in our necks waiting for the depth charges. Then, long before the first bomb came down, something happened. There were two explosions ahead of us . . . good solid explosions that seemed to be pushing the whole Pacific Ocean back on top of us.

"One of the officers looked at me and gasped.

" 'My God!' he said in a squeaky voice. 'What's that?'

"So I looked at him sternly.

" 'You naturally wouldn't know,' I said to him. 'But that, sir, is the noise of two torpedo bursts.'

"He looked almost as if he didn't understand what I was talking about.

" 'Then,' he said, 'we must have hit something.'

"The cans started to plaster hell out of us just about then but we hardly noticed."

They heard some more torpedo bursts after that, including a couple that probably sank a cruiser. But Tex, still on his theme that a submarine-skipper's life is not a happy one, didn't remember many of the details.

"I thought I'd seen about everything there was to see in the way of trouble," he said. "But then we ran into a typhoon. There are two schools of thought about what you ought to do in a typhoon. Some skippers ride them out. Some stay under them and that's what I did. But so many things had happened to the zero fighter that I was almost afraid to try it. There is always a moment as a boat surfaces when she is unstable and virtually out of control, and I didn't like to think of being in that spot in a high wind. I thought the chances were pretty good we might be blown down for keeps. But in the end we did go down and we stayed there. We took a bad battering.

"When we got up the sea was still pretty rough and the sky was overcast and visibility bad. Out in the haze I caught sight of a ship that seemed to be alone. I made an approach and saw she was a hospital ship. I suppose she was taking a lot of malaria patients up and down for a ride in the sea air."

It was obvious he didn't think much of malaria as a disease. No submariner does, probably because malaria-carrying mosquitoes haven't yet found a way to break through steel hulls.

"I let her go by," he said. "Then as I was watching her go over the horizon a patrol escorting another ship came along. I cut in past the patrol ships, intending to get one of the parade, and just as I was ready to fire I saw another red cross. I let that one go by, too. And then, when I was drawn off position, a naval auxiliary ship went past in another lane. Nobody will tell me all this wasn't done deliberately. . . ."

The other officers agreed with him. One recalled the recent patrol report of a particularly exasperated skipper.

"I came up in bright moonlight," this captain had written. "I felt as if I were walking up Main Street without any clothes on. A ship came over toward me and I went after her. I was pretty close before she turned her lights on and I saw she had the labels of a hospital ship. Maybe she was a hospital ship. I had my doubts. I let her go by."

"I almost got another one in a rain squall that obscured her markings," Tex remembered. "If it had been a little later in the day when the light was poorer I'd never have seen them at all. And I had another experience with that sort of business. One night I was off a port in the Solomons when I saw a ship near me showing hospital lights. I thought it was funny because he was running 90 degrees off his proper course so I went in to investigate. It was a patrol boat but before I found that out I'd come in so close they could almost look down the hatch. I swung off and came in again to take a crack at it. But when I got there the second time a destroyer was waiting. I fired a fish at the destroyer and it didn't go off. I dived and destroyers dropped everything they had on me.

"We did hit a couple of ships when we finally got out of that mess. I know we hit because everybody in the boat could hear the noises. But we couldn't stay on the surface to watch them sink so we didn't get any credit for them.

"Toward the end of this unlucky business we ran into a formation up north of Guadalcanal—a couple of cruisers, a carrier and some destroyers. It looked impossible for us to do anything against a setup like that. But for that matter everything was beginning to look impossible so that was no excuse for not making a try. We came boring in and none of the stuff up ahead heard or saw us. Before I could believe it had happened we were in range and just a little ahead of the beam of the carrier. I fired two torpedoes at her and we heard them both go off as we dived.

"We didn't sink her. She was the *Hyoso* and she was so badly damaged that she had to go back home—and that took the last Japanese carrier out of the attack on Guadalcanal."

Unofficially most of the submariners concede that he sank the probables he talked about. And pondering that I asked Captain Cassedy once more about his dismal inventory.

"Well," the captain said, "I'll tell you a parable that you probably have heard. Do you remember the old story about the drunk and the talking horse? In case you don't I'll remind you of it.

"The drunk was on his way home when he saw the horse standing at a curbstone and, without thinking, spoke to him. He was greatly surprised when the horse said 'Hello' and asked him how he was feeling. He may have been drunk but he was polite, so he stopped to chat with the horse and eventually the horse told him his life history—how he had been born in Lexington, Kentucky, and how he had run around in the Blue Grass region, how he had won the Kentucky Derby in 1930 or some such time, and how after that things had gone from bad to worse until finally he developed arthritis and had to take on a milk wagon to keep out in the open air.

"Well, so this story goes, the milkman came out of a house just about time the story was done and the drunk turned to him and said, 'I've just had a very interesting conversation. Did you know that your horse can talk?'

"And the milkman says:

"'Of course he can talk. But don't let him give you any of that nonsense about the Kentucky Derby.'"

47

LUCK IS WHERE YOU FIND IT

According to Captain Hiram Cassedy, firing torpedoes is something like shooting dice. You need a little skill and daring but you also need something else. And he makes out a good case for his theory.

The skill and daring and something else have combined very well to produce a fine record for Captain Cassedy. He has had a wider variety of experience than comes to most submarine skippers even in so strange a war as the one they designed for themselves in the Southwest Pacific. He fought a little, ran a little ferry service, hauled ammunition with the rest of the fleet to Corregidor, lived a melodrama like a chapter out of *Treasure Island* in his rescue of marooned Australian aviators, sank a lot of Japanese ships, and eventually brought his boat back to the United States without the loss of a man. One might think that all his days were filled with stormy action and his nights with wild exhilaration. But if you did you'd be wrong. His first weeks in the Java Sea were deadly, not on account of perilous missions but because of a hundred discouragements through which his weary crew moved steadily toward an enervating boredom. And if luck rode with him at all it was a stowaway completely disguised.

"We had a couple of unproductive patrols," he says, describing this period. To a submarine officer no further detail seemed necessary. An "unproductive patrol" apparently sums up almost everything that can come to plague a skipper, from ash cans and tempests to daily losses at acey-deucy. Anyway they had little to their credit in the way of sunken Japanese shipping when they found themselves assigned to a strait.

If they had had no luck previously they could see no prospect for improvement when they took up their station. They were in a narrow strip of water outside a port with land on two sides of them and quite close. Two channels led to the harbor entrance and no amount of finesse or calculation did them any good when it came time for them to choose which channel they were going to cover.

They'd stay three or four days in one only to see the enemy ships steaming in and out through the other. They'd change over. So would the ships.

"Our luck was just out," Captain Cassedy summarized it. "But we were more than a month proving it."

Surprisingly, nobody came to molest them during those days of increasing dullness. On the way into their area one night Lieutenant Francis D. Walker (now Lieutenant Commander), the executive, saw a target dead in the water ahead of him. It was a fairly big freighter, and had he been able to see that she was beached he probably would not have wasted a torpedo on her. But the darkness was behind her and all about her, and her dim silhouette seemed to rise straight and tall from the swirling black water under her stern. So he tossed a fish at her and blew her up. There was roaring excitement ashore as the submarine slipped past into the straits.

Again, a few days later, at the opposite end of the area, Captain Cassedy picked up a German naval auxiliary. A lot of Nazi vessels seem to have ventured freely into Asiatic waters in those days. Diplomats returning on the exchange ship have told of seeing German officers in Tokyo. Haupt, the Chicago saboteur, was taken to Germany on a blockade-runner that he boarded in Japan. This ship, possibly, had come out to deliver instruments to the Japanese and was returning with a load of rubber. The Japs hadn't bothered to provide her with an escort so Captain Cassedy proceeded in a leisurely fashion to blow her apart.

One might have thought that these evidences of American submarine activity in the straits would have brought out a detachment of patrol boats immediately. But none came. The submarine went on with a futile dance from channel to channel, unmolested and so far from actual participation in the war that the sweating crew might have welcomed the novelty of a depth charge. Finally, after several weeks of this, Captain Cassedy saw a ship coming in that looked as if she might justify the risk of going into the channel. She was a naval auxiliary tanker and, like most of the tankers that came into that region, well loaded.

The submarine was on the surface along about midnight when she came by—as usual in the other channel. The captain started after her.

Daylight caught him before he was well inside the port, and he had to make a cautious approach in still, clear water. But he crept in slowly and altogether unsuspected. There wasn't much activity in the harbor at that time. A few dock hands stood about waiting for the tanker to come up to her pier. A few smaller ships lay anchored to buoys, with no signs of life on them. The tin-roofed warehouses beyond the white quay were closed and seemingly untenanted. For just a moment the captain was indignant. Something must be wrong with a war that didn't make the Japanese show more energy than this.

The tanker sidled up to the dock and threw out her lines and was tied up. By that time Captain Cassedy was almost alongside her. In the forward torpedo room all the tubes were loaded and ready for firing. All the crew stood at battle stations and not a man moved or spoke.

The captain put up his periscope for a few seconds to check his observations and as he did he saw a procession moving along the dock. A lot of little Japanese naval officers in dress uniform were moving toward the tanker's gangway, dragging long swords on the pavement behind them. The fish he had been about to fire stayed in the tubes as he waited for another observation. Officers and men, unaware of what he had seen, looked at him in puzzlement. He was the captain, of course, and he knew what he was doing, but what was it?

Two or three minutes later he pushed the periscope up again for a flash and saw a reception at the head of the gangway. The ship's officers were in stiff formation bowing to the last of the shore establishment who, presumably, had come aboard for breakfast.

The captain muttered, "They should have stayed at home," and fired three torpedoes. The ship blew up. The visiting naval officers and a large part of the dock went with her.

A TRANSPORT GOES WEST

Two torpedoes did this. The submarine which blasted this Japanese ship was so close that the target more than covered the periscope scale.

TAKE HER DOWN

This is how a submarine's bow looks a moment before the water begins to break over the deck.

The harbor woke up after that and the submarine shivered under the ash cans. It took little calculation to determine where the boat had dived.

"It was a bad pounding," the captain recalled. "Not until we could get up to the surface late that night did we find out that we hadn't been seriously damaged. But we knew that a lot of little things had happened to us. We had the usual muck of broken glass and such stuff on the decks."

So far as they could see everything was working all right. Things were quieter when they started out. Trouble came to them from an unexpected source. Nothing was in sight on the surface near them as they approached the entrance. Sound could pick up no propeller noises. Then a bombing squadron came over low and began to spread the sea with bombs.

"Take her down," ordered the captain and the diving officer made a sickening discovery. The bow planes wouldn't rig out.

"That looked like curtains," the captain says of it. "We stuck a little more angle on the stern planes and dived anyway. I thought we were never going to get the boat down. I lived a hundred years just about then. But the diving officer had a good trim and he got her down in almost normal time, and he leveled her off without a hitch at the bottom of the dive. I've never heard of a thing like that happening before or since. . . ."

They got out of that area without further mishap but mechanical trouble was never far from them. On the next patrol they had a bad fire and had to be towed in.

"We were unlucky to have the fire," said the captain. "It was a bad one and left us without power. On the other hand we were lucky to survive a thing like that and we were certainly lucky to get a tow. I suppose luck is not only where you find it but also in the way you look at it.

"For one thing we'd figured they'd be waiting for us with everything they had when we got into the straits after sinking the tanker. But nothing happened.

"On another patrol all our electrical cables were shot and we kept getting serious shorts. We were in a spot then where we couldn't ask for any tow, and I was afraid we might have another fire any minute. Lieutenant Walker and I talked over what we'd do about it if we did, and we talked about a plan to beach the ship and get the crew off and blow her up. The crew didn't know about that."

All things considered, however, luck as the submariners interpret it seemed to have changed for the better with the blasting of the tanker. On a later patrol Captain Cassedy, cruising on the surface, discovered some masts over the horizon. The night was dark but somehow there was enough visibility for him to make out details of the convoy he was approaching—a destroyer, a corvette, a mine layer close together and traveling almost in echelon, a supply ship and some other sort of auxiliaries behind them.

Captain Cassedy came around the end of this formation with all the speed he could get out of his engines, and closed in on what now seemed like a solid wall of ships. Into this mélange he threw five torpedoes, all of which hit. He saw a destroyer break in two and dive while bits of a shattered corvette were still coming down. A big ship that looked to be a transport was afire, and the flame gave a momentary glimpse of other ships listing or plunging or slewing about in the water.

He got credit for the destroyer and the corvette, the only ones whose finish he had time to supervise before the rest of the escort chased him down. But Frank Walker thinks the transport was undoubtedly sunk, and very likely the mine layer and a supply ship.

He went from there to a Japanese island base and pecked at the convoys.

"When we went up there it was virgin territory," the captain said dryly about this adventure. "No submarines had been up there ahead of us and the Japs seemed to know about it.

"They were playing their third-string team with the convoys. When we'd been up there a little while they began to put in the first team. But in the meantime we annoyed them a lot. . . ."

One incident of the nuisance campaign that the captain does not set forth in detail was an audacious attack on a convoy almost across the bows of a corvette. The commander of the corvette may not have been very alert when the attack began. The submarine slipped in behind him in the night, came close to a cargo carrier and demolished it with two torpedoes. Before the ship had plunged, however, he had brought his mind back to his job, turned his ship around and was streaking back toward where the white wake of the torpedo was still visible enough to give him directions. Captain Cassedy watched him come and made a quick mental calculation of his speed and bearings.

"Hell," he said, "he doesn't know where he's going. He'll pass us."

So the corvette passed and began to drop ash cans diligently but in the wrong place.

"Keep track of him," the captain ordered. "I want to know when he starts to move this way." After which he closed in on the convoy again and sank another ship. He slipped out then into still waters while the frustrated corvette captain went on and on with his useless work.

All of the men who came back to the United States for new ships after that first weird year under the Pacific will tell you that the records they established are being smashed daily by the skippers who succeeded them. There is the recent and so far undetailed record of Captain Dudley W. ("Mush") Morton who sank 16 Japanese ships in a row. There are stories less well authenticated but probably true of ships that have been piling up smaller tonnages but with greater regularity and over a longer period. It is beginning to be apparent that despite a frantic increase in Japan's precautionary measures against U. S. submarines these boats are blasting her shipping at a steadily mounting rate. The day seems near when a bag of two or three ships will look like a routine matter unworthy of mention in dispatches.

You wonder, of course, what sagas this year's skippers will write when they, in turn, get home. And yet you doubt that their reports of a more perfect technique in maneuver and torpedo fire will take anything much from the glamorous record of the men who pioneered this fantastic war under the sea. What science they had was theoretical. The techniques of maneuver that they made effective were those that they evolved themselves. If they felt the need of luck they had the instinct to find it. And having found it, they did pretty well with it.

In the new order it seems hardly likely that submarine skippers are going to do much chasing through the war zones on the surface in daylight as Lieutenant Commander McKinney had to do when he first went out of Manila. Captain McKinney himself has undoubtedly worked out a less suicidal strategy. But it seems to me that scientific knowledge and experience and better equipment are likely to take out of submarine warfare some of the spectacular elements that the McKinneys and Cassedys and Fennos and Wrights and Coes and Willinghams and Brockmans and Warders and others of their period put into it.

There comes to mind the picture of McKinney's attacks on cruisers near Java. When he met the first one he was pursuing the only policy he knew—a policy that so far had piled up a lot of wrecks on a lot of different coral bottoms—get in close and get in fast.

It was dusk and he may not have been detected but at any rate he did come in fast and he did come in close. He ignored a couple of destroyers that circled behind him to investigate, fired three torpedoes at the cruiser and dived. He heard his three torpedoes go off and it is reasonable to suppose that he sank his target. The cans were on him immediately and held him down so long that he could not check on his handiwork—which is not remarkable when you think that they might reasonably have kept him down forever.

Again, he came upon a cruiser and destroyers. Even in so short a time he had become warier. But for all that he did jockey himself between the destroyers into a suitable spot and fired his fish at the cruiser.

Three of them hit and the ship bent in the middle and blew up.

"It was a terrifying spectacle," he said. "Not many men ever see a thing like that—that big, powerful ship crumpling up like tinfoil, fire roaring out of her, her turrets sliding off. . . .

"I called the quartermaster over and let him take a look at it. And he turned sick. 'My God!' he said. 'What a way to earn a living!'"

The captain could never understand the quartermaster and it is likely that the quartermaster could never understand the businesslike detachment of the captain. Captain McKinney is one of the most gentle and sensitive men I have ever met. But he was like the others in his service on the morning when the Japs came over to bomb Manila; he was automatically a pioneer plunging into a new life in which few of the standards and professional directives of the old one were going to have any place or meaning. He and others like him went out to meet the Japs, convinced that they were going to be killed. Whatever else happened could be no surprise to them nor much of a shock.

There may or may not have been giants in the earth in those days. There certainly were under the sea. . . .

48

APPENDECTOMY UNDER THE ASH CANS

THE Pulitzer prize story which George Weller, Chicago *Daily News* war correspondent in the Southwest Pacific, gave to the world concerning the appendicitis operation which Pharmacist's Mate Wheeler B. Lipes of Newcastle, Virginia, performed under the keels of the Japanese patrol fleet to my mind will continue to rate as one of the classic bits of reporting of this war long after the war is finished. It was not only the first graphic narrative of life aboard a submarine to reach the upper air but, what seems more important, it was the first account of a brand of miracle which submerged pill-dispensers seem to be able to repeat at will.

Weller's story, as you may have gathered from the name of the talented amateur surgeon, had as its setting the incredible bedlam of "the Old Red Submarine," although he did not mention that in dispatches. The patient, Dean Rector, of Chautauqua, Kansas, was himself one of the "Red Pirates," albeit a pretty sick one. Somewhere in the midst of the lambasting that they had been taking after a successful raid along the Indo-Chinese coast he had fallen unconscious on the deck, and Pharmacist's Mate Lipes ("We generally call 'em 'Quack' but I wouldn't mind calling Lipes 'Doc' if it'd make him feel any better. . . . He was certainly a savvy dude.") Lipes had diagnosed his trouble as acute appendicitis.

You get some inkling of the status of Lipes aboard the ship from the fact that nobody among the officers or crew thought of questioning his diagnosis. He had taken the Navy hospital course in San Diego and thereafter had served three years in the service hospital in Philadelphia. He had qualified as a laboratory technician with a special rating as a cardiographer. In his hospital course he had assisted at numerous operations and had seen scores of appendectomies. But of course he had never performed an operation and had never dreamed that he would ever have to perform one. He didn't want to perform one when he picked up the prostrate Dean Rector. But the boy, who had just passed his nineteenth birthday, was running a high temperature and his heart was making a last stand, and even the laymen who looked at him could see death in his face. Lipes made a quick report to the captain, Lieutenant Commander W. B. Farrell of Pittsburgh.

"His appendix is about to burst," he said, "if it hasn't gone already."

"Well," said the captain, "what do you do now?" High-speed screws were beating overhead but so far the Japanese hunters had not picked up the submarine's scent.

"He'll die if he doesn't have an operation right away," said Lipes. "And that's the flat of it." The captain for a moment forgot about the menace of the Japs.

"Can you operate?" he wanted to know. Lipes made a quick decision.

"Yes, sir," he said. "I can do it. But the chances are slim that he'll come out of it."

"You can only do what you can do," said the captain. "Get rigged for it. We'll take her down to stiller water. Pick what crew you need. Then, if he's conscious, ask him what he thinks about going on with it."

So they carried Dean Rector into the little wardroom—which in the Old Red Submarine is so small and so cramped for headroom that you have to bend your knees to get into it—and they laid him out on a table just long enough to hold him. Lipes designated as chief assistant surgeon, Lieutenant Norvell Ward of Indianhead, Maryland, "because he is cool and dependable." Lieutenant Franz Hoskins, communications officer, was named anesthetist. Engineer Officer Lieutenant Charles C. Manning of Cheraw, South Carolina, was "circulating nurse," assigned to keep up the supply of sterile dressings and boiling water. All the operating staff dressed for their work in pajama coats turned backward.

They had a scalpel without a handle. Lipes made a handle for it. His rubber gloves didn't fit. The finger were too long. But he made them do. They had hemostats—clamps for closing off blood vessels and arteries—but they had no muscular retractors. They made retractors by bending spoons in the shape of wishbones. They made an ether mask out of a tea strainer and rigged up a searchlight to light the operating theater. They mixed torpedo alcohol with water and boiled it to sterilize their instruments. They made an antiseptic powder by grinding up sulfanilamide tablets. The captain and the cook both counted sponges as they went into the patient and as they came out.

With everything ready, Lipes spoke to Dean Rector, roused him and told him what was going on.

"I've never done anything like this before," he said. "And if you don't think I ought to do it, you're the one to say so."

"I know how it is, Doc," Rector said. "Let's get on with it."

So Lipes operated on Rector while the men on the planes held the ship level and men on watch at stations in other compartments heard a play-by-play account passed back to them by observers from the crew, who stood peering into the forward battery room.

It was a long operation but eventually the appendix came out. The sponges and retractors were counted and checked. Lipes sewed up the incision with catgut. Dean Rector recovered and is back in the submarines again. Surgeons throughout the United States congratulated Lipes on his success against terrific odds and cited him as a fine example of the thoroughness of Navy training. And that, in brief, is the substance if not the form of the story George Weller told.

One might have thought with considerable reason that here was one episode that would remain unique in the tumultuous history of the submarines. You didn't feel that things like that could ever happen twice. It seemed possible perhaps that there should be two such gifted pharmacist's mates as Lipes in the service but that the other talented one might be cast for a similar role in similar circumstances was something that should have been taken care of by the law of averages.

In a business where death threatens in such a variety of guises you might think that it would never bother to wear the same mask twice. But it does and the submariners have a few words on that phenomenon, too.

"The postman always rings five or six times," one of the crew of the Old Red Submarine told me. And he quoted an ancient Irish bull: " 'Where there's two, there's one.' "

So nobody should have been surprised when, just about the time that the country was nominating Mr. Weller's report for first position among the best war stories of the year, a duplicate appeared in the patrol report of another submarine operating in the same area. So far as I know, this story never got far out of the official records and it may be appearing here for the first time. But in any case it is worth repeating if only as a striking vindication of the submariners' belief that all good miracles repeat themselves, presumably in an endless succession.

It would appear that some time after Dean Rector arose from his bed of pain and went back to his duty among the torpedoes, another Dean Rector fell to the deck of the USS *Fish*, another submarine in the same area, and another Wheeler B. Lipes interpreted all the deadly signs. So close was the parallel between this and the story already in print that one might be disposed to dismiss it with the short notation that the operation was successful and the patient lived to feel glad about it. But it seems that there were some important variations.

In the first place the patient's condition wasn't discovered until some time after his collapse, because everybody was too busy to notice him. The *Fish* had just torpedoed a tanker and had dived, as usual, just ahead of the ash cans. She stayed submerged for about four hours before there was any appreciable lull. And then she stayed submerged for an even longer period because she could hear the antisubmarine patrols still crisscrossing overhead in search of her.

During the first respite, however, somebody went looking for a cup of water and stumbled over the patient.

One may well skip the details of the first part of this story, inasmuch as Mr. Weller has written them down for all time. In brief it was pure repetition. The pharmacist's mate was another lad who knew his business. The patient was already on the verge of death. An operation was the only thing that could possibly save him. The PM volunteered to do the work, the captain gave his permission and the patient said it was all right with him.

So they prepared the wardroom table and the officers reversed their pajama coats and put them on, and they made a sterilizer out of a pot in which they boiled a mixture of water and torpedo alcohol. They gave the captain a job counting sponges and instruments. They broke out the dressings and sulfanilamide tablets and hemostats, and they bent the spoons to make retractors. But they didn't have to make a handle for the knife. Their knife already had a handle.

There was some slight difference in the operating technique. They had been submerged for several hours and the air was already pretty foul. The PM talked it over with the captain and decided that it would be better not to risk polluting the air further with ether fumes. So he administered a local anesthetic, stuck his thumb in the patient's umbilicus and little finger on the hip bone, and stretched his forefinger to determine the place of incision. The preliminary cutting was neatly done.

Then slight complications developed. This man, it seems, had an adhesion, and the amateur surgeon hadn't planned any routine for taking care of adhesions. From that point until he got the appendix clear enough to remove it he proceeded largely by instinct. One unforeseen thing in an operating room naturally leads to another. As time ran on the effectiveness of the first hypodermic shot wore off and they had to administer another. That took more time and threw the sweating pharmacist's mate off his stride still farther. The second anesthetic wore off and there was no more novocaine left to make possible another one.

The PM reported to the captain and the captain of course said, "Well, we'll close off the compartment and give him the ether."

The closing off of the compartment meant just literally that, because the ventilation system was cut off at the intervening bulkheads. The operating crew were shut up in a box like a somewhat enlarged oxygen tent and in a few minutes they were all breathing nearly as much of the ether fumes as the patient.

The pharmacist's mate got the appendix out by sheer will power and thereafter stayed on his feet longer than the rest. But one after another, the officers and men of his operating staff slid onto the deck at his feet. For a time he tried running out to the control room where the ether was less concentrated, but he gave that up when he found out how much trouble he had making his legs carry him back. When the last of his helpers had passed out he got the door to the forward torpedo room open, the unconscious men were hauled out to revive in clearer air, and another relay came in to take their places. When they collapsed, and with them the pharmacist's mate, another crew came in from the after battery room and went on with the job.

Fortunately by the time this relay arrived, the job was virtually done save for the removal and check of sponges and hemostats and retractors. The captain had left a written record of how many they were expected to find so this part of the work gave them no trouble. A volunteer sewed up the incision with what he described afterward as "a baseball stitch." It seemed to be adequate if unorthodox.

After that the doors were opened and the air, such as it was, allowed to circulate again. A lieutenant revived sufficiently to scatter soda-lime absorbent about the ship and bleed in oxygen from the supply of the Momsen rescue lungs. An entirely fresh relay took the patient to his bunk, and another relay got to the controls under the depth gauges just as the men on the diving planes were about to slide to the deck.

Thirty minutes later all of the personnel were in circulation again and able to do their work, although a bit groggily. This, it was admitted later, was the biggest piece of luck in all the performance. The patient was just coming out of the ether and starting to sing when the questing destroyers up above got a new sound bearing on them and the first of a string of ash cans came down on them. Thereafter for hours they never had a minute's peace.

The second charge was close. It lifted the ship up by the stern and heeled her over almost on her beam-ends. She shivered and creaked and everything loose in her went clattering. The circuit breakers came out and gauges smashed and thick darkness blotted out the roaring turmoil.

When they got power again, the sailors had to move about in a chaos of debris—cork insulation from the hull lining, chunks of glass and crockery, the contents of disrupted bunks and lockers. Nothing in the ship seemed to be in its proper place except what had been bolted down. The removable sections of the wardroom table were out in the battery-room passageway. So were the books from the library cupboard and a lot of phonograph records and pencils and ink and navigation books and charts.

It took the better part of an hour to get enough of the wreckage pushed aside so the men actually running the boat could stand up to their work. And during it all new blasts came to shake them and shake down more debris from broken instruments and cracked bulkhead linings.

It was hours before the final blast came down and the diminishing noise of screws told them that for the time at least the attack was finished. The actual work of putting the submarine into proper running order again was long and arduous, the more so because by that time the ether-filled air was thick and unbreathable and the crew moved about in it with the feeling one has in dreams of being unable to lift one's feet off the ground.

The shock of the ash-can barrage had numbed their brains to all thought and they worked like automata without much idea of what they were doing. Instinctively, they knew that they must clean up the boat and instinctively they went about it but with no plan or organization. Each man was his own trash-removal squad. You picked something up. You put it somewhere else. You got it out of your way and if it was in somebody else's way he piled it up in front of you again.

Despite this confusion the ship eventually got straightened out principally because submarine crews are trained to do things right even when they are only partly conscious. The captain, who knew that order would presently be restored and that the men would be functioning normally as soon as the shock wore off, paid little attention to these details. Up in the conning tower he considered his situation and gave thought to the time when he would be able to surface for at least long enough to get some fresh air in the boat. Then he heard the voice of the chief of the boat who, apparently, had just picked up one of the bent spoons.

"My God!" said the chief. "Everything in the ship has been dumped on the deck. . . . And we left that poor guy in his bunk and he wasn't strapped in. . . ."

The crew had got halfway out of their torpor by that time. The chief's voice brought them the rest of the way out. Heavy feet came up off the deck with new energy and there was a rush aft as half a dozen men at once started to find out what had become of the forgotten patient. The captain turned on the communicator to get a report and received his biggest surprise of the day when he heard it.

"Why, he's in his bunk just where we left him," came the chief's startled voice. "He's the only thing in the ship that's still in place. . . ."

Night came as it must even on a hot corner. The submarine surfaced and pumped out the ether. The patient opened his eyes and murmured something coherent. The pharmacist's mate who had been watching by his side since the end of the attack leaned over him.

"You're all right," he said. "You're lucky, too. We had a hell of a lambasting and you're the only thing on the ship that didn't go onto the deck."

"The hell I didn't," mumbled the patient. "I lit on the deck right on my knob. But I thought it might spoil my operation if I stayed there. So I got up and crawled back in here again. . . . Did I do right?"

I wonder what the next submarine appendectomy is going to be like.

49

END PAPER

You may judge from all of this that the complete story of the submarine war can never be told until it is over. You may listen to a few returning warriors and think that you have heard all that is to be said of daring and skill and human endurance . . . and the next day somebody else does something to prove how wrong you were. You live with the submariners in an atmosphere of unfinished business and bewildering anticlimax. Yesterday a commander came back to port with a record of ships sunk. Tomorrow another skipper may turn in a report of twice as many. There seems to be no end to it.

Yet even in a world of constantly changing values you may suddenly be brought face to face with the truth that there are heights beyond which no man in any service is ever going to rise—some deeds that heroes themselves will discuss in awe as long as lives are sacrificed to war. So it is fitting to close this inadequate record of the submarines with the story of Commander Howard W. Gilmore of New Orleans who accomplished the ultimate.

Commander Gilmore at forty was one of the oldest captains in the service and his record was one of the best. He was given the Navy Cross twice—the first time for a raid on a Japanese harbor, the second time for the destruction of 25,000 tons of enemy shipping.

He was not only a skillful technician but one of those who have acquired the particular hate of the Japanese navy by persistent attacks on warships. His theory of operation got him into more than the average trouble with cruisers, destroyers and patrol boats generally. But in the end it was none of these but an armed sampan that brought him to greatness.

He was on the surface, charging batteries, one cloudy night when he ran into it. There was virtually no visibility and the first warning the lookout got of the Japs' presence was when it loomed out of the murk close aboard. The first sight Captain Gilmore got of it was when he saw it driving forward at full speed to ram him.

The captain, with no other course open to him, swung hard left rudder at seventeen knots and charged, trying to ram the sampan. The boats were only a few feet apart when a 20-millimeter gun swept the bridge. The sampan yawed, and the submarine struck her only a glancing blow as the order was passed to stand by for a dive. Gilmore was wounded and his legs buckled under him as he started for the hatch down which his quartermaster had already fallen. Men came scrambling up the ladder from the conning tower but he waved them back while another murderous blast struck the bridge.

"I can't make it," he said. "Close the hatch."

And then he gave his last order.

"Take her down."

He was still on the bridge as the boat dived.

APPENDIX

DIFFICULTIES OF THE SUBMERGED LIFE

In case you don't realize what perils beset the submariner aside from depth bombs and leaks, you may possibly learn something from the appended letter of Captain J. W. Coe who apparently lived in dire straits, not to say want, for several months. This document occupies a place in the Navy's Ready Letter Writer, as the prize exhibit of its kind:

USS SUBMARINE

#3s184/L8   S36-1   June 11, 1942

FROM: The Commanding Officer
TO: Supply Officer, Navy Yard, Mare Island
VIA: Commander Submarines, Southwest Pacific

SUBJECT: Toilet Paper

REFERENCE: (a) (4608) USS *Holland* (S184) USS *Submarine*
                     Req. 7042 of July 30, 1941
                (b) SO NYMI Canceled invoice No. 272836

ENCLOSURE: (A) Sample of canceled invoice.
                (B) Sample of material required.

1. This vessel submitted a requisition for 150 rolls of toilet paper on July 30, 1941, to USS *Holland*. The material was ordered by *Holland* by supply officer, Navy Yard, Mare Island, for delivery to USS *Submarine*.

2. The supply officer Mare Island on November 26, 1941, canceled Mare Island Invoice No. 272836 with the stamped notation "Canceled. Cannot Identify." This canceled invoice was received by *Submarine* June 10, 1942.

3. During the eleven and a half months elapsing from the time of ordering the toilet paper to the present date, USS *Submarine* personnel, despite their best efforts to await delivery of the subject material, have been unable to wait on several occasions, and the situation is now acute, particularly during depth-charge attacks by the "back stabbers."

4. Enclosure (B) is a sample of the desired material provided for the information of the supply officer, Navy Yard, Mare Island. The commanding officer of USS *Submarine* cannot help but wonder what is being used at Mare Island as a substitute for this unidentifiable material once well known to this command.

5. Boat's personnel during this period has become accustomed to the use of ersatz in proportion to the vast amount of incoming paper work generally nonessential, and in so doing feels that the wish of the Bureau of Ships for the reduction of paper work is being complied with, thus killing two birds with one stone.

6. It is believed by this command that the stamped notation "Cannot Identify" was possibly an error, and that this is simply a case of shortage of strategic war material, USS *Submarine* probably being low on the priority list.

7. In order to co-operate in the war effort at small local sacrifice USS *Submarine* desires no further action be taken until the end of the current war, which has created a situation so aptly described as "war is hell."

(Signed) J. W. COE

THE BADGE OF SERVICE

The emblem of the submarine service—a winglike arrangement of twin dolphins placed head to head with the bow of a submarine between them—has connotations other than the generally known one that the wearer is assigned to duty with the submarines. It is awarded, as a gold badge to an officer, an embroidered sleeve patch to an enlisted man, only after he has undergone long training and passed a rigorous examination. To qualify for it any officer must be able to do the work of any other man, commissioned or enlisted, aboard the boat. . . . Similarily an enlisted man must be able to take over the job of any other enlisted man. Admirals long out of service with the pig boats will still wear it with conscious pride.

NAMES OF SUBMARINES

In the U. S. service the first submarine was the *Holland*, named after John P. Holland, its inventor. Later acquisitions were given letters and numbers. This system obtained until the building of three of the largest of such ships in the world which were called the *Argonaut*, *Narwhal* and *Nautilus*. More recently all submarines have been named after fish, some of which, such as the *Mingo* and the *Harder*, nobody but the piscatorial experts of the American Museum of Natural History had ever heard of.

DECK GUNS

There has long been a controversy among submarine designers over the uses of the deck gun. A couple of our big boats were put out with a pair of six-inch guns apiece, enough armament to give them advantages over any armed merchantman they were likely to meet and something of a chance in a surface action with a destroyer. However, the antagonists of such artillery point out, a submarine is so extremely vulnerable that one hit would probably ruin her, and, therefore, should not be considered or armed as a surface fighter. Against that, big-gun advocates argue that submarines frequently have to dispose of small patrol boats and sampans which are not worth a torpedo and which themselves may have better artillery than that with which a majority of the world's submarines are now equipped. If you have to fight on the surface, they say, it is better to have something that you can do damage with.

SUPERSTITIONS

The submariners are not generally a superstitious lot but they are firm believers in a "change nothing" policy. If you got out of a bad depth-charge attack while wearing an old suit of overalls, it seems best that you should continue to wear the same suit for every depth charge thereafter, presumably so your luck won't be confused.

Mascots, from baby shoes to toy dogs, are a common part of torpedo-room equipment. One that happens to be hung on one of the torpedo tubes when the ship makes a successful approach is likely to stay there forever.

And there is always the submariner's conviction, which may rate as superstition or merely as common sense, that if you keep your mouth shut and mind your own business trouble from brass hats or enemy destroyers will be longer finding you.

UNIFORM

Ashore, if and when they have any clothes left after a long patrol, submarine crews wear the same uniform as other sailors and are as neat or, if possible, neater. Aboard ship, however, they wear what they please from skivvy shorts or nothing at all to college sweaters and crew pants. They keep the ship clean and habitable but do none of the work for work's sake or work for discipline's sake that is done on surface ships. They are selected for—among other virtues—habits of personal cleanliness. But they polish no buttons.

SEA PRESSURES

The water pressure with decks awash has been figured at about 45 pounds to the square inch of hull. This increases about 45 pounds to the square inch at each additional hundred feet of depth. The pressure on the hull of an 800-ton submarine—a type which the Germans have been building in large quantities—would total somewhere around 60,000 tons.

Submarines, including some of our own trainers, have actually been crushed by getting out of control on a dive and going too deep. So the increased safety of modern ships, which as warships go are little more than an ingenious arrangement of tin plate, is a marvel of engineering. Compartment bulkheads serve not only to block off damaged sections of the boat as a means of saving the rest of it but to give a rigidity to the whole structure. They are braced to take stresses equal to those exerted on the pressure hull.

Normally the submarine operates with its interior at surface atmospheric pressure. The pressure inside the boat does, however, get somewhat higher as she submerges, inasmuch as the weight of water actually compresses her and, at the same time, the air inside her. This phenomenon has to be taken into consideration in a dive, as it makes the ship less buoyant.

ACTION OF DEPTH CHARGES

The layman generally assumes that the depth charge wrecks the submarine by hitting it directly with a blast of explosive. As a matter of fact few submarines have ever suffered direct hits. Depth charges as well as torpedoes get their effect through the incompressibility of the water in which they explode. When they burst, the pressure of the explosion travels in all directions. When they burst near a submarine or the submerged hull of a ship, the force, blocked in all other directions by the water, exerts itself on the hull.

THE GERMAN SUBMARINES

Jane's *Fighting Ships* and other authorities on naval construction divide the Nazi submersible fleet into four classes: (a) Coastal and training type, 250-300 tons; (b) Home-operational type, 517 tons; (c) Ocean-going type, 750 tons; (d) Mine-laying submarines, 1,060 tons.

It is generally believed that at the beginning of this war Hitler could muster between forty and sixty boats of the ocean-going class and early in 1940 the Allies were reasonably certain that they had destroyed nearly all of them. Hitler, starting over again, stopped virtually all other naval construction and began to turn out Type C in quantities. Just before Pearl Harbor it was believed that he had around 450 submarines capable of transatlantic operation.

Class A, despite its design for training purposes, can still be deadly in its own waters. It is 136 feet long with a speed of thirteen knots on the surface and seven submerged. It carries five torpedoes—three in bow tubes and two spare. It carries one .79-caliber automatic rifle. Complement 23 men.

Class B, designed for coast defense, is 206 to 220 feet long and is given a bulky appearance by saddle tanks fitted externally to each side of the hull. Its maximum speed is sixteen to eighteen knots on the surface; eight submerged. It carries nine torpedoes— four in bow tubes, one in a single stern tube, four spare. Its deck guns are one 4.1 inch and two .79 inch. Complement 35 men.

Class C, the submarine of the wolf packs, is a double-hulled boat similar in many ways to some of our own types. It is 244 feet long and has a thin outer casing which extends almost to the keel. Maximum speed on the surface is eighteen knots; submerged eight knots. Normally it carries nine torpedoes, four bow and one stern in tubes and four spare, but the number of spares inside the boat or in recesses between the outer casing and the pressure hull has undoubtedly been increased. Guns: one 4.1 inch and two .79 inch. Complement 40 men.

Class D, the mine layers, are not believed to be operating extensively at present. They are the largest of the Nazi U-boats, 275 feet long and bulky. They have a speed of sixteen knots on the surface and seven submerged and carry the same armament as Class C. Complement 45 men.

Unlike most others of the world's submarines the German U-boats have a distinctive profile, a long flush deck rising to the bow. The stem is sloping. They are generally painted in an over-all neutral tone that blends with the seascape.

The mine layers are believed to have a range of about 8,000 miles, the B-type (517 tons) about 10,000 miles, C-type (740 tons) about 14,000 miles without refueling if operated during the entire cruise at economical speed. The mine layers and 740-ton boats seldom stay out longer than a month on a cruise but the latter class could probably stay out two months if not too greatly harassed. The 300-ton training boats can make fairly long ocean patrols if necessity requires. Saddle tanks containing fuel give them a possible range of 4,000 miles at slow speeds.

The U-boats run as do our own submarines with Diesel engines on the surface and on battery-powered electric motors submerged. There has been some report of a new all-purpose Diesel which would do away with the storage batteries and motors, supplying its own air by cracking water into its components of oxygen and hydrogen. U.S. submarine engineers discount these reports on the ground that the water-cracking apparatus would probably be too cumbersome and any reciprocating engine, such as the Diesel, too noisy for use in submerged operations.

SAMPANS

The term "sampan" applied by laymen to any small Japanese boat cannot but be confusing to the layman. A sampan originally was a fishing boat under sail. Recent enlargements of this craft were fitted with Diesel motors and had a long range. Some of them were as large as 400 tons. Many of them have been converted to war work and used in combination scouting-and-fishing jobs, some of them far from Japan. Some of them are heavily armed.

THE LITTLE DAVID

At least two boats which might be considered prototypes of the submarine were built for the Confederate Navy during the war. The first was called *Little David*, designed by a physician, Dr. St. Julien Ravenal, at the suggestion of one Theodore D. Stoney of Charleston. The *Little David*, which hit the Federal ship *New Ironsides* with a spar torpedo and severely damaged it in 1863, ran awash but had many of the characteristics of a submersible ship. After her success the Confederates tried to build a true submarine and turned out the *Hunley*, which later was rebuilt and also named *David*. The *Hunley* sank five different times before she blew up the *Housatonic*, in which action she was herself blown up, and established a record for having drowned 600 percent of her crew.

PLANE-CARRYING SUBMARINES

Several nations have experimented with plane-carrying submarines but most of them have given up the notion. The Japs had a few of the type at the beginning of the war but so far as is known they have not been used. Difficulties in launching and picking up planes in rough sea apparently have restricted their use. Submarines designed for such purposes have generally been overlarge, heavy on top and sluggish in maneuver.

THE SUBS HAVE A WORD FOR IT

Air Manifold. Series of valves through which compressed air at 600 pounds' pressure can be fed into tanks at reduced pressures.

Amps a Side. ("Fourteen hundred amps a side.") A measure of motor speed by means of current consumption on older types of boats.

Angle on the Boat. The angle of the keel from the horizontal.

Ash Cans. Depth charges.

Battle Surface. A surfacing operation during which the submarine is made buoyant by blowing suitable tanks and then held down by the bow and stern planes and motor power until she leaps upward. Ships thus handled come up flat, or nearly flat, instead of bow first, and suddenly.

Beach. Anything that isn't sea water. In this service it frequently describes a submerged extension of the shore.

Black Gang. Engine-room crew—although there is no record of there having been a coal-burning submarine.

Bleed In. (To "bleed in" air or water.) To let in a small amount of air or water.

Blow Ballast. To force water from tanks into sea with compressed air.

Boiler. Synonym for pig boat, sewer pipe, submarine.

Boot. As in the surface ships, a recruit.

Bow Planes or *Stern Planes*. Fins that determine the submarine's angle of dive.

Broach. To surface without intent. To stick the bow out of the water when rising to periscope depth.

Can. The storage battery: "The can is empty." "We had to surface to fill the can." Also short for *Tin Can*.

Captain. Any officer of any rank in command of the boat.

Chief of Boat. A chief petty officer in charge of personnel.

The Christmas Tree. Panel of red and green lights which denote whether valves and vents are open or closed.

Crash Dive. A term generally out of use among submariners inasmuch as all dives nowadays are crash dives. A crash dive primarily is a dive made through the momentum of the Diesel engines, which are not shut off until the ship has started under water.

Dove. In the submarine service the past tense of the verb dive.

Eye-Port. A small, thick, glass window in watertight doors and also in the conning tower.

Fan. See *Spread.*

Fireman. See *Black Gang.*

Flat. (Of a battery). Discharged. "The can is flat."

Flood Down. Fill tanks till the decks are awash. See *Trim Down.*

Foo-Foo. Anything with a pleasant odor noticeable after weeks on patrol.

Foo-Foo Dust. Talcum powder.

Ganomie. A strange creature who fouls things up—a seagoing Gremlin.

Gas Boats. Gasoline-driven submarines of the era before Diesel engines.

Going Hot (Of torpedoes). Properly directed toward the target and, as a matter of course, hitting. "All our torpedoes went hot."

Hard Dive. Dive at maximum angle.

The Head. A highly complicated toilet.

Jam Air. To compress air.

Jamoke. Coffee.

Kingston. A valve from the bottom of a ballast tank to the sea.

Ladder Chancre. Shin bruises caused by collisions with ladders and comings, a common ailment.

Lash-Up. Any kind of an arrangement or setup. "That was a bum lash-up."

Lung. The Momsen escape lung, an oxygen mask whose use makes possible escape from wrecked submarines.

Minnie the Mermaid. A much-discussed character who turns out to be a submerged mural in the diving tower at the New London Submarine School.

Old Man. The skipper who is generally a lieutenant commander about thirty-two years old.

On the Coral. On the bottom, which in most spots in the South Pacific is the same thing.

Periscope Depth. That depth at which the periscope is sticking out of the water two or three feet.

Pig Boat. The old-fashioned submarine, so called from its appearance alongside a tender. The term fitted the living conditions of the boat quite well also.

Pogey Bait. Here, as up there—candy.

Pressure Hull. Internal hull which is cylindrical and built to withstand heavy pressure, as against the thinner external hull which holds the ballast tanks.

Pull the Plug. To submerge—take her down.

Quack. The pharmacist's mate who prefers, generally, to be called "Doc."

Ride the Vents. To proceed with valves at bottom of ballast tanks open and air vents closed.

Ring the Bell. To hit. As: "They almost rang the bell on us."

Rugged. A bit of civilian high-school slang taken over by the submarines as an all-inclusive description of anything tough, dangerous or inconvenient, from depth charges to bad weather.

Sewer Pipe. Another local name for a submarine.

The Silent Service. A poetic name for the submarine business that the submariners themselves will have none of.

Sitting Pigeon. Unarmed enemy ship proceeding slowly without escort.

Sound. The man who works the sound devices. Similar to "Chips" or "Sparks," both of whom are to be found unchanged in the sub service.

Spread. A number of torpedoes fired at the same time but at different angles.

String. Similar to *Fan* or *Spread* except that it applies to a number of depth charges dropped in a single run of the patrol ship at regular intervals.

Those Guys up There. The Japanese.

Tin Can. Common enemy of the subs. Below, as on the surface, the term describes a destroyer.

Tin Fish (or just *Fish*). Torpedoes.

Topside. The deck.

Trim Down. Reduce buoyancy until the ship is running virtually awash.

U-Boat. A German submarine.

Up on Top. The surface.

Valve-Turners. Experimenters who twist controls to find out what will happen—a short-lived race.

Vent. An opening at the top of a ballast tank.

Walk Around. (As "Walk the periscope around!") To turn the periscope in a 360-degree sweep of the horizon.

Wardroom. On new boats a compact, well-furnished little room; on old ones a place to sit down.

Water Slug. Water taken into torpedo tube after firing, to compensate for loss of weight of torpedo.

Working Over. Usual description of a depth-bomb barrage: "They certainly gave us a working over."